SOY *of* COOKING

Easy-to-Make Vegetarian, Low-Fat, Fat-Free,
and Antioxidant-Rich Gourmet Recipes

Marie Oser

CHRONIMED
PUBLISHING

Soy of Cooking: Easy-to-Make Vegetarian, Low-Fat, Fat-Free, and Antioxidant-Rich Gourmet Recipes ©1996 by Marie Oser.

Library of Congress Cataloging-in-Publication Data

Oser, Marie
Soy of cooking: easy-to-make vegetarian, low-fat, fat-free, and antioxidant-rich gourmet recipes / by Marie Oser.

     p.   cm.

Includes index.

ISBN 1-56561-086-5; $15.95

Editors: Jolene Steffer and Jeff Braun
Cover Design: Terry Dugan Design
Text Design: Liana Raudys
Production Artist: David Enyeart
Photography: John Strange Photography
Art/Production Manager: Claire Lewis
Printed in the United States

Published by
Chronimed Publishing
P.O. Box 59032
Minneapolis, MN 55459-9686

10   9   8   7   6   5   4   3

Dedication

With much love and gratitude to my husband, Lanny, whose steadfast support of my work makes everything possible.

And our children, Kyra and Justin. They are my light and my inspiration.

NOTICE:
Consult a Health Care Professional

Readers are advised to seek the guidance of a licensed physician or health care professional before making any changes in prescribed health care regimens, as each individual case or need may vary. This book is intended for informational purposes only and is not for use as an alternative to appropriate medical care. While every effort has been made to ensure that the information is the most current available, new research findings, being released with increased frequency, may invalidate some data.

Grateful acknowledgment to:

Everyone at Chronimed Publishing, especially David Wexler, who "really, really, really" wanted to do this book.

Jeff Braun, my editor, whose skillful eye, warm humor, and good nature made this project a joy to complete.

Tom McReynolds, a.k.a. "Tommy Tofu," a gifted writer and exceptional country music talent, for his valued input and ongoing support. While a great title is worth a thousand pictures, when I "hit a wall" looking for just the right segue, I know I can depend on Tom.

Ellen Tarantino, my personal assistant, who is always there for me, doing whatever is needed, without complaint. She is a jewel.

Mary Lisardi, my computer maven, and Pat Moore, my personal cheerleader, who have provided me with indispensable encouragement.

Judy Rae, Dale Hallcom, Mimi Clark, and Rosemary Campagna for valued recipe testing, tasting, and input.

The many nutrition professionals, food scientists, and biochemists who have shared research and lent their expertise to this work, among them:

Mark Messina, Ph.D., for his ongoing distinguished efforts in disseminating valuable information regarding the beneficial effects of including soyfoods in the diet. And Ginny Messina, R.D., M.P.H., whose considerate and thoughtful manner make speaking with her a pleasure.

The American Soybean Association, especially Susie Oberdahloff, for providing a wealth of data for my soy endeavor.

William Shurtleff of The Soyfoods Center, for information and advice that have contributed to this effort.

Scott Sanders, Ph.D., of Creative Food Consultants, and Russ Bianchi, Ph.D., of LSI Specialty Products, who are always generous with their time, and have allowed me free rein to pick their considerable brains.

◆ *v* ◆

Contents

Foreword

The soybean's tiny size belies the power within. For decades, white-coated investigators have teased this tiny legume apart seeking to explain its strength against cancer, heart disease, and day-to-day annoyances, like hot flashes. And they have found hundreds of natural compounds hidden in the soybean that drive cholesterol levels down, put hormones into balance, activate toxin-destroying enzymes, and work other wonders.

A second group of white-coated explorers are discovering the bean's magic in the kitchen. Just as carbon can turn into diamonds or pencil lead, the diverse manifestations of the soybean are no less remarkable. It is steamed in the pod as an appetizer and turned into tempeh to replace burgers or sausage. When transformed into tofu, it becomes the most versatile ingredient ever to find its way into the pantry. Soy also becomes hot dogs, sloppy joes, tacos, pizza topping, and spaghetti sauce.

Soy of Cooking is a treasury of recipes that are quick, easy, and wonderfully tasty. The heartiest meal remains low in fat, and none has even a speck of cholesterol.

Marie Oser has done a wonderful job in bringing together this extraordinary compilation. May you enjoy these delicious foods in the very best of health.

Neal D. Barnard, M.D.
President, Physicians Committee for Responsible
Medicine, Washington, D.C.

x

Preface

Soyfoods are hot! Nutrient-rich soybeans are proving to be an important dietary staple. Recent findings show that substances found exclusively in soybeans can lower cholesterol and help prevent disease. Numerous studies attest to the role soyfoods can play in preventing many forms of cancer, heart disease, and osteoporosis, and in controlling diabetes. How can you take advantage of the unique properties of this wonderpod? If the only soyfood you know is tofu, then read on.

Adding soy to your diet has never been easier. There is a great variety of new and lighter soy products, which I have used to create these delectable dishes. Although widely available, some of these wonderful soyfoods may be unfamiliar to some cooks. Not to worry, though, just turn to the Soyfoods Pantry (page 17) to learn about both new and traditional soy products. While the majority of ingredients used in *Soy of Cooking* are found in supermarkets and health food stores across the country, the Quick Guide to Ingredients and the Resource Guide will help you locate products.

Soyfoods are delicious! The new meat analogues defy detection by even the most skeptical and can help to recreate your favorite traditional meals, healthfully. Lite silken tofu and soymilk lite are very low-fat and versatile ingredients that add richness and creaminess to dips, quiches, soups, sauces, cakes, and pies. When you are looking for something to "sink your teeth into," the flavorful, chewy texture of soy tempeh will surely fill the bill. Using easy, innovative techniques and marinades, you can change the texture of tofu to a richly flavored, meaty consistency. Soy flour and soy grits are used to boost the nutrition of baked goods while adding a pleasant nuttiness.

These are only a few of the many wonderful soyfoods I have used to create this collection. There are 31 tasty ingredients derived from soybeans listed in the Soyfoods Pantry, and this is only the beginning. You'll be amazed by the number of innovative soy products that continue to enter the market every day.

The new and lighter soyfoods offer the health conscious cook the ability to create exciting meals—delicious meals with many added health benefits; enticing meals without the high-fat and cholesterol-laden ingredients offered at virtually every meal by, as John Robbins refers to it, the Great American Food Machine. *Soy of Cooking* speaks to the role that soyfoods can play in replacing unhealthy foods. It is a cookbook that can help you move toward a well-balanced diet that is low in fat, high in fiber, rich in phytochemicals, and cholesterol free. All this is made easy because soyfoods, especially lower-fat ones, are now widely available.

Soyfoods play the starring role in *Soy of Cooking,* but there is a terrific supporting cast of hearty whole grains, luscious fruits, vegetables, and legumes, all rich in nutrients and phytochemicals. In fact, the recipes here contain no food products from animal sources—no meat, fish, eggs, or dairy products. They are completely vegetarian meals. You will find that your opportunity to reap the impressive health benefits of replacing animal products with soyfoods is enhanced exponentially by including the many other important plant foods in your diet.

I will show you how to create an enticing variety of delectably satisfying meals, from appetizer to dessert, while always keeping fat to a minimum. No recipe exceeds 5 grams of fat per serving. Indeed, they average about 3 grams of fat.

The extra good news is that these guiltless, low-fat dishes are as delectable as they are healthful. Family and friends will marvel at the diversity of flavors and presentations you can achieve using the ingredients and techniques outlined here for the health conscious cook. *Soy of Cooking* is more than a cookbook. It holds the key to what most enlightened physicians and nutritionists consider the optimal diet. Using this book daily will lead you to a more healthful lifestyle.

Soy of Cooking is your guidebook for expanding your culinary repertoire. The recipes are easy to follow and the recommended ingredients are wholesome and of high quality. Each recipe is a delicious opportunity to incorporate soyfoods into your diet. My hope is that these luscious gourmet dishes will inspire you to include this important staple in your diet. Join me and explore the amazing world of soy. Your heart will thank you for it!

Marie Oser

One more thought: Regarding the type of diet presented in *Soy of Cooking,* I am certainly not the first person to promote vegetarian-centered cuisine. However, if I have piqued your interest, I heartily recommend the books of John Robbins, president of the EarthSave Foundation (see Recommended Reading, page 249). Robbins' book, *Diet for a New America,* an international bestseller that was nominated for a Pulitzer Prize, has had a tremendous impact. First printed in 1987, it has changed the lives of many. My son Justin, now 16, read the book when he was 10 and has been vegetarian ever since. *May All Be Fed,* a more recent work from Robbins, is a beautifully written guide to eating and to understanding how our food choices affect our health and the planet. John Robbins' wisdom and compassion can also encourage you toward a more healthful lifestyle.

Introduction

Times are rapidly changing. Just look around. Veggie burgers are turning up on restaurant menus—not to mention supermarket shelves, next to the vegetarian hot dogs. And don't be surprised if the next time you ask someone what they are planning to make for dinner tonight, they say, "tempeh sloppy joes," "tofu stir-fry," or "vegetarian chili over rice."

Soy of Cooking is riding the crest of a wave—the movement toward a plant-based diet. A 1992 Yankelovich survey sponsored by *Vegetarian Times* magazine found that almost 7 percent of American adults are making an effort to eat less meat and identify themselves as vegetarians. That same year, the National Restaurant Association conducted a survey that found that 20 percent of restaurant-goers are looking for a meatless entrée when they eat out.

The movement toward a plant-based diet isn't just a fad—it's a permanent lifestyle shift. No wonder. Driving the shift is a mountain of scientific research linking plant-based diets with lower rates of coronary artery disease, several types of cancer, obesity, high blood pressure, and adult onset diabetes. Even severe atherosclerosis has been shown to be reversible in some cases, without the use of drugs or surgery, when a low-fat vegetarian diet is eaten.

The benefits of a plant-based diet are difficult to ignore. Foods of plant origin contain fiber, vitamins, minerals, and phytochemicals, substances that protect against disease. Soyfoods, for instance, have been determined to contain isoflavones, phytochemicals which may have cancer-fighting properties.

In contrast, animal products—meat, eggs, and high-fat dairy products—are devoid of fiber and contain saturated fat and cholesterol, substances that are disease-promoting in the amounts eaten by most people in Western countries. Animal products contribute greatly to the overabundance of protein and total fat in the diet, as well.

We are learning more about the complexities of nutrition and the links between diet and health every day. What now appears to be clear is that increasing the ratio of plant to animal products in your diet is a smart move. That means making fruits, vegetables, grains, and legumes (dried beans and peas) the foundation foods of your diet. It also means cutting way back on your consumption of foods of animal origin—all types of meat, eggs, and fatty dairy products.

In its 1993 position paper on vegetarian diets, The American Dietetic Association acknowledges that "vegetarian diets are healthful and nutritionally adequate when they are appropriately planned." In fact, foods of animal origin are not necessary at all for good health. Assuming that reasonable attention is paid to basic principles of nutrition (junk-food junkies, that caveat is meant for you), then a diet comprised of fruits, vegetables, grains and grain products, and legumes can provide you with all of the nutrition you need while helping you avoid the dietary excesses that characterize the typical Western diet.

If you do choose to eat animal products, however, they should be a minor part of your meals. If you eat them, think of meats, eggs, and dairy products as condiments or side-dishes—minor ingredients in a dish—rather than the focal point of the plate.

How does soy figure into the picture? Soyfoods can help ease the transition to a more plant-based diet. Soy products such as tempeh, tofu, soymilk, textured vegetable protein, and others make great substitutes for meat, eggs, and dairy products in traditional recipes. Need something fun to take to a summer cookout? Try veggie burgers and tofu hot dogs. They taste great. Have a hankering for quiche, scrambled eggs, or egg salad sandwiches? They can all be made with tofu instead of eggs—deliciously. Your favorite dip. Soups. Sauces. Casseroles. You name it. Almost all of your favorite recipes can be modified by using soy products in place of animal products.

Soy of Cooking will show you how delicious, nutritious, and versatile soy foods can be. By integrating low-fat soy foods into your daily diet and substituting them for animal products, you'll benefit two ways. You'll get the good qualities of soy, packed with vitamins, minerals, and phytochemicals. At the same time, you'll displace the biggest sources of fat, saturated fat, and cholesterol in your diet.

You may find that you have more variety in your diet, as well. Dishes made with soy products can be an introduction to cuisines of other cultures, many of which have vegetarian traditions. You'll discover a whole new world of dishes based not only on soy but on other legumes, grains, vegetables, and fruits. Some people think that when one reduces or eliminates meat, the diet becomes more limited. Most vegetarians, however, would say the opposite is true. When meals are based on foods of plant origin, the variety is nearly endless.

Enjoy the delicious, health-supporting recipes in *Soy of Cooking* and learn how to incorporate versatile soy foods into your meals. Above all, let *Soy of Cooking* help you take the first steps away from yesterday's "meat and potato" ways, to swap old traditions for new, and to make the transition to a healthful, satisfying plant-based diet.

Suzanne Havala, M.S., R.D., F.A.D.A.
Registered dietitian and author of Shopping for Health: A Nutritionist's Aisle-by-Aisle Guide to Smart, Low-Fat Choices at the Supermarket *and* Simple, Lowfat & Vegetarian

SOY *of* COOKING

◆*2*◆

Soyfood for Thought

How can you adopt a diet that will meet your nutritional needs and protect health? Is there a nutrition plan to prevent heart disease, lower the risk of cancer, even help you lose weight? Is there a practical and appealing approach to a more healthful eating style? These are just a few of the questions that have spurred scientists and physicians to investigate the plant kingdom in a quest for the optimal diet.

A number of prominent medical professionals recommend a diet based on four food groups that may surprise some readers. The food groups are grains, legumes, vegetables, and fruits. Neal Barnard, M.D., is president of Physicians Committee for Responsible Medicine (PCRM), in Washington, D.C., and a well known author. He cites overwhelming evidence that this approach to a more wholesome lifestyle can help prevent disease and promote health. He presents this powerful menu as an ideal prescription for lowering cholesterol, staying slim, preventing cancer, and maybe even slowing the effects of aging. In his latest book, Dr. Barnard's nutrition strategies are offered as a defense against the chemical assaults that are fundamental to the aging process. Though we have not yet discovered the "fountain of youth," it is the power of your food choices that will counteract the effects of aging. Make healthy food choices and you will aid the body in strengthening bones, cleaning arteries, dissolving fat, rejuvenating skin, and boosting the immune system.

The New England Journal of Medicine, The Journal of the American Medical Association, and many respected professional groups all link nutrition and lifestyle to health. They report that there are substances in vegetables, not only vitamins and minerals, which appear to have a protective effect against certain diseases, and that nutrition can play a vital role in the prevention, treatment, and cure of a variety of ailments.

MOVING FROM MEAT TO SOY

The counterpoint to the high-fat, fiber-barren American diet is a naturally low-fat, high-fiber, plant-based diet. Even the government endorses plant-based diets.

The latest Dietary Guidelines for Americans, released by the U.S. Department of Agriculture early in 1996, endorses vegetarian diets for the first time since it started issuing dietary guidelines in 1916. The guidelines are the official blueprint for school lunches and all other federal nutrition programs. The revised guidelines, championed by PCRM, won the support of top medical authorities, such as the famed pediatrician Benjamin Spock, M.D., Colin Campbell, Ph.D., of the China Health Study of Oxford and Cornell, and Henry Heimlich, M.D., who invented the lifesaving technique that has saved over 50,000 lives in the last 25 years. The Dietary Guidelines Advisory Committee endorsed the safety of vegetarian diets and pointed out that the failure to include vegetarian diets in the past was a serious oversight.

Dean Ornish, M.D., is another physician and author who makes a strong case for setting aside the traditional meat and potatoes approach to eating. Dr. Ornish's Preventive Medicine Research Institute has been enormously successful in reversing heart disease through its Life Choice Program. The program uses no cholesterol-lowering drugs or surgery; instead it focuses on a low-fat vegetarian diet, stress management, smoking cessation, moderate exercise, and emotional support. In the first randomized, controlled clinical study of its kind, the "Lifestyle Heart Trial" demonstrated that arteries that have become clogged with fatty deposits actually respond to lifestyle and dietary changes. Though the major focus of the research was on preventing and reversing heart disease, participants in the Ornish program lost an average of 22 pounds while eating abundantly. Dr. Ornish's program was a revolutionary approach that the medical establishment has recognized as both sensible and well founded.

A study published recently in the *Journal of the American College of Nutrition* showed that patients following a very low-fat, plant-based vegetarian diet (no eggs or dairy products), experienced a significant lowering of serum cholesterol and blood pressure in only 12 days. John McDougall, M.D., the study's principal investigator and medical director of The McDougall Program, conducted the study with colleagues at St. Helena's Hospital and Health Center in Deer Park, California. They examined 500 patients with high cholesterol who participated in an intensive 12-day live-in program focusing on dietary modification, moderate exercise, and stress management over six years, between 1986 and 1992. (The program's criteria for high cholesterol is any measurement over 200 mg/dl, and participants are encouraged to continue working toward a goal of 150 to 160 mg/dl when they finish the 12-day program.) Participants were fed a vegetarian diet that was 5 percent fat, 12 percent protein, and 83 percent carbohydrate.

The results were very encouraging. On average, participants in the short-term program reduced their total serum cholesterol by 11 percent and blood pressure by 6 percent. If they continued over many years to observe the dietary and lifestyle changes learned during the live-in program, this reduction would translate into a 22 to 33 percent decrease in risk of dying from coronary heart disease. While more comparative studies are needed regarding the effects of the plant-based, very-low-fat diet on triglycerides as well as total and HDL cholesterol, the researchers concluded that dietary and lifestyle changes prescribed by the McDougall Program are an effective way to lower total serum cholesterol and blood pressure.

It seems as though a new study is released every day that emphasizes the need to reassess the meat-centered diet that has been the gold standard most of this century. But how does one make the necessary changes in diet and lifestyle without sacrificing the flavor, texture, and protein in familiar dishes? Is there an easy way to make the transition? Enter the soybean.

THE HEALTH BENEFITS OF SOY PROTEIN

Soybeans are nutrient-rich legumes. And replacing animal protein with soy protein makes good sense. Soy protein is considered essentially equal in quality to animal protein, like that in meat, milk, and eggs, and is recognized by the U.S. government as a protein alternative equivalent to meat.

Typically, the average American diet contributes twice the amount of protein necessary—approximately 70 percent—from animal sources. In China, protein intake averages only about two-thirds of what it is in the West, and only about 10 percent of the total protein intake is from animal sources. Contrary to general impression, an abundance of quality protein is available in the plant kingdom. Furthermore, including a variety of wholesome grains, legumes, vegetables, and fruits in your daily diet will ensure well-balanced nutrition.

A vegetarian diet provides plenty of protein without any careful planning, provided it is drawn from a variety of foods. The concept of "protein complementing," requiring various food combinations at each meal to assure adequate protein, has been discarded, as dietitians have found that any varied diet of plant foods provides more than enough protein.

Soybeans are much more than an excellent source of high-quality protein. They are also rich in calcium, iron, zinc, and many of the B vitamins. A healthy diet is important for strong bones. Would you guess that green leafy vegetables provide a better source of calcium than milk? Well, they do because the calcium in vegetables such as kale is more easily absorbed. The calcium in soyfoods is also well absorbed by the body, and there is evidence that soy protein may ward off osteoporosis by improving calcium utilization. Some brands of tofu are excellent sources of calcium because they are coagulated with calcium salt. Depending on how it is processed, a half cup of tofu can provide between 80 and 435 milligrams of calcium.

CALCIUM IN SOYFOODS

Soyfood	Calcium
Soybeans, mature, 1/2 cup	80 mg.
Soybeans, green, 1/2 cup	130 mg.
Tempeh, 1/2 cup	77 mg.
Tofu, 1/2 cup	130 mg.
TVP, 1/2 cup prepared	85 mg.
Soymilk, 1 cup	80 mg.
Soymilk, fortified, 1 cup	250-300 mg.

REDUCING THE RISK OF CANCER AND MORE

Beyond the excellent nutritional quality of soyfoods, consider that an impressive amount of research has shown that substances found almost exclusively in soyfoods can have an impressive effect on our health. There is a class of non-nutritive components found only in plant foods called phytochemicals (which actually means plant chemicals). These phytochemicals have been investigated by the scientific community in recent years because of the beneficial way in which they can affect our health. Many plants contain plant estrogens or phytoestrogens, and soybeans contain high levels of a unique type of phytoestrogen called isoflavones. It is the isoflavones in soybeans that are credited with the role that soyfoods play in cancer prevention and reducing the risk of osteoporosis.

In the mid 1980s, studies began to suggest that an isoflavone in soybeans, genistein, could be an effective weapon against many types of cancer. A number of scientific studies conducted in China and Japan have shown that frequent consumers of tofu and soymilk have a lower cancer risk than those who rarely consume these foods.

Early in 1994, the first international symposium on the "Role of Soy in Preventing and Treating Chronic Diseases" was held in Phoenix, Arizona, and chaired by Mark Messina, Ph.D., a leading authority in the area of soyfoods and a former program director at the National Cancer Institute. Forty speakers presented papers with topics that included studying the effect of soyfoods in lowering blood cholesterol levels and reducing the effects of chemical carcinogens. Almost 30 other studies were also presented. The consensus at the conference was that if people consumed more soyfoods, they would reduce their risk of heart disease and some forms of cancer.

Some of the more intriguing studies dealt with the role of soyfoods in the reduction of bone mineral loss and minimizing some of the unpleasant effects of menopause. It seems that there is no Japanese phrase for "hot flashes," and that Japanese women who consume a traditional diet high in soy experience a mild menopause. Bones tend to be stronger in Asia and broken hips and spinal fractures are less common. Western women consume much more meat and four times as much fat as do women on traditional Asian rice-based diets, but they consume only one-fourth to one-half the fiber. Women who enter menopause on a low-fat vegetarian diet often breeze right through it, with mild or even nonexistent symptoms.

Researchers investigating the relationship between soyfood consumption and cancer prevention at the National Cancer Institute found that soyfoods are rich in anticarcinogens. It was reported that genistein, the main isoflavone found in soybeans, not only can inhibit cancer cell growth, it can also cause cancer cells to differentiate— that is, to go from cancer cells to normal cells, actually reversing the cancer process. In addition, researchers indicate that genistein inhibits angiogenesis, the growth of blood vessels that allows tumors to grow beyond a very small size.

In 1995 alone, more than 300 scientific papers were published attributing potent cancer-fighting characteristics to genistein. But how much isoflavone, particularly genistein, is needed each day to make a difference? That's difficult to say because cancer is affected by many factors. However, based on epidemiological studies, Mark and Ginny Messina (authors of *The Simple Soybean and Your Health*) recommend one serving of soyfoods a day—which provides approximately 25 to 40 milligrams of isoflavones—in order to reduce the risk of cancer.

Isoflavones, unlike vitamins, are not destroyed by conventional cooking methods. The following is the isoflavone content of selected foods:

SOYFOOD	ISOFLAVONE
Soymilk, 1 cup	40 mg.
Tofu, 1/2 cup	40 mg.
Tempeh, 1/2 cup	40 mg.
TVP, prepared, 1/2 cup	35 mg.
Miso, 1/2 cup	40 mg.
Soy flour, 1/2 cup	50 mg.
Soybeans, cooked, 1/2 cup	35 mg.
Soynuts, 1 oz.	40 mg.

Another interesting benefit of a soyfoods-based diet is its effect on glucose control. Recently, scientists have become interested in the role of soyfoods in controlling diabetes. A number of studies indicate that a healthful diet and exercise are the keys to managing diabetes. A diet that is abundant in complex carbohydrates and very low in fat is especially important. Soybeans have a low glycemic index, which is a measure of how much blood sugar rises when a particular food is consumed. Foods with a low glycemic index produce a smaller rise in blood glucose, which is helpful in controlling diabetes. Soybean's low glycemic index (lower than any other bean) may occur because soybeans are high in compounds called phytates and tannins. These substances slow the absorption of the starch in soybeans.

While weight loss is fundamental in treating type II diabetes, which does not require insulin, scientists have found that in both types of diabetes, soluble fiber can be helpful in glucose control by delaying the absorption of nutrients into the bloodstream. Soybeans and some soyfoods like tempeh, textured soy protein, and soy flour are rich in soluble fiber. To control blood sugar, many people plan their meals and snacks using the Exchange Lists for Meal Planning, developed and published by the American Dietetic Association and American Diabetes Association. Soyfoods can be included in this menu planning approach using the following exchanges:

S O Y F O O D	E X C H A N G E
Soybeans, 1/2 cup	1 protein
Tofu, 1/2 cup	1 protein
Tofu hot dog, 1	1 protein
Tempeh, 1/4 cup	1 protein
Roasted soynuts, 1/4 cup	1 protein
TVP, prepared, 1/4 cup	1 protein
Soy cheese, 1 oz.	1 protein, 1 fat
Low-fat soymilk, 1 cup	1 milk
Regular soymilk, 1 cup	1 milk, 1 fat

F I G H T I N G   C H O L E S T E R O L

Heart disease is still the number one killer in this country, and no one disputes the fact that elevated cholesterol levels sharply increase the risk of heart disease and stroke. At the same time, an impressive amount of research has shown that eating soyfoods can dramatically lower cholesterol levels in the blood. Soy may prevent heart disease in many ways. Certainly, reducing blood cholesterol is an important factor, however, there are many other factors that affect the risk of heart disease. Though it is not yet clear that soy protein inhibits cholesterol oxidation (which occurs when cholesterol that has been exposed to oxygen undergoes structural changes and, as such, can damage the arteries), genistein has been shown, in test tubes, to inhibit the growth of cells that form the plaque that lines arteries. Genistein may also inhibit the formation of blood clots.

♦9♦

In August of 1995, the *New England Journal of Medicine* published a study by James Anderson, M.D., which concluded that adding soy protein to a low-fat diet appears to be one of the most potent cholesterol fighters. This study suggested that moderately high to high levels of cholesterol are significantly lowered by introducing soy protein into the diet. They found that an average of 47 grams of soy protein per day can decrease low-density lipoproteins (LDL)—the bad cholesterol—by 12.9 percent in just one month, while leaving the high-density lipoproteins (HDL)—the good cholesterol—alone. Most intriguing, they found that the higher the concentration of cholesterol in the blood the greater the power of soy to reduce it. At 300 milligrams per deciliter of blood, the cholesterol level plunged by 20 percent. Although these effects of soy are considered speculative, they indicate that eating soyfoods is a wise choice and may help protect against heart disease.

10

A Healthy Kitchen

Healthy meals and snacks start with healthy ingredients. In *Soy of Cooking*, you will find that added fat is kept to a minimum, and butter, shortening, and margarine are never used. Butter is unnecessary in my approach to gourmet food; it is very high in fat and cholesterol and is an animal product. Shortening and margarine are hardly health foods since they contain unwanted trans-fatty acids produced by the addition of an extra hydrogen atom. They are hydrogenated, like many oils, which are labeled as "partially hydrogenated." Hydrogenated oils should be avoided because several studies have suggested that the trans-fatty acids created in this process make them physically equivalent to animal fats. Unenlightened commercial bakers like to use hydrogenated oils because they extend shelf life. The baked goods found in this cookbook are heavenly without added fat.

OLIVE OIL

You will note that in those recipes that use oil, vegetable oil cooking spray and olive oil are listed. Pump action sprays made with canola oils are wonderful for lubricating baking pans, or anywhere a little oil is needed. Canola oil is very low in saturated fat and has a neutral flavor. Olive oil is largely monounsaturated fat and, as such, lowers the LDL (bad) cholesterol, and raises the HDL (good) cholesterol. Studies of the traditional Mediterranean diet conclude that regular olive oil consumption lowers arterial blood pressure and reduces the risk of stroke. Olive oil contains antioxidants that guard against free radical damage to cells—the type of damage that precipitates cancers and the unwanted effects of aging. This is not to say that you should increase the amount of fat in your diet. What is recommended here is to replace the unhealthy fats with monounsaturated fat, while reducing the overall amount of fat in the diet.

The olive oil I prefer to use is extra virgin olive oil. It is the finest grade, and therefore the most expensive, but it has a rich, full-bodied flavor and a lovely fruitiness. I feel the same way about using the best quality olive oil as I do about using a good quality wine in cooking. These ingredients impart a special flavor and a distinctive gourmet character to the finished dish. Some would say that it is a waste to use extra virgin olive oil for cooking, but even in small amounts it makes a difference. In addition, because it is used in small quantities, a bottle will last a long time. Virgin olive oil is somewhat similar to extra virgin in flavor, though it is slightly more acidic. It is less expensive than the higher grade and may be substituted with good results.

GARLIC

The most often combined ingredients in my kitchen are onions, olive oil, and garlic. It is a marriage made in heaven, not only because of the superior flavor, but because of their special protective qualities. Garlic is actually a member of the lily family and is closely related to the onion. When you cook with these gourmet treasures, you might well be getting more than just great flavor. The potential health aspects of fresh garlic and its cousins are an added incentive to the generous use of these aromatic ingredients.

While there has been much myth and magic surrounding garlic, the evidence about garlic is almost as stunning as the folklore. Potent compounds in garlic appear to retard heart disease, stroke, cancer, and a wide variety of infections. Garlic contains the amino acid allicin, which has antibiotic and bactericidal effects, according to scientists. This compound renders raw garlic more powerful than penicillin and tetracycline. Hundreds of studies confirm garlic as a broad spectrum antibiotic effective against a long list of microbes that spread disease. How much? A mere half clove of raw garlic a day can improve the blood clot dissolving activity that helps prevent heart attacks and strokes.

Interestingly, garlic is also good for dogs. I keep a jar of chopped garlic in the refrigerator for my beautiful black Labrador retriever, Colby. Adding a teaspoon to his food keeps fleas at bay. I think he likes the "gourmet" touch, too.

Garlic unleashes at least 100 sulphur-containing compounds, which are linked to its medicinal uses. "Undisturbed, the garlic bulb has limited medicinally active compounds," says Eric Block of the State University of New York at Albany, who is an authority on garlic's chemistry. "Cutting triggers the formation of a cascade of compounds that are quite reactive and participate in a complex sequence of chemical reactions." He adds, "Chopping, steaming, and food processing do miraculous things to garlic. Ultimately, an amazing array of chemical compounds are produced."

TOMATOES

Tomatoes are an excellent source of potassium, vitamin C, and fiber. Each tomato contains about 22 milligrams of vitamin C and 1 gram of fiber. Tomatoes also contain a carotene (carotenoids are pigments) that is different than other vegetables. It is called lycopene, the substance that gives tomatoes their distinctive red color. Lycopene has been shown to lower the risk of several forms of cancer, including cancers of the pancreas, cervix, and bladder. Most recently, a study published in the Journal of the American Cancer Institute indicated that lycopene intake was associated with a lowered risk of prostate cancer. Not only available in raw tomatoes, lycopene is present in processed products like tomato paste and tomato juice.

PEPPERS

Peppers are a most flavorful and frequently used ingredient in my kitchen. Bell peppers are very high in vitamin C and sweet peppers are a good source of beta carotene. Chilies are the spicy peppers used liberally in Mexican and South and Central American cuisine, among others. I have not often used whole chili peppers, such as jalapeños, in this collection; however, many times I will season the oil at the start of a sauté with crushed red pepper. This quick "hit" of added spice seems to become a bit milder with longer cooking. Capsaicin is the substance that gives hot peppers their heat and is very evident in the crushed pepper and cayenne used in my dishes. Capsaicin has been found to be an effective pain reliever, and can boost metabolism, causing the body to burn calories faster. Spicy foods have been known to clear up stuffiness, making a rather tasty nasal decongestant! Also thought to be useful in clearing arteries, capsaicin seems to prevent excessive stickiness that leads to blocked arteries.

CARROTS

Carrots are root-imentary in my repertoire. Making soup without colorful chunks of carrots is almost unthinkable, and what vegetable melange doesn't profit from the addition of its delightfully sweet flavor. Carrots are part of the unbelliferae family. Characterized by their lacy, feathery leaves, celery, fennel, dill, and parsley are all relatives of the carrot.

The health benefits of carrots have been touted for many years, and of all fruits and vegetables, carrots are the highest in beta carotene. Remember when you were told to eat your carrots for good eyesight? Well, their high level of beta carotene (one carrot contains 13,500 IU of beta carotene) makes carrots a powerful ally in the prevention of premature aging and cataracts. This is in addition to counteracting the oxidizing effects of free radical damage to cells in the body. Furthermore, this fiber-rich vegetable is high in a type of soluble fiber that has been shown to reduce cholesterol. The average carrot contains 2.3 grams of fiber, and researchers recommend eating two carrots a day to reduce cholesterol levels by as much as 20 percent. One carrot contains enough beta carotene to meet your total daily allowance requirement of vitamin A.

I'm fond of using what is commonly referred to as "baby carrots." True baby carrots are very young, slender carrots, generally sold in bunches. The baby carrots in my recipes are those that the industry calls "baby cut carrots." These are mature carrots that have been peeled, cut, and bagged. Mature carrots contain more beta carotene than the young variety, and should have a healthy reddish-orange color. It is interesting to note that cooking does not destroy beta carotene, and that the beta carotene in cooked vegetables is more easily assimilated in the body.

POTATOES

While once considered a lowly starch, potatoes are now recognized as a nutritious, beneficial vegetable to be included in every balanced diet. A 7-ounce baked potato has 5 grams of protein, 26 milligrams of vitamin C, 20 milligrams of calcium, an incredible 844 milligrams of potassium, and only 220 calories. Potatoes are also high in water-absorbing fiber that makes one feel more satisfied and less hungry. Not only great tasting, inexpensive, and nutritious, potatoes are virtually fat free. Sweet potatoes are nutritional powerhouses, bursting with beta carotene. A 6-ounce sweet potato contains 265 milligrams of potassium, and 26,082 IU of vitamin A, and only 136 calories.

Potatoes are an excellent source of complex carbohydrates, the body's best energy source. Complex carbohydrates are far superior to simple carbohydrates, like those found in sugars and refined products that tend to give a quick lift. Complex carbohydrate foods like potatoes deliver a slow release of energy, thereby keeping the blood sugar level steady longer. A high-carbohydrate meal can actually boost metabolism and speed the burning of calories—ideal for weight control.

CRUCIFEROUS VEGETABLES

Cruciferous vegetables such as cabbage, broccoli, cauliflower, and brussels sprouts are rich in the cancer-fighting chemical, sulforaphane. Researchers at Johns Hopkins

University and the National Cancer Institute have found that sulforaphane appears to protect against some forms of cancer, particularly of the colon, stomach, and rectum.

Broccoli, because it is a dark green vegetable, is also an excellent source of beta carotene. A good source of fiber, this tasty vegetable also contains a considerable amount of vitamin C, potassium, folic acid, calcium, and selenium. In addition to sulforaphane, snowy white cauliflower is also high in B vitamins, vitamin C, and fiber and is a source of essential minerals like calcium, potassium, and phosphorus. Brussels sprouts look like tiny cabbages and, as the name implies, are native to Belgium. They contain the most fiber of all vegetables—7 1/2 grams per cup. Rich in antioxidants, they are every bit as high in vitamin C as citrus fruits and are a source of vitamin E and beta carotene.

The Soyfoods Pantry

Which country produces the largest crop of soybeans in the world? Is it one of the Asian countries, which are well known for their use of soybeans? After all, the Chinese have been using soybeans in a myriad of foods that have sustained them in robust health for over 5,000 years. And in Japan, tofu and miso are an integral part of the daily diet. Asia might well be a logical answer, given the history of the soybean; however, if you chose anywhere in Asia, you are mistaken. The United States is by far the largest producer of soybeans in the world; 29 states grow soybeans on more than 62 million acres of soil.

How do Americans treat this nutritional treasure growing in their own backyard? They use soybeans as the basis of cattle and hog feed. Animals destined for the slaughterhouse actually enjoy a healthier diet than people in this country. Despite the American penchant for traditional meat-based diets and a generally cavalier attitude toward those concerned with achieving sound health through a wholesome diet, consumer interest in the many new healthy food products made from soybeans is quite high. Soy is truly the magic bean, with the ability to play a part in any course, any meal, any time of the day!

The following is a summary of the variety of soyfoods that play important roles in many of the delightful recipes in this collection. Use this book as your guide. In no time you will count these versatile soyfoods among the essentials on your shopping list. No need to change your diet! Clever use of ingredients like creamy lite silken tofu, hearty tempeh, and the many ingenious soy-based meat analogues will allow you to recreate your favorite dishes with a much healthier bottom line. Bon appétit!

Baked Tofu—A delicious form of precooked and ready-to-eat tofu that can be sliced and added to salads and sandwiches right from the package. Available in three varieties from The Soy Deli: Savory Baked Tofu, Five-Spice Baked Tofu, and Hickory Smoked Tofu, each having a flavor reminiscent of smoked meat or roast duck. Tree of Life also makes a baked and savory baked tofu. These versatile ingredients are quick, high-protein additions to stir-fry and baked dishes and are available at health food stores nationwide.

Barley Miso, Country Barley Miso—Reddish brown in color, with a chunky texture and rich flavor. This flavor of miso is strongly preferred by the American macrobiotic community. Mellow barley miso is similar in color to mellow white miso, but not as creamy.

Bragg Liquid Aminos—A mineral-rich liquid seasoning derived from soybeans. Though not fermented, this tasty flavoring is used in the same way as soy sauce, and it contains many of the essential amino acids. Available in health food stores nationwide from Live Food Products.

Dressings made with soy—There are some terrific salad dressings on the market that are made using tofu, miso, or shoyu. My favorites are sold under the brand names Nasoya and Simply Delicious. They are available in health food stores nationwide.

Firm Nigari Tofu—A very firmly pressed tofu with a dense texture that is somewhat lower in fat (3 grams per 4 ounces) and vacuum-packed. Vacuum-packed tofu will keep unopened in the refrigerator for up to 2 months. Once opened it should be used in a few days. Made from organic soybeans and sold under The Soy Deli brand name, this tofu has a subtle sweetness and handles well because of its firm texture.

Gimme Lean—This wholesome meat alternative is available in sausage and ground beef style, and sold in the refrigerator or freezer section of most health food and specialty stores. This easy-to-use product is exceedingly authentic in flavor, texture, and appearance, and holds together well when making patties or "meat" balls. Made by Lightlife Company, with a combination of textured soy protein and wheat gluten.

Green Vegetable Soybeans, in the pod (Edamamé)—These green or immature soybeans are harvested at about 80 percent maturity. They are available, usually frozen, in health food stores, Asian markets, and some supermarkets. They are quite flavorful, with none of the stronger "beany" taste associated with mature beans, and they make a nutritious snack or a delicious addition to an appetizer buffet.

Hatcho Miso—This richly flavored miso is a dark cocoa brown with slight overtones of chocolate. Hatcho means "eighth street" and takes its name from this location in Okazaki, Japan (near Nagoya).

Lean Links Italian—This is a low-fat vegetarian sausage link product from Lightlife that duplicates the taste and texture of Italian sausage. Available at health food stores and specialty stores nationwide.

Lite Silken Tofu—A very low-fat tofu (1 gram of fat per 3 ounces), lite silken tofu has a rich-tasting, smooth texture and a custard-like consistency. It is widely available in aseptic packages in supermarkets and health food stores nationwide as Mori Nu Silken Tofu Lite. Because of its award-winning packaging, this is the only tofu that can be eaten right from the box. It is a time-saving ingredient for dips, spreads, and dressings, because it does not need to be precooked. Its creamy versatility makes it an excellent substitute for eggs and dairy products in baked goods and cream sauces.

As this book neared completion, Mori Nu announced it was changing the package size of lite silken tofu. For this reason, recipes were rewritten to reflect volume rather than weight. The original package size (10.5 ounces) equals 1 1/4 cups of lite silken tofu; half the original package size equals 1/2 cup plus 2 tablespoons.

$\bullet$ *19* $\bullet$

Mellow White Miso—Pale beige color with a subtle, sweet fragrance, this highly versatile miso has a rich, creamy texture. This rich-tasting miso has many applications in soy-centered cuisine.

Miso—This savory, fermented soybean paste has a consistency somewhat like peanut butter, and may be aged for several years. A mainstay of Japanese cuisine for centuries, miso is a living natural food, rich in enzymes and beneficial bacteria. Miso is easily digested and highly nutritious, and adds depth of flavor to soups, sauces, marinades, dips, salad dressings, and main dishes. Available in health food stores and Japanese markets, miso should be kept refrigerated.

Nayonaise—The brand name for the tofu-based mayonnaise I always use in place of traditionally prepared mayonnaise. Made by Nasoya, this tasty, wholesome alternative contains no eggs and therefore no cholesterol, and is also much lower in fat.

Ready Ground Tofu—This ready-to-use meat analogue can be used in many dishes or added to a colorful vegetable mélange for texture. Its loose consistency makes it perfect for sloppy joes, tacos, pot pies, etc. However, it does not hold together for patties or "meat ball" type applications. Made by Tree of Life, it is available in three styles (original, hot and spicy, and savory garlic) at health food stores nationwide.

Shoyu—A naturally brewed, high-quality soy sauce. Processed in the traditional Japanese method, it is aged 2 to 3 years without coloring, additives, or preservatives. Shoyu is true soy sauce and is available in Asian markets and health food stores.

Smoked Tofu—Smokehouse-style tofu that has the texture and flavor of smoked cheese. This exciting product can be used as a spread or sliced and tossed into a salad. It's available from at least two manufacturers, each in two styles: Tree of Life makes hot and spicy, and original, and Wildwood Natural Foods makes garlic teriyaki and mild Szechuan. All are delicious and available at health food stores.

Soy Boy Ravioli—Prepared, frozen ravioli stuffed with tasty fillings, all made with organic tofu. These low-fat products are available in three flavors: ravioli (plain pasta with a ricotta-like filling), ravioli rosa (tomato pasta with roasted pepper filling), and ravioli verde (spinach pasta with garden herb filling). These products are made by Northern Soy, Inc. and can be found in health food stores.

Soy Flour—A finely ground flour made from soybeans that is very high in protein (35 percent—twice that of wheat flour) and low in carbohydrates. Generally mixed with other flours, especially in baking, as it contains no gluten. Soy flour may also be used to bind sauces and replace eggs in baked goods. Soy flour is available in 1 1/2 pound packages from Arrowhead Mills, in health food stores across the country.

Soy Grits—Whole soybeans, lightly toasted then cracked into small pieces. They are great for boosting nutrition while adding texture and consistency to baked goods. I have added soy grits to bread crumbs when breading or making a crusty gratin. Cooked soy grits can be used in many recipes in place of whole cooked soybeans. They cook a good deal faster than whole beans (less than 15 minutes without presoaking) and are somewhat lower in fat than whole soybeans. Soy grits are to be added to recipes uncooked, unless otherwise specified. (Fearn Soya Granules are soy grits and are available in health food stores nationwide.)

Soy Sauce—A generic term for the dark salty sauce made by fermenting boiled soybeans and roasted wheat or barley. Most soy sauce sold in the United States is artificially colored and processed from defatted soybean meal and wheat mixed with chemicals.

Soybeans, whole—This delicious legume is available as a dry bean, which needs to be presoaked and cooked for 3 hours. Once precooked, soybeans are a delicious ingredient ready to be used in many recipes. Arrowhead Mills organic soybeans are sold in 1-pound packages in health food stores nationwide.

Soymilk—A nondairy product made by pressing ground, cooked soybeans. Higher in protein than cow's milk, soymilk is cholesterol free and low in fat and sodium. It can replace cow's milk in any recipe.

Soymilk Lite—An organic, 1 percent fat soymilk that is sold under the name Westsoy Lite Nondairy Soy Beverage and made by Westbrae Natural Foods. Widely available in supermarkets and health food stores across the country, this is the soymilk of choice in my kitchen. Aseptically packaged, this soy beverage has a long shelf life and needn't be refrigerated until opened. It has a clean, wholesome taste—not "beany" like some soymilks—and is a versatile ingredient in baked goods and cream sauces.

Soynuts—These roasted, crunchy snacks are similar to peanuts and can be found in many grocery stores. See page 60 for a quick and easy way to make homemade soynuts that are fresher and tastier than the store-bought variety.

Tamari—A natural soy sauce made only with soybeans. Tamari is similar to shoyu. Its mellow flavor is slightly stronger than shoyu. You will find tamari in health food stores and Asian markets. Imported tamari is far superior to the domestic variety and is well worth the higher price, as its darker, richer flavor will go farther. For this reason I prefer the imported variety, which I have used in formulating these recipes. Tree of Life tamari is made with organic soybeans and is found in health stores nationwide.

Tempeh—Fermented from whole soybeans, tempeh is an easily digestible, live cultured food. It has a chewy texture and a distinctive nutty flavor, contains more protein than tofu, and is the best known source of vitamin B12 for vegans (strict vegetarians). Because tempeh is made from the whole bean, it is richer in flavor and nutrients than tofu. Tempeh can be found in the refrigerator or freezer section of health food stores as tempeh burgers or as the cultured soyfood ingredient used in many recipes in this collection. Tempeh is available under the brand names, Pacific Tempeh, Lightlife, and Soy Power, among others.

Textured Vegetable Protein (TVP)—TVP is made from defatted soy flour. Once rehydrated, TVP is a very credible low-fat meat substitute and an excellent soyfood to introduce your family to the goodness of soy. It is trademarked by the Archer Daniels Midland Corp., and available in ground beef, chicken chunk, or steak strip styles, among others. (The recipes in this collection use only the unflavored variety.) Because dry TVP has such a low fat content, it has a long shelf life. A wide selection of this extremely economical, high-protein food source is available through the Harvest Direct Catalog or The Mail Order Catalog (see Resource Guide, page 245). TVP is sold in health food stores, generally in the flavored ground beef style.

Tofu—Soybean curd made from coagulating soy milk with nigari (seaweed) or calcium chloride in much the same way cheese is made from milk. High in protein, low in saturated fats, and cholesterol free, tofu's blandness and ability to absorb flavors make it a very versatile ingredient.

Tofu Mayonnaise—(see Nayonaise)

Tofu Wieners—A wholesome alternative to traditional hot dogs, these are very authentic in taste and appearance. Available in health food stores nationwide, they are sold under the brand names, Yves Veggie Wieners, Not Dogs by Northern Soy, and Smart Dogs, made by Lightlife.

Yves Veggie Canadian Bacon—This is a very authentic meat analogue; very close to Canadian bacon or ham in appearance and taste. It is made with soy protein and wheat gluten and can be enjoyed right out of the package. Used in sandwiches and salads, it is also a delicious ingredient in stir-fry and baked dishes, adding protein and carbohydrates, but very little fat.

Yves Veggie Pepperoni—Another authentic meat analog from Yves, it's terrific in sandwiches and colorful salads. Yves also makes a vegetarian deli slices (bologna).

A Quick Guide to Ingredients

The ingredients in *Soy of Cooking* are easy to use and generally available in health food stores and supermarkets. However, some ingredients may be unfamiliar to some cooks. Here is a brief description of those ingredients. For more information, including manufacturers of soyfoods and other products, check the Resource Guide (page 245).

Agar Flakes (Kanten or Agar Agar)—This vegetable gel, derived from seaweed, is colorless, odorless, tasteless, and calorie free. It has been used for over 1,000 years. Agar is also available as bars; however, recipes in this collection use agar flakes.

Applesauce—In recipes that call for applesauce as a fat replacer, you should use unsweetened applesauce. It is widely available in supermarkets and health food stores.

Arrowroot—This powder can replace tapioca flour or cornstarch where a thickening paste is required.

Baking Powder—Nonaluminum, double-acting baking powder is available nationwide at health food stores and many supermarkets. Rumford, Featherweight, and Cellu baking powder are all nonaluminum.

Balsamic Vinegar—Slightly sweet and fragrant with a distinctive depth of flavor, genuine balsamic vinegar is aged at least 6 years and produced in the Modena area of Italy.

Basmati Rice—An aromatic, long-grain rice, scented with a faint nutlike flavor and aroma. Many cooks consider this high-quality rice to be the world's finest. The recipes here calling for basmati rice use white basmati. It is also available in brown basmati rice varieties, which take longer to cook. Check package for cooking directions.

Couscous—Found in Middle Eastern cuisine, these tiny grains of pasta are made from milled wheat. Sold in this country presteamed, couscous needs only to be added to boiling water or broth, stirred, removed from heat, and set aside for 5 minutes to absorb the liquid.

Date Pieces (sometimes called Date Nuggets)—These are chopped dates that are rolled in oat flour rather than sugar. They are available in health food stores and specialty stores.

Egg Replacer Powder—EnerG Egg Replacer is a dry product made from tapioca starch and leavenings. A most effective ingredient in baked goods, it is sold in health food stores, and is also available through the EnerG catalog (see Resource Guide). Recipes in this collection that use egg replacer were created with this product.

Florida Crystals—This is an unbleached and minimally processed sugar, which is light in color and finely granulated. It can be substituted on a 1:1 basis for refined white sugar.

Fruitsource—A wholesome sweetener made from grapes and grains. Though available at natural food stores in both liquid and granulated forms, I have used only the liquid Fruitsource for the recipes found in *Soy of Cooking*. Fruitsource also acts as a fat replacer in baked goods, because it is a source of pectins. Fruitsource is widely used in commercial baking under the name Fruitrim.

Garbanzo Beans—I have used low-sodium garbanzo beans, available from Eden Foods, in these recipes with great results. They are flavored with kombu and contain no added salt. Available at health food stores and some supermarkets nationwide.

Gingerroot—A knobby root with an aromatic, spicy ginger flavor. Fresh gingerroot is peeled and grated before adding to the recipes in this collection. Gingerroot is found in supermarkets and grocery stores across the country.

Granulated Garlic—Textured into grains like sugar, this form of garlic is far superior to garlic powder in flavor and aroma. Available at health food stores.

Jasmine Rice—Distinctly fragrant rice that is at the center of Thai cuisine.

Kombu—A dark green deep-sea vegetable harvested in cold northern waters. Kombu is used to tenderize dry beans and tempeh as they cook and as a flavor enhancer in soup stocks.

Mashed Potato Flakes—I use Barbara's Mashed Potatoes, made from whole, unpeeled Idaho potatoes and distributed by Barbara's Bakery.

Mirin—Lower in alcohol than Japanese saké, mirin is a sweet, rice wine that tenderizes and enhances sautées.

Nutmeats—A number of my recipes, particularly baked goods, use nuts for added crunch and flavor. Nuts are a good source of protein (almonds have 30 grams of protein per cup), but are also high in fat. I have found that 1/3 cup of nuts will add just the right crunch and impart plenty of flavor. Plus, my recipes are so low in fat, you can afford a bit of "nutty indulgence."

•25•

Nutritional Yeast—Available in health food stores, these delicious flakes are very high in protein and B vitamins. Not to be confused with brewer's yeast, which has a characteristically bitter taste, nutritional yeast adds a rich, cheese-like flavor and creaminess. It is also an effective thickening agent in dairy-free cream sauces and soups.

Oat Bran—A fiber rich bran derived from oats that adds a distinctive hearty flavor to baked goods. Available at health food and specialty stores.

Oil Cooking Spray—A pump action, nonaerosol canola oil product used to oil baking pans or wherever reduced fat is desired, such as sautées. Pam and Wesson make pump-action oil sprays, which are available in supermarkets and health food stores nationwide.

Onion Soup Mix—I always use Mayacamas brand, which is made with natural ingredients (including soy protein) and contains no preservatives. It is available nationwide at health food stores and supermarkets.

Orange Blossom Water—The distilled essence of orange blossoms used to perfume sweets in eastern Mediterranean cuisine. It is used sparingly, and will fill your home with its fragrance.

Orzo—A light and delicious rice shaped pasta that is perfect in soups or as an innovative ingredient for the creative cook. Widely available.

Phyllo Pastry—These paper-thin leaves of dough are available in the freezer section of most supermarkets.

Prune Purée—Puréed prunes are a very effective fat replacer in baked goods. Prepared prune purée is available in supermarkets across the country and can be found with the Kosher foods or in the baking aisle. Brand names include Solo, Lekvar, Baker, and Sokol. See Techniques for a simple recipe for homemade prune purée.

Rose Water—The distilled essence of rose petals, used to perfume sweets in eastern Mediterranean cuisine. Like orange blossom water, it is used sparingly, and will fill your home with its fragrance. Folklore says the soothing flavor of rose water will put you in a happy mood.

Sea Salt—Salt derived from evaporated sea water, which retains some natural trace minerals and contains no additives.

Semolina Flour—Semolina is a coarse-textured flour ground from durum wheat. Pastas made with semolina flour are higher in protein and have a firm texture. I use Semolina Flour Mix by Arrowhead Mills, a blend of organic semolina flour and organic kamut flour, to make all my pastas.

Shallots—Used extensively in French cuisine, this mild member of the onion family combines the flavor of onion and garlic.

Shiitake Mushrooms—Available both fresh and dried, these distinctive mushrooms are used in stir-fries, soups, and salads.

Soba Noodles—Sold in health food stores, specialty stores, and Asian markets, this dried pasta is traditionally made from buckwheat.

Sucanat—A granulated form of unrefined cane sugar; made from cane juice. Sugar in this form is a whole food and therefore retains all of the vitamins and minerals found in nature. Sucanat is stirred into the dry ingredients when making baked goods, because it does not emulsify with creamed ingredients. It imparts many of the same characteristics as brown sugar (which can be substituted for Sucanat on a one to one basis), and is found in health food stores nationwide.

Sun-Dried Tomatoes—Ripe tomato halves that have been oven dried, giving them a uniquely intense flavor. I use only the dry variety, which is reconstituted in boiling water, never those that have been packed in oil. Organic sun-dried tomatoes are available in the Sonoma brand.

◆*27*◆

Sunspire Chocolate Chips—Real chocolate chips that are wholesome and dairy free. They have several varieties, but my favorites are the new Organic Dark Chocolate Chips. These chips are knock-your-socks-off delicious! They are sold in health food stores nationwide.

Tapioca Flour—This flour made from tapioca is an effective thickening agent. It may be substituted for arrowroot.

Veganrella—This vegetarian cream cheese is made from Brazil nuts and imparts texture to chilled dishes. It's available in plain and flavored varieties. I have used only the plain Veganrella in the recipes included here.

Vegetable Broth—Beef- or chicken-flavored vegetarian broth powder is used to reconstitute unflavored TVP. These products are available in some health food stores and through the Harvest Direct and The Mail Order catalogs.

Wheat Gluten—The natural protein derived from wheat and used in bread baking to enhance the rise and flavor, improve the shape, and extend freshness. It is widely used by the baking industry to produce consistent, uniform breads.

White Wheat Flour—A new variety of whole grain flour, produced from hard white wheat. It combines all the fiber of traditional whole wheat and the sweeter, milder taste and baking performance of unbleached flour. White wheat flour is available from King Arthur's Flour Baker's Catalog; organic white wheat flour is available from Arrowhead Mills in healthfood stores nationwide.

Whole Wheat Pastry Flour—The best whole grain flour to use in cakes and quickbreads, this finely milled flour is made from soft wheat. It has a low gluten content and is not used in yeast breads. Organic whole wheat pastry flour is available from Arrowhead Mills in health food stores and some supermarkets.

Wonderslim Cocoa—This is real cocoa, and lower in fat than low-fat regular cocoa. Even better, it is caffeine-free, with the caffeine extracted using a natural process. This cocoa is available in supermarkets and health food stores nationwide. You may use this cocoa in any recipe that calls for cocoa.

Substitutions

Throughout this book, I have indicated some substitute ingredients for those that might be unfamiliar. For instance, brown sugar may be substituted for Sucanat, sugar may replace Florida Crystals, and honey may replace liquid Fruitsource.

Other acceptable substitutions on a one to one basis include dry sherry for mirin; beaten egg whites for EnerG egg replacer powder and water; low-fat cream cheese for Veganrella; and chopped dates instead of date pieces.

To substitute egg whites for egg replacer, use 1/4 cup of beaten egg whites in place of 1 tablespoon of egg replacer powder and 1/4 cup of water. You may also replace any nutmeats listed in a recipe with another you may have on hand. For instance, pecans might replace cashews or walnuts in a quick bread or muffins with tasty results. When substituting honey for liquid Fruitsource, a one to one ratio is a good rule of thumb. However, honey may vary in taste and texture, and honey does not contain the pectins that are present in Fruitsource. Be aware of these variances when substituting honey for the preferred listed ingredient.

These substitutions are offered to make *Soy of Cooking* as user-friendly as possible. However, the nutrition analyses are calculated according to the original ingredient listed, not the substitute ingredient. The original ingredient is the ingredient of choice and the one I recommend for the delectable dishes in this collection. I encourage you to use the suggested ingredients when making these recipes. I do not endorse the use of eggs, refined sugar, or honey. These substitutions are offered solely for your convenience.

◆*30*◆

Spices:
The Variety of
Kitchen Life

Spices have long been added to food for flavor and variety. In the past decade, herb and spice consumption has been on the rise. The popularity of ethnic foods and the interest in lowering the fat in our diets has encouraged some of us to try new and unusual herbs and spices. Herbs and spices can be used artfully to boost the flavor of a dish and substantially reduce the amount of fat at the same time. The flavor and aroma of fragrant herbs and spices reduces the need for fat and salt in cooking. Anyone who appreciates fine food, well presented, knows that the clever use of herbs and spices adds depth and dimension to even the most basic assemblage of ingredients.

There are no strict rules governing the use of herbs and spices in cooking—the best route is to experiment. Learning to recognize the particular flavors, aromas, and attributes that distinguish each herb and spice is necessary in order to appreciate the qualities they contribute to a dish. Gourmet cooks know that spice is the variety of kitchen life and the clever use of herbs and spices will make your efforts more appetizing, appealing, and digestible.

Using spices and herbs with confidence is the key to developing interesting menus and enlivening simple fare. Confidence comes from familiarity, and the best way to get to know any spice or herb is by cooking with it. The challenge is that many of us become accustomed to using several herbs and spices with which we are familiar, and we avoid others. We rely on tried and true favorites or blends rather than risk trying something new.

Fresh herbs are a wonderful addition to any dish, and most supermarkets stock the more common herbs like parsley, cilantro, basil, oregano, mint, dillweed, and chives. Specialty markets and ethnic grocers can supply the adventurous cook with more exotic varieties. When using fresh herbs, you will find that they are milder than the dried variety and you can safely substitute three to five times times the amount of dried herb (depending on the strength of the herb) called for in the recipe.

GUIDE TO SPICES AND HERBS

The term "spice" refers to all aromatic plants used to season foods. However, herbs are the leaves of low-growing, non-woody plants or shrubs; spices are generally derived from the bark, root, fruit, or berries of perennial plants and trees. Both spices and herbs may produce aromatic seeds.

Allspice—Pungent spice of a reddish-brown berry found in Central America and the West Indies. Used in pumpkin dishes, spice cakes, applesauce, chutney, and fruits, it has the flavor of cinnamon, nutmeg, and cloves.

Anise—Small, oval shaped, grayish-brown aromatic seed grown in Spain and Mexico. Used in stews, cakes, fruit pies, sweet rolls, Italian coffee, and liquors.

◆ *32* ◆

Basil (Sweet Basil)—A powerful herb with a rich and pungent flavor, heady aroma, and an adaptable taste. Indispensable in Italian and Mediterranean cookery, it is native to the Near East and is used in cuisines around the world.

Bay Leaf—Native to the Mediterranean, there are several varieties sold as bay or bay laurel. Ninety percent of all bay leaves sold in this country are of Mediterranean origin because of its smoother, full flavor. Used in sauces, soups, stews, and pickling spices.

Bouquet Garni—Several herbs tied together in a small cheesecloth bag so the herbs can be easily removed. Parsley, thyme, and bay leaf are the basics, but basil, rosemary, chervil, tarragon, or celery leaves can also be included.

Capers—The bud of a bush that grows wild in the Mediterranean, pickled and preserved in brine, vinegar, or salt. It has a sharp, pungent flavor and is used with tomatoes, sauces, gravies, and eggplant dishes.

Caraway—Small, brown, crescent-shaped seed with a mild licorice taste, found in central Europe. Used in rye breads, cabbage and turnip dishes, soups, stews, and pickling spices.

Cardamom—Native to India, and also found in Guatemala and Sri Lanka, cardamom is a perennial of the ginger family. It produces green seedpods that are harvested by hand. Pungent and aromatic, it is a bit like mild ginger with an interesting flowery sweetness. Used extensively in India, it is found in sweets and curry dishes. It is also popular in Scandinavia, where it is used in breads, baked goods, and sweet potatoes.

Cayenne—Dried and ground from the tropical capsicum plant native to Latin American countries. Once processed, a dash of this bright scarlet, very hot chile will bring out the natural flavor in many Mexican, Indian, Latin American, and Cajun dishes.

Celery Seed—Small, light brown aromatic seed with the flavor of celery, found in India and southern France. Actually a member of the parsley family, celery seed is used in stuffing, salad dressings, coleslaw, pickles, soups, and potato dishes.

Chervil—Bright green feathery leaves, resembling parsley, but with a subtle slightly licorice flavor. Used more extensively in France, it is considered a blending herb.

Chili Powder—A ground blend based on a combination of spices and herbs typically including: chili peppers, cumin, coriander, garlic, cloves, paprika, oregano, turmeric, and black pepper.

Chive—A delicate onion-flavored herb with long green tubular leaves, that is available fresh, minced, dried, or frozen. Can be used with baked potatoes, and in dips, soups, salads, and dressings.

Cilantro—Pungent and peppery aroma and flavor, with round, delicately fringed leaves. Sometimes called fresh coriander or Chinese parsley, it adds a sharp, distinctive flavor and is essential to many Mexican, Oriental, and Mediterranean dishes.

Cinnamon—Produced in southern China, Sumatra, Sri Lanka, and Indochina, cinnamon is at the same time sweet and mildly hot. Found in eastern Mediterranean, Indian, and Mexican dishes, and used extensively in baked goods and beverages, it is widely available in powdered and rolled bark (cinnamon sticks).

Clove—The dried, unopened buds of a tropical evergreen native to Indonesia, clove has a strong, sweet, and pungent flavor. Available in whole and ground form, it is widely used in cakes, cookies, custards, pickled fruits, and hot cider.

Coriander—Aromatic seed with a warm, slightly musty taste, somewhat like sage, and a lemon-like undertone. Native to Yugoslavia and French Morocco, coriander is available whole or ground. It's used extensively in Indian cuisine to flavor vegetable dishes or in preparing curry powder.

Crushed Red Pepper—Sometimes referred to as red pepper flakes, it has a hot, strong flavor. It is quite useful in seasoning the oil at the outset of sautéeing, and its heat diminishes somewhat during cooking. These spicy flakes are used sparingly.

◆ 34 ◆

Cumin—Strongly aromatic and reminiscent of caraway with a very agreeable flavor, this yellowish-brown seed is ridged and slightly curved. Found in French Morocco and Iran, cumin is available whole or ground. Cumin is an essential ingredient in chili powder and most curries, adding a warm, heady, and robust flavor to many dishes.

Curry Powder—A prepared blend of six or more of the following spices: turmeric, cumin, coriander, ginger, cloves, pepper, fenugreek, mustard, and cardamom.

Dill—Found in California, the seeds are small and tan, and the leaves are feathery light green with a tangy flavor resembling caraway. Used in breads, salads, sauces, and pickling spices.

Fennel—Native to India and Rumania and available as chartreuse seeds or fresh as short, rounded, celery-like bulbs. Having a pronounced licorice flavor that diminishes somewhat as it cooks, fennel is used in casseroles, sweet pickles, and Italian breads and rolls.

Fenugreek—Native to Asia, fenugreek is available as a smooth, red, aromatic seed or in the ground form. It's used in chutneys and curry powders.

Ginger—Contributing a clean, hot, spicy-sweet flavor and a pungent aroma, fresh gingerroot is cultivated extensively in most semitropical regions. Native to Southeast Asia, Jamaican ginger is considered to be of the highest quality. Peel back the skin before grating. It is also available in the more familiar ground form.

Mace—Found in the Moluccas Islands of Indonesia, mace is processed from the fibrous covering of the nutmeg shell. Mace has a flavor similar to nutmeg but it's somewhat milder. It's used in cherry pies, pumpkin breads, pound cakes, and puddings.

Marjoram—Found in France and Portugal, marjoram is actually a member of the mint family. It has a musky flavor, similar to oregano. Available fresh or dried, and it is used in tomato dishes, with green vegetables, in salads, stuffings, and casseroles.

Mint—Found in Belgium, France, and Germany, this herb has emerald green leaves and a warm, menthol flavor. It's available fresh, dried, and as an extract. Mint is used in desserts, cold beverages, hot teas, and jellies, and with chilled fruits.

•*35*•

Mustard—Available as whole seeds or ground, mustard has a tangy, biting quality. The seeds can be white, brown, or black. Black mustard seeds are commonly used in Indian cooking. Sautéed in hot oil until they pop, they add a pungent quality to vegetable, rice, and legume dishes.

Nutmeg—Grown in hot, moist regions of the tropics, like Malaysia and Java. Nutmeg is the oval shaped, dried seed of an apricot-like fruit of an evergreen tree that bears for more than 50 years. Available in whole or ground form, the spicy-sweet flavor is best when using freshly grated nutmeg. Used in desserts, quick breads, cakes, vegetable dishes, and some cream sauces.

Oregano—Stronger and heavier in aroma and flavor than marjoram, this herb adds zip to pizza, pastas, tomato dishes, and vegetables. Another strain of this popular herb is Mexican oregano, an essential ingredient in chili powder.

Paprika—Native to Central America but grown commercially in California, paprika is the dried, stemless pod of a sweet red pepper. Most of the paprika used in the United States is mild and slightly sweet and used as a garnish. Hungarian paprika is more pungent and lighter in color.

Parsley—The curly leaf variety is grown chiefly in California and is the main source of dehydrated parsley flakes. Either fresh or dried, it is used generously to flavor and garnish most foods, sweets being the exception. It has a pleasant mild odor and an agreeable taste. Flat leaf parsley, sometimes called Italian parsley, has a stronger flavor.

Rosemary—A delightfully sweet, fragrant herb, its spiky leaves resemble miniature pine needles. Used in breads (Rosemary Foccacia is one example), or sprinkled on boiled potatoes or green beans, this herb imparts a distinctive flavor and aroma.

Saffron—Widely used in French, Spanish, and Indian dishes, saffron is native to the Mediterranean, primarily imported from Spain. This pleasantly bitter spice is the most expensive spice in the world. It is the whole dried stigma of the saffron crocus. It requires 75,000 blossoms or 225,000 stigmas to make one pound of saffron. It is orange-yellow and used for color as much as flavor. It is used sparingly—a pinch or two will go a long way.

Sage—Native to Albania and the Balkans, sage is available as silver tipped, grayish green leaves or in the ground form. Sage has a slightly bitter and strongly astringent flavor and is used in stuffings, baked dishes, dressings, and stews.

Sesame Seed—The dried hulled fruit of a tropical plant, sesame seed is the source of a cooking oil used widely in the East. This smooth, creamy-white oval-shaped seed is one of the most versatile of the seeds. Its rich, nut-like flavor enhances breads, cookies, noodles, vegetables, salads, and more. When ground into a paste, it is called tahini, which is widely used in Middle Eastern cuisine.

Tamarind—Used in Southeast Asia, India, the Middle East, and Latin America, this flavoring adds a tasty prunelike sourness to curries, chutneys, pickles, and hot and sour soups. It's available in ethnic groceries. You may substitute lemon juice.

Tarragon—A distinctive herb with uniquely sharp, spicy, and aromatic flavor, with undertones of licorice and mint. The word tarragon comes from the French word for little dragon, and the herb grown for culinary use is of the French variety. It's available dried and ground.

Thyme—A strong flavored herb with a heavy, spicy aroma and a pungent clove-like taste. This versatile herb blends well with other herbs, and is found in bouquet garni.

Turmeric—Turmeric is the root of a tropical plant of the ginger family. Used extensively in Indian cooking, turmeric is best known as an ingredient in curry powder, and is available in ground form in supermarkets and Indian groceries. It has a musky, slightly bitter taste. Like saffron, a little turmeric adds a rich golden color to cooked dishes or baked goods.

Vanilla Bean—Long, dark, slender seed pods with a pleasant sweet flavor. Available as whole beans or as an extract, it is used extensively in sweet dishes, baked goods, puddings, and chilled and frozen confections.

◆*38*◆

Techniques

Here are some useful directions for preparing various ingredients and foods used in *Soy of Cooking*.

BAKING WITHOUT ADDED FAT

I use no added fat in my baked goods. For the most part, I make use of the pectins and sorbitols that are naturally present in fruits. Unsweetened applesauce and prune purée are most effective in replacing the fat in my baked desserts, breads, and muffins. Miso can also be used in essentially the same way to replace fat in yeast breads and savory dishes. A mildly-flavored miso is best in this application; I generally use mellow white miso, as it has a rich natural flavor and a subtle, sweet fragrance. I also use liquid Fruitsource to replace both fat and honey. These ingredients and innovative techniques help to slash fat and calories dramatically.

BLANCHING TOFU

To blanch tofu, drop cakes or cubes into boiling water, and simmer 5 minutes. This will help keep tofu firm and more absorbent. It also keeps it from diluting what it is added to. Placing tofu in the microwave for 2 to 3 minutes after it is cut or mashed into the desired shape will achieve the same, if not better, results.

CHESTNUTS

To blanch: Place chestnuts in boiling water for 2 minutes. Remove a few chestnuts at a time, allow them to cool slightly, and use a paring knife to peel the shell from the nutmeat. If some shells are particularly difficult to remove, boil an additional 2 minutes.

To roast: Preheat oven to 400°. With a sharp knife, cut an "X" through the shell on the flat side of the chestnuts. Spread the chestnuts, cut side up, on a baking sheet. Roast chestnuts until tender, about 20 minutes. Test tenderness with a fork.

DRIED BEANS

Dried beans are of all varieties need to be rehydrated before use. They should be rinsed thoroughly and sorted. Lentils and split peas don't need to be presoaked, but other types of dried beans should be soaked with one of two equally effective methods. The preferred method is to soak the beans overnight. In the case of soybeans, place the bowl in the refrigerator so the beans will not ferment. The second method is to bring the rinsed and sorted beans to a boil, remove from heat, and let stand for an hour, then proceed with cooking. Most dried beans will cook in 1 1/2 to 2 1/2 hours; soybeans and chickpeas require more time. Never salt the beans or add acidics like tomatoes or vinegar during the precooking process, as this will prolong the cooking time.

It is a good idea to discard the soaking water and cook the beans in fresh water for the first 30 minutes, then discard this water and continue the cooking process with fresh water. This will address the digestive problems some associate with consumption of beans. It is also true that as you start to eat beans more often, these digestive problems tend to disappear. A University of California-Berkeley study reported participants had greater tolerance after three weeks of eating beans regularly. It seems that the more often you eat beans, the better the chances of developing the enzymes needed to handle it.

FROZEN TOFU

Freezing tofu can produce excellent results, yielding a "meatier," chewy, coarse textured ingredient, like that of cooked chicken or veal. Freezing will radically change the structure and basic character, as frozen tofu is highly concentrated and readily absorbs flavors, sauces, and marinades much like a sponge.

For frozen tofu, I use firm or extra firm tofu; *regular* silken tofu is not recommended because it tends to disintegrate into a mushy substance. Each recipe specifies the type of tofu best suited for that recipe; however, vacuum-packed nigari tofu and extra firm *lite* silken tofu are generally indicated.

When freezing tofu, remove it from its original packaging and drain slightly, then pat with a paper towel. It's generally best to slice the tofu into cutlets or cubes at this stage to hasten thawing. Wrap the cutlets, cubes, or blocks individually in plastic wrap and place packages in a plastic bag, pressing out the air. I like to use the zipper type, because of their heavier weight. During freezing the color will change from creamy white to yellow and resemble a block of cheese. The longer tofu is frozen the better the texture, so you will want to freeze it for at least a week or two; you can safely freeze tofu for more than six months.

In tofu, water makes up about 85 percent of the weight, and freezing tofu turns the water into ice crystals. When the ice thaws, it leaves a firm network of concentrated protein and solids. I prefer to defrost tofu in the microwave, especially when it has been precut in the cutlets or cubes. Just place the frozen tofu in a bowl, cover, and microwave it, checking it every 2 or 3 minutes, so that it does not cook. Tofu can also be thawed by pouring several quarts of boiling water over the blocks set in a pan. Thawing takes about 15 minutes this way and can be hastened by slicing the block into smaller pieces when partially thawed. I generally replenish the hot water halfway through, which also quickens the process. Frozen tofu can also be thawed in the refrigerator for several hours or overnight.

Some recipes call for shredded tofu after it has been defrosted. Before freezing, the block of tofu should be cut thirds or pieces 1-inch wide. Then, after thawing, squeeze out as much water as possible by gently pressing it between your palms. Gently run the times of a fork through the tofu to produce the desired shape.

Once as much water as possible has been squeezed out, you will have a super absorbent form of tofu. It is in this sponge-like state that tofu fully absorbs flavorful sauces and marinades. At this stage, slice the tofu to the desired size and place it in a bowl that will allow the pieces to be submerged in the marinade. Set it aside for as little as 15 minutes, several hours, or overnight (as indicated in each recipe) and turn occasionally.

LEEKS

Leeks can be very gritty. They often retain sand between their many tight layers, especially where the white bulb joins the tender green shaft. Thorough cleaning is essential in order to avoid unpleasant residue. First, cut off and discard the roots and tough green top. Then, without cutting all the way through, slice the leek in half lengthwise. Fan the layers open, but do not pull the leek apart. Rinse the leek thoroughly under running cold water. Finally, soak the rinsed leeks in a large bowl of cold water, changing the water several times until no grit appears at the bottom of the bowl.

LITE SILKEN TOFU

Lite silken tofu is aseptically packaged. This means that it can be eaten right from the box or incorporated into a chilled recipe without precooking. Always drain tofu

◆ *41* ◆

by cutting the side flaps where marked and pouring off the liquid. Remove from box, wrap in paper towels of double thickness, and set aside until ready to use.

Always blend lite silken tofu until smooth, before adding other ingredients to the food processor or blender.

(Note: To accurately measure tofu, stir with a fork to break down, and measure as you would flour, leveling with a knife.)

M I N C I N G   G A R L I C

The best way to mince garlic is to place an unpeeled clove on a cutting board. Lay the flat side of a large, wide-bladed knife over the clove and strike a few times with the heel of your hand; remove the peel. Mince with short chopping motions, grasping both ends of the knife carefully.

M I S O   S O U P

Miso soup has four basic elements: dashi, vegetables, miso, and garnishes. The preparation of miso soup begins with a traditional stock called dashi. Made with kombu (dried seaweed), a fragrant and flavorful dashi is a fundamental ingredient in good miso soup. I make my dashi with kombu and a combination of western-style vegetables. After simmering the dashi, I generally remove the solids and press them against a wire strainer in order to extract optimal flavor.

Next, I like to add flavored vegetable broth and seasonings. There are many varieties of miso that can be used in miso soup. Using a combination of different miso flavors produces a delightful balance of flavor and aroma. Miso is always mixed with a liquid, most times a ladle or two of hot broth, before being added to the soup. To "cream" the miso, place a cup or so of liquid gradually and blend with a small wire whisk or fork. The soup is then allowed to simmer for several minutes but is never allowed to come to a boil. To do so would destroy the microorganisms and enzymes for which miso soup is so highly prized.

N U T M E A T S

I generally purchase nutmeats either whole or in large pieces. I always measure the nuts first and then place them in a plastic bag. I place the closed bag on the kitchen counter and rap it a number of times with the edge of my rolling pin. This enables me to crush nuts smaller than available commercially. I think it makes them go further and seems to increase the volume.

PASTA

Pasta should be cooked in a large pot of boiling water, with at least 4 quarts of water per pound of pasta. Place a tablespoon of oil in the water along with a teaspoon of salt, to help keep the strands from sticking together. Cooking times will vary according to the thickness of the pasta, with filled pastas generally cooking longer. Keep a close watch on boiling pasta, being careful not to overcook. Frequent testing by biting or pinching a test piece is the best method. Pasta has reached what is considered the perfect texture, "al dente," when it is firm but flexible; pasta is gummy when it's overdone.

PEARL ONIONS, PEELING

First blanch the onions by plunging them into boiling water for 2 minutes. Drain immediately, and plunge them into ice water. With a sharp knife, cut off the root and stem ends. The remaining skin should slide off easily with the knife.

PHYLLO DOUGH

Sometimes spelled filo, this versatile pastry is available in the freezer section of most supermarkets. Remove the package from the freezer and place it in the refrigerator overnight. Remove the package from the refrigerator and place it on the kitchen counter, unopened, for 2 to 4 hours before opening. This will bring the dough to room temperature. Remove the number of sheets needed, and freeze the remainder.

Work quickly with each individual layer, keeping the remaining dough covered with a damp cloth. I like to use a water spritzer, like the typical indoor plant sprayer, to keep the cloth from drying while I'm working. Spray lightly; do not drench the cloth or the dough will become gummy, especially around the edges.

Always make the filling for phyllo dough before removing it from its wrapper. If the filling has been cooked, it should be cooled a bit before mounding it onto the prepared layers in order to avoid sogginess. Flavored bread crumbs are sometimes sprinkled between the layers to promote crispness.

If you've never worked with these leaves of dough, you might think they are sheets of translucent paper. They are very delicate and dry out easily, so handle them gingerly. Generally the leaves of dough are brushed with melted butter before placement to promote flakiness. In my approach to low-fat cuisine, I use an oil cooking spray instead. There are flavored mists on the market that will impart the flavor of butter or garlic, however this is not absolutely necessary, especially if butter is not

♦ *43* ♦

something you normally include in your diet. The use of oil sprays has proven to be a very adequate fat-busting ally.

P I Z Z A   D O U G H

Pizza dough is always made with bread flour, which has a high gluten content and allows the yeast maximum rise. The yeast used in this book is baker's yeast, which is sold in jars in supermarkets across the country. Red Star and Fleishman are two popular brands. This type of yeast is measured in teaspoons rather than packets. A package of yeast contains two and a half teaspoons, and the yeast called for in these recipes is not rapid rise. I keep yeast in the refrigerator to maintain maximum freshness.

I use the food processor to make pizza dough. However, if you prefer to make the dough by hand you may proceed with the standard method:

In a small glass measuring cup, warm the water with the sweetener called for to no more than 110° in the microwave. Sprinkle the yeast into the water and set aside to proof. If the yeast is good, it should foam. In a large bowl, stir together the flours and salt. If a cooked potato is needed, it should be riced before adding to the flour. Make a well in the center of the flour and pour in the yeast mixture. Mix well and knead for 10 to 12 minutes, adding more flour as needed to make a smooth dough. To knead by hand, place the dough on a lightly floured surface and sprinkle the top lightly with flour. Using the heel of your hands, press down and away, and then fold the dough back onto itself. Repeat this action, turning the dough around a little each time. Add only enough flour to prevent the dough from sticking. When the dough is smooth, elastic, and springy, it is ready to rest. At this point, proceed with the recipe.

P R U N E   P U R É E

Homemade prune purée is a snap: Simply place 2 cups of pitted prunes in a food processor or blender with 3/4 cup of water and 4 teaspoons of vanilla extract. Blend until smooth, then cover and refrigerate. Prune purée will keep in the refrigerator for more than two weeks.

" S N I P P I N G "   I N G R E D I E N T S

Sometimes a recipe will call for an ingredient to be "snipped." I use my kitchen shears to cut herbs or dried fruits. For basil, I roll the leaves into a tight bunch and cut them into strips. For dried fruits or sun-dried tomatoes, I snip them into halves or thirds, as indicated in the recipe.

SOY BUTTERMILK

Adding lemon or cider vinegar to soymilk lite creates a low-fat ingredient that imparts the same characteristics as traditional buttermilk to baked goods, dressings, and sauces. This marvelous ingredient is easy to make and rich in phytochemicals. It has the same thick texture and tangy flavor as traditional buttermilk.

Simply place soymilk in a glass measuring cup. Add the souring ingredient called for in the recipe, and set aside while assembling remaining ingredients.

Sensational Starters

How do soyfoods find their way into the first course? By using exciting new products that are widely available and easy to use, you can create first-rate appetizers. Here, heart heavy ingredients like sour cream, eggs, and meat products that are high in fat and cholesterol are replaced with heart healthy alternatives. Available in natural food stores and supermarkets across the country, these wholesome alternatives will introduce you to a low-fat, high fiber, and dairy-free cooking style.

Using some of the newest soyfoods on the market and creative techniques, the health conscious cook can replace unhealthy ingredients with those that mimic familiar tastes and textures. Delight your guests with the scrumptious Spanakopitta, a gorgeous Greek spinach pie fashioned from phyllo pastry. You can wrap it up with style making the enticing Sausage Roll-Ups. Adding versatility with a minimum of fuss is easy: just blend, chill, and serve Chick-Pea Dip, Savory Spinach Dip, or Spicy Roasted Pepper Dip with Pita Crisps or crudités.

Whether planning a festive buffet or an intimate dinner, the enticing hot and cold appetizers in this exciting collection will greet your guests with an irresistible invitation to dine. The first course is primarily designed to stimulate the appetite and serve as a prelude to the rest of the meal. When planning your menu, focus on the taste, texture, and color of your choices and how they will be complemented by succeeding courses. Whatever you select, you can be sure these tasty openers are both healthful and delicious. ◆

Chick-Pea Dip With Pita Crisps

Dramatically lower in fat than traditional hummus,
this exceptional appetizer tastes rich and delicious.

◆ ABOUT 4 CUPS ◆

DIP

1 1/4 cups lite silken tofu, drained
2 cloves garlic, peeled
15-oz. can garbanzo beans, drained
4 scallions, tops only

2 Tbsp. tahini
1 Tbsp. tamari
1 Tbsp. Dijon mustard

Place tofu in food processor, and blend. Add garlic, and blend. Add remaining ingredients; blend until smooth. Chill until ready to serve.

PITA CRISPS

Vegetable oil cooking spray
12 whole wheat or oat bran pita
   pockets

granulated garlic

◆ 48 ◆

Preheat oven to 400°. Line a baking pan with foil, then coat the foil with cooking spray. Cut each pita pocket into eighths, and place on prepared pan. Coat the top side of each pita lightly with cooking spray, then sprinkle with granulated garlic. Bake 10 minutes. Place under the broiler 3 to 4 minutes; broil until lightly browned. Place dip in a small bowl in center of platter or tray, and surround with pita crisps. Serve immediately.

NUTRITION ANALYSIS
(PER SERVING: 1/3 CUP DIP + 4 PITA CRISPS)

Protein 10 gm., Carbohydrate 31 gm., Fiber 5 gm., Fat 3 gm.,
Cholesterol 0, Calcium 23 mg., Sodium 258 mg.

Calories 186
From protein: 20%; From carbohydrate: 65%; From fat: 15%

Colorful Guacamole

Serve this easy-to-make starter with blue corn chips.

◆ 1 2   S E R V I N G S ◆

2 large ripe avocados
juice of 1 plump lime
2 cloves garlic, minced
1/3 cup sliced scallions
1/3 cup chopped red bell pepper

14 1/2-oz. can diced tomatoes with
   jalapeños (drained)
1/4 cup snipped fresh cilantro
2 tsp. Bragg liquid aminos

Slice avocados in half and remove pit. Use a melon baller to remove flesh. Place in a medium bowl and mash. Drizzle generously with lime juice. Add garlic, scallions, and bell pepper. Add drained tomatoes and cilantro; mix thoroughly. Cover and chill until ready to serve.

N U T R I T I O N   A N A L Y S I S
(P E R   3   1 / 2 - O Z .   S E R V I N G)

Protein 2 gm., Carbohydrate 24 gm., Fiber 1 gm., Fat 5 gm.,
Cholesterol 0, Calcium 9 mg., Sodium 116 mg.

Calories 68
From protein: 4%; From carbohydrate: 67%; From fat: 29%

◆ *49* ◆

Cocktail Nibbles

*Chunks of broiled tofu hot dogs or squares of lite silken tofu
are speared with toothpicks for dipping in a tasty sauce.*

◆ 8 SERVINGS ◆

2 12-oz. pkg. tofu hot dogs, cut to
  1-inch pieces (see Soyfoods Pantry)
  OR
2 pkgs. lite silken tofu* (extra firm),
  drained and cubed
  DIPPING SAUCE:
1 cup fruit-sweetened ketchup

2 Tbsp. dry sherry
1 clove garlic
2 scallions, sliced
3 Tbsp. tomato paste
3 Tbsp. Dijon mustard
1 Tbsp. grated gingerroot

Blend sauce ingredients until smooth (a hand-held blender works best). Place the
cut hot dogs under the broiler and cook, turning frequently, about 3 to 4 minutes.
Pierce hot dogs with toothpicks. Serve immediately.

◆50◆ SILKEN NIBBLES

Place the cubed tofu on a plate around a bowl of sauce. Diners can spear tofu with
toothpicks, dip in sauce, and enjoy.

*Only Mori Nu, aseptically packaged tofu, can be used right from the package. If you're
using water packed or vacuum packed tofu, it should be steamed for 10 minutes, then
cooled and cubed.

COCKTAIL WIENERS NUTRITION ANALYSIS
(PER 4-OZ. SERVING)

Protein 21 gm., Carbohydrate 18 gm., Fiber 3 gm., Fat 1 gm.,
Cholesterol 0, Calcium 5 mg., Sodium 429 mg.

Calories 174
From protein: 51%; From carbohydrate: 42%; From fat: 6%

SILKEN NIBBLES NUTRITION ANALYSIS
(PER 4.5-OZ. SERVING)

Protein 7 gm., Carbohydrate 10 gm., Fiber 0, Fat 1 gm.,
Cholesterol 0, Calcium 6 mg., Sodium 500 mg.

Calories 77
From protein: 36%; From carbohydrate: 52%; From fat: 12%

Cold Noodles Szechuan

A popular first course at Chinese restaurants,
this delightful dish is easy to make at home.

◆ 6 SERVINGS ◆

1/4 cup rice vinegar

3 Tbsp. peanut butter

1 1/2 Tbsp. tamari

1 1/2 tsp. hot pepper sesame oil

1/2 tsp. toasted sesame oil

2 cloves garlic, minced

3 Tbsp. chopped shallots

2 Tbsp. hot water

8 oz. soba noodles

1 cup sliced scallions

1 to 3 Tbsp. Szechuan chili sauce—
to taste

In a 2-cup glass measuring cup or small bowl, blend together the first 8 ingredients
to prepare dressing. Set aside in refrigerator. Cook noodles according to package directions.
Drain noodles and rinse with cold water. Place noodles in a 2-quart. bowl and toss with
dressing and scallions. Mix well. Add chili sauce according to taste. Serve immediately.

◆ *51* ◆

NUTRITION ANALYSIS
(PER SERVING)

Protein 8 gm., Carbohydrate 33 gm., Fiber 1 gm., Fat 5 gm.,
Cholesterol 0, Calcium 19 mg., Sodium 509 mg.

Calories 201
From protein: 15%; From carbohydrate: 62%; From fat: 23%

Dilled Artichoke Dip

This creamy dip is delicious served hot from the oven or chilled.

◆ A B O U T   5   1 / 4   C U P S ◆

1 cup soymilk lite

1 tsp. cider vinegar

1 1/4 cups lite silken tofu (firm), drained

1/2 cup sliced scallions

3 cloves garlic, peeled

2 13.75-oz. cans quartered artichoke hearts, drained

1 Tbsp. dried dillweed, separated

2 Tbsp. very dry sherry

1/4 cup nutritional yeast

1 Tbsp. Dijon mustard

◆ 52 ◆

Preheat oven to 350°. Place soymilk in a small measuring cup; add vinegar, and set aside. Place tofu in food processor, and blend. Add scallions and garlic, and process. Add artichokes and soymilk; process. Add 1 tsp. of the dried dillweed along with remaining ingredients. Process to mix. Pour into a 2-quart casserole dish. Sprinkle generously with reserved dillweed. (At this point you may cover and refrigerate for up to 24 hours.) Bake in preheated oven for 35 minutes or until lightly browned and firm to the touch at the center. Serve garnished with fresh dill, with pita crisps (see page 56).

NUTRITION ANALYSIS
(PER 1/3-CUP SERVING)

Protein 4 gm., Carbohydrate 5 gm., Fiber 1 gm., Fat 0,
Cholesterol 0, Calcium 7 mg., Sodium 101 mg.

Calories 38
From protein: 40%; From carbohydrate: 50%; From fat: 11%

Especially Onion Dip

This dairy-free variation on a classic is creamy and delicious.

◆ ABOUT 3 CUPS ◆

1 1/4 cups lite silken tofu (extra firm), drained

3 Tbsp. Veganrella cream cheese or low-fat cream cheese

1.75-oz. pkg. dry onion soup mix

3 cloves garlic, peeled

8-oz. can sliced water chestnuts, drained

3 scallions, sliced

1/4 cup soymilk lite

Place drained tofu in a food processor, and blend until smooth. Add cream cheese and blend. Add dry soup mix and garlic; blend. Add water chestnuts, scallions, and soymilk. Pulse, just to mix, leaving a chunky consistency. Serve with crudités.

NUTRITION ANALYSIS
(PER 2-OZ. SERVING)

Protein 3 gm., Carbohydrate 6 gm., Fiber 1 gm., Fat 1 gm.,
Cholesterol 0, Calcium 10 mg., Sodium 408 mg.

Calories 46
From protein: 21%; From carbohydrate: 54%; From fat: 25%

◆ 53 ◆

Marvelous Mushroom Pâté

"Meaty" portobello mushrooms and tempeh lend
an authentic quality to this fabulous pâté.

◆ 12 SERVINGS ◆

1 1/2 tsp. olive oil

1/4 tsp. crushed red pepper

1 cup sliced scallions

6 cloves garlic, minced

6 oz. portobello mushrooms, cubed

6 oz. cremini mushrooms

4 oz. seasoned tempeh, cubed

3 Tbsp. very dry sherry

1 Tbsp. egg replacer powder*

1/4 cup water

1/3 cup tomato paste

2 Tbsp. Dijon mustard

1 tsp. granulated garlic

2 tsp. rubbed sage

1 Tbsp. tamari

1/4 tsp. ground allspice

1/8 tsp. ground cloves

dash cayenne pepper

◆ 54 ◆

Heat oil and crushed red pepper 1 minute, over medium high heat. Add scallions and garlic; sauté 2 minutes. Add the next 3 ingredients and cook, stirring, 5 minutes. Add sherry, and simmer 10 minutes. Cool slightly, then pour mixture into food processor. Whisk egg replacer powder with water in a small bowl until foamy. Add to mushroom mixture along with remaining ingredients. Blend until thick and smooth. Spoon into loaf pan and garnish with fresh basil. Chill 3 hours or overnight. Serve with pita crisps (see page 56).

*Do not substitute with beaten egg whites.

NUTRITION ANALYSIS
(PER 3-OZ. SERVING)

Protein 4 gm., Carbohydrate 6 gm., Fiber 1 gm., Fat 1 gm.,
Cholesterol 0, Calcium 14 mg., Sodium 80 mg.

Calories 52
From protein: 29%; From carbohydrate: 48%; From fat: 23%

Grilled Marinated Portobellos

These tender, flavorful mushrooms are sometimes described as "vegetarian steak."

◆ 4 SERVINGS ◆

4 portobello mushrooms (about 12 oz.)
Vegetable oil cooking spray
  MARINADE:
1/3 cup balsamic vinegar
4 Tbsp. tamari

3 Tbsp. very dry sherry
6 cloves garlic, minced
1 tsp. dried thyme
3 Tbsp. minced shallots
1 Tbsp. olive oil

Remove and discard stems from mushrooms. Wipe caps with damp paper towels and divide in half. Set aside. Whisk together marinade ingredients in a large glass measuring cup. Place mushroom caps in a single layer in a zipper lock plastic bag (1-gallon size). Pour marinade in bag, close, and turn bag several times to soak mushrooms. Set aside, allowing mushrooms to marinate at room temperature for at least 2 or 3 hours. Turn bag every 30 minutes, if possible.

Spray a broiler pan with cooking spray, and place mushrooms in preheated broiler. Broil mushrooms 3 to 5 minutes on each side. Lightly spray second side when turning them over. Check mushrooms often. Remove mushrooms, slice thinly, keeping slices together, and serve.

◆55◆

NUTRITION ANALYSIS
(PER SERVING)

Protein 4 gm., Carbohydrate 9 gm., Fiber 1 gm., Fat 4 gm.,
Cholesterol 0, Calcium 27 mg., Sodium 816 mg.

Calories 83
From protein: 18%; From carbohydrate: 42%; From fat: 40%

Pita Crisps

These low-fat alternatives to chips are terrific with any dip.

◆ 12 SERVINGS ◆

Vegetable oil cooking spray
12 whole wheat or oat bran pita pockets
granulated garlic

Preheat oven to 400° Line a baking pan with foil, and spray with cooking spray. Cut pita pockets into eighths, and place on prepared pan. Lightly spray the top side of the pita bread, and sprinkle with granulated garlic. Bake 10 minutes. Place under the broiler 3 to 4 minutes or until lightly browned. Serve immediately.

NUTRITION ANALYSIS
(PER SERVING: 8 PITA CRISPS)

Protein 5 gm., Carbohydrate 25 gm., Fiber 3 gm., Fat 1 gm.,
Cholesterol 0, Calcium 15 mg., Sodium 172 mg.

Calories 122
From protein: 15%; From carbohydrate: 77%; From fat: 8%

Spicy Roasted Pepper Dip

This is a delicious, savory dip that is low in calories and fat.

◆ 3 CUPS ◆

1 1/4 cups lite silken tofu (firm), drained

1/3 cup tofu mayonnaise (see Soyfoods Pantry)

4 cloves garlic, peeled

3/4 cup roasted sweet red and yellow peppers (drained)

2 Tbsp. red wine vinegar

1/2 tsp. Tabasco sauce

2 tsp. tamari

1/2 tsp. dried basil

1/2 tsp. dried marjoram

Place tofu in food processor, and blend. Add tofu mayonnaise, garlic, and peppers; pulse to mix. Add remaining ingredients, and pulse until blended but chunky. Refrigerate several hours or overnight. Serve **well chilled** with crudités and pita crisps (see page 56).

◆57◆

NUTRITION ANALYSIS
(PER 3-OZ. SERVING)

Protein 2 gm., Carbohydrate 4 gm., Fiber 1 gm., Fat 1 gm.,
Cholesterol 0, Calcium 20 mg., Sodium 69 mg.

Calories 28
From protein: 24%; From carbohydrate: 51%; From fat: 25%

Sausage Roll-Ups

These roll-ups are so authentic in taste, appearance, and texture, you could fool even the most avid meat eater. You can make them in advance, if you wish, then reheat and slice just before serving.

◆ 24 HORS D'OEUVRES ◆

FILLING:

1 1/2 tsp. olive oil

1/8 tsp. crushed red pepper

1 medium, sweet onion (Vidalia, Texas, Maui), chopped

5 large cloves garlic, minced

14-oz. pkg. Gimme Lean, sausage flavor

10-oz. pkg. frozen spinach, thawed, drained, and pressed in colander

1/4 cup very dry sherry

1 tsp. thyme

DOUGH:

1/2 cup soymilk lite

2 Tbsp. lemon juice

2 cups whole wheat flour

1/2 tsp. salt

2 1/2 tsp. baking powder

1/3 cup lite silken tofu, drained

1 Tbsp. liquid Fruitsource or honey

1 1/2 tsp. olive oil

◆ 58 ◆

Preheat oven to 350°. Heat oil and crushed pepper in a 10" frying pan over medium-high heat for 1 minute. Add onions and garlic, and sauté 3 minutes. Add Gimme Lean and well drained spinach; mix thoroughly. Sauté 10 minutes, stirring frequently. Add sherry and thyme, and lower to simmer. Combine soymilk and lemon juice in a cup; set aside. Place next 3 dough ingredients in food processor; process to mix. Add tofu, and process to crumb. Add Fruitsource; blend, then add soymilk through feed tube while processing.

Place dough on floured board. Oil hands lightly, and knead dough 5 minutes, until elastic. Divide dough in two, and roll 1/2- to 1/4-inch thick. Spread 1 1/2 cups filling on dough, and roll up, tucking in ends as you go. Repeat with second half of dough and remaining filling. Place roll-ups in a baking pan coated with cooking spray. Bake 20 minutes, then serve immediately, or wrap in foil, and refrigerate. Reheat in foil 15 minutes at 325° before serving.

NUTRITION ANALYSIS
(PER SERVING)

Protein 5 gm., Carbohydrate 12 gm., Fiber 2 gm., Fat 1 gm.,
Cholesterol 0, Calcium 25 mg., Sodium 142 mg.

Calories 73
From protein: 25%; From carbohydrate: 65%; From fat: 10%

Soybeans in the Pod

*One of my favorite ways to enjoy soybeans is to eat them right out of the pod.
Hold one end of the pod between two fingers, place the pod between your teeth
and pull gently. The delicious soybeans will slide out. Discard the pod.
They're so tasty, you won't be able to stop eating them.*

◆ 4   S E R V I N G S ◆

5 quarts water
1 tsp. salt
16-oz. pkg. green vegetable soybeans (Edamamé)

Bring water to boil in a large saucepan. Add salt and frozen pods. Do not defrost
pods before cooking. Simmer pods for 5 minutes. Drain, and serve hot or cold.

NUTRITION ANALYSIS
(PER SERVING)

Protein 14 gm., Carbohydrate 15 gm., Fiber 3 gm., Fat 4 gm.,
Cholesterol 0, Calcium 82 gm., Sodium 272 mg.

Calories 142
From protein: 36%; Calories from carbohydrate: 39%; From fat: 24%

Soynuts

Roasted soynuts are easy to make in your own kitchen. They make a great snack and a deliciously crunchy addition to an hors d'oeuvres buffet.

◆ 2 1 / 2 C U P S ◆

1 cup dried soybeans
1 quart cold water

Vegetable oil cooking spray
1/2 tsp. salt

Rinse beans thoroughly. Sort and discard any stones or debris that remain. Place beans in a bowl, and cover with cold water. Soak beans 3 to 4 hours on the counter or overnight in the refrigerator. Drain the beans, and pat dry with paper towels.

Preheat oven to 350°. Spray a baking sheet with cooking spray. Place beans in a single layer on the baking sheet. Bake 35 to 45 minutes, stirring often, until well browned. Place in a bowl, and salt to taste. Serve warm, or store in a covered container in the refrigerator. You may reheat at 325° until hot, if desired.

NUTRITION ANALYSIS
(PER 1-OZ. SERVING)

Protein 9 gm., Carbohydrate 7 gm., Fiber 3 gm., Fat 5 gm.,
Cholesterol 0, Calcium 68 mg., Sodium 57 mg.

Calories 102
From protein: 33%; From carbohydrate: 27%; From fat: 40%

(The percentage of calories from fat seems high
because the calories are so low.)

Spanakopitta

This savory Greek pie made with flaky phyllo
pastry is as delectable as it is beautiful.

◆ 1 6   S E R V I N G S ◆

16-oz. pkg. phyllo pastry

Vegetable oil cooking spray

2 1/2 cups lite silken tofu (extra
  firm), drained and patted dry

1/2 cup nutritional yeast

2 Tbsp. mellow white miso

2 Tbsp. mirin

4 10-oz. pkg. frozen spinach, thawed,
  drained, and pressed in a colander

6 cloves garlic, minced

2/3 cup chopped scallions

2 tsp. dried dillweed

1/4 tsp. ground nutmeg

1/4 tsp. lemon pepper

1/2 cup whole wheat bread crumbs

Prepare phyllo pastry using techniques on pg. 43. Preheat oven to 350.° Spray a
9" x 13" pan with cooking spray. Place tofu in a large bowl. Use a potato masher to
mash it into curds. Stir in nutritional yeast. Blend miso with mirin in a small bowl until
smooth. Add to tofu mixture. Add drained spinach, and mix thoroughly. Mix in garlic,
scallions, dill weed, nutmeg, and lemon pepper. Set aside.

Gently place one pastry leaf across the bottom of the pan, leaving an overlap. Spray
lightly with cooking spray and sprinkle with bread crumbs. Repeat until half of the
phyllo leaves are used. Spread spinach mixture over dough, then fold the pastry in
over the filling. Top with the remaining pastry, using the cooking spray and bread
crumbs between the leaves in the same way. Trim the pastry around the edges to a one
inch overhang. Then tuck the top pastry in down the sides, using a rubber spatula to
make room. Use a sharp knife to make a diamond pattern cutting just through the top
pastry. Bake for one hour; serve warm.

◆*61*◆

NUTRITION ANALYSIS
(PER SERVING)

Protein 12 gm., Carbohydrate 32 gm., Fiber 2 gm., Fat 2 gm.,
Cholesterol 0, Calcium 112 mg., Sodium 274 mg.

Calories 170
From protein: 24%; From carbohydrate: 66%; From fat: 10%

Spinach Balls

These delicious hors d'oeuvres are easy to make. They can be assembled in advance and popped into the oven just before serving.

◆ A B O U T 5 0 S P I N A C H B A L L S ◆

Vegetable oil cooking spray
1 1/4 cups lite silken tofu (extra firm), drained
2 Tbsp. mellow white miso
1 1/2 Tbsp. very dry sherry
2 Tbsp. egg replacer powder
1/4 cup water

1 Tbsp. Dijon mustard
1/4 cup nutritional yeast
1 tsp. granulated garlic
1 tsp. dried parsley
1 tsp. tamari
10-oz. pkg. frozen spinach, thawed and well drained

Preheat oven to 350.° Spray 2 baking sheets with cooking spray. Place tofu in food processor, and blend. Add miso and sherry, and blend. Whisk egg replacer powder and water in a small bowl until frothy; add to the mixture. Add the next 5 ingredients, and blend. Add the spinach, and pulse to mix. Place rounded tablespoonfuls of the spinach mixture on the prepared baking sheets. Bake for 15 minutes, then broil until brown. Serve hot.

NUTRITION ANALYSIS
(PER SERVING: 4 SPINACH BALLS)

Protein 4 gm., Carbohydrate 4 gm., Fiber 1 gm., Fat 1 gm., Cholesterol 0, Calcium 8 mg., Sodium 80 mg.

Calories 34
From protein: 48%; From carbohydrate: 40%; From fat: 12%

Savory Spinach Dip

A most popular dip at get-togethers, this creamy, flavorful, and rich-tasting dip is low in calories and fat. Serve with crudités and pita crisps to rave reviews.

◆ 4 1/2 CUPS ◆

1 1/4 cups lite silken tofu (extra firm), drained

1.75-oz. pkg. onion soup mix

1/2 cup tofu mayonnaise

3 large cloves garlic, peeled

10-oz. pkg. frozen, chopped spinach, thawed, drained, and pressed in a colander

8-oz. can sliced water chestnuts, drained

1/4 cup thinly sliced scallions

Drain tofu, and pat with paper towels. Place tofu in food processor, and blend until smooth. Add dry soup mix, mayonnaise, and garlic; blend. Add spinach, and blend. Add water chestnuts and scallions; pulse just until chunky. Refrigerate for at least an hour before serving.

•*63*•

NUTRITION ANALYSIS
(PER 2.25-OZ. SERVING)

Protein 2 gm., Carbohydrate 4 gm., Fiber 1 gm., Fat 2 gm.,
Cholesterol 0, Calcium 30 mg., Sodium 103 mg.

Calories 42
From protein: 21%; From carbohydrate: 41%; From fat: 38%

Savory Stuffed Mushrooms

*The hearty filling for these popular appetizers can be made
in advance, refrigerated, and then stuffed just before baking.*

◆ 8 SERVINGS ◆

Vegetable oil cooking spray
30 large mushrooms
1 1/2 tsp. olive oil
1/8 tsp. crushed red pepper
1 1/2 cups chopped red onion
1 cup finely grated carrot
  (1 large carrot)
1 cup dry TVP granules,
  ground-beef style

1/3 cup water
1 Tbsp. vegetable boullion powder,
  beef flavor
1/2 cup white wine
1 tsp. granulated garlic
1/4 cup nutritional yeast
1 Tbsp. Bragg Liquid Aminos

Preheat oven to 375.° Spray a baking pan lightly with cooking spray. Rinse, brush or damp-wipe mushrooms, then dry thoroughly. Gently remove stems; chop, and set aside.

Heat oil and crushed pepper in a 10" frying pan over medium-high heat for 1 minute. Add onion, carrot, and chopped mushroom stems. Sauté 5 minutes. Stir in dry TVP granules. Cook 2 minutes. Add water, boullion, and wine. Lower heat to simmer, then add garlic, nutritional yeast, and liquid aminos. Simmer 5 to 8 minutes, stirring occasionally. Mound filling into mushroom caps, and place on prepared pan. Bake for 12 minutes, then broil for 3 minutes or just until browned. Serve hot.

◆ *64* ◆

NUTRITION ANALYSIS
(PER SERVING)

Protein 10 gm., Carbohydrate 51 gm., Fiber 4 gm., Fat 1 gm.,
Cholesterol 0, Calcium 11 mg., Sodium 134 mg.

Calories 106
From protein: 15%; From carbohydrate: 79%; From fat: 5%

Chili 'n Chips

*Serve this spicy filling with pita crisps or blue corn
chips, and Colorful Guacamole (page 49).*

◆ 1 6   S E R V I N G S ◆

1 1/2 tsp. olive oil

1/8 tsp. crushed red pepper

1 cup chopped red onion

6 cloves garlic, minced

1/3 cup chopped red bell pepper

1 cup zucchini, cut into
   julienne strips

1 1/2 cups chopped carrots

1 cup chopped mushrooms

2 10-oz. pkgs. Ready Ground Tofu,
   Hot & Spicy

15 1/2-oz. can chili beans with
   chipotle peppers

14 1/2-oz. can diced tomatoes and
   jalapeños

1 tsp. dried thyme

1 tsp. Mexican oregano

1 tsp. ground cumin

1/3 cup snipped fresh cilantro

◆65◆

In a 4-quart saucepan, heat oil and crushed pepper for 1 minute over medium-high heat. Add the next 3 ingredients and sauté 2 minutes. Add zucchini, carrots, and mushrooms. Cook 5 minutes, stirring frequently. Stir in tofu. Lower heat to medium and cook 3 minutes, then add remaining filling ingredients. Lower heat and simmer 10 minutes, stirring frequently. Keep warm until ready to serve.

NUTRITION ANALYSIS
(PER 4 1/2-OZ. SERVING)

Protein 5 gm., Carbohydrate 10 gm., Fiber 2 gm., Fat 2 gm.,
Cholesterol 0, Calcium 15 mg., Sodium 179 mg.

Calories 69
From protein: 27%; From carbohydrate: 49%; From fat: 25%

Sweet and Sour "Meatballs"

*This delicious dish is always a crowd pleaser. Serve it as
an appetizer or as a main course over rice or noodles.*

◆ 16 APPETIZER SERVINGS
OR 8 MAIN-COURSE SERVINGS ◆

SAUCE:
1 Tbsp. olive oil
1/8 tsp. crushed red pepper
1 Tbsp. grated fresh gingerroot
3/4 cup chopped red onion
1/3 cup chopped red bell pepper
5 large cloves garlic, minced
2 28-oz. cans crushed tomatoes
1 large bay leaf
2 Tbsp. cider vinegar
1 tsp. tamari
1/2 tsp. ground ginger
2 Tbsp. liquid Fruitsource or honey

1/4 cup frozen apple juice concentrate, thawed
2 Tbsp. lemon juice
"MEATBALLS":
2 14-oz. pkg. Gimme Lean, ground
beef style
1/2 cup ketchup
2 Tbsp. egg replacer powder
1/2 cup water
1/4 cup whole wheat bread crumbs
1 1/2 tsp. ground allspice
2 tsp. granulated garlic
Vegetable oil cooking spray

Heat olive oil and crushed pepper in a 4-quart saucepan over medium-high heat. Add the next 4 ingredients, and sauté 3 minutes. Add the tomatoes and bay leaf, and simmer 5 minutes. Whisk together the next 6 ingredients in a small bowl; add to the sauce. Cover, and simmer, stirring occasionally.

Preheat oven to 400°. Place the Gimme Lean in a large bowl with ketchup, and mix with a fork. Place egg replacer powder and water in a small bowl. Whisk until foamy. Add remaining meatball ingredients; mix thoroughly. Coat a baking pan with cooking spray. Form meatball mixture into about 30 balls (2 to 3 inches in diameter) and place on prepared pan. Spray meatballs lightly with cooking spray. Bake 15 minutes. Place under broiler to brown during the last few minutes of baking. Place browned meatballs in the sauce, and simmer 30 to 45 minutes or until ready to serve.

NUTRITION ANALYSIS
(PER APPETIZER-SIZE SERVING)

Protein 10 gm., Carbohydrate 22 gm., Fiber 3 gm., Fat 1 gm.,
Cholesterol 0, Calcium 35 mg., Sodium 410 mg.

Calories 129
From protein: 29%; From carbohydrate: 63%; From fat: 8%

Veggie Nachos

*Your guests will be incredulous to learn that there are no meat or
dairy products in this intensely flavorful and appealing Southwestern treat!*

◆ 12 SERVINGS ◆

TVP LAYER

3 cups TVP, ground beef style

1 1/2 cups beef-flavored
vegetable broth, boiling

1 1/2 tsp. olive oil

1/2 cup chopped red onion

1/4 cup chopped green pepper

3 cloves garlic, minced

2 15-oz. cans Mexican-style
stewed tomatoes

1/4 cup tomato paste

1/4 cup burgundy

1 tsp. ground cumin

1/4 cup chopped
fresh cilantro

BEAN LAYER

1 1/2 tsp. olive oil

1/2 cup chopped red onion

1/4 cup chopped green pepper

1 clove garlic, minced

2 15-oz. cans black beans

6 Tbsp. tomato paste

1 bay leaf

1 1/2 tsp. ground cumin

1/2 tsp. ground coriander

dash cayenne pepper

CHEESE SAUCE

1 1/4 cups lite silken tofu
(extra firm), drained

2 Tbsp. lemon juice

2 cloves garlic, peeled

3/4 soymilk lite

1/3 cup nutritional yeast

1 tsp. Bragg Liquid Aminos

1 10-oz. bag blue corn tortilla chips

1 avocado, sliced into wedges, drizzled with 2 Tbsp. lime juice

TVP LAYER

Place TVP in a medium bowl, cover with boiling broth, stir, and set aside for 10 minutes. Heat oil in a 10" skillet over medium-high heat. Sauté the next 3 ingredients for 3 minutes. Add reconstituted TVP and sauté mixture 10 minutes, stirring frequently. Add remaining TVP layer ingredients, and continue to cook over low heat 10 minutes or until ready to assemble. Stir occasionally.

BEAN LAYER

Heat oil in a medium saucepan over medium-high heat. Add the next 3 ingredients and sauté 3 minutes. Stir in the beans and cook 2 minutes. Add remaining bean layer ingredients. Lower heat and simmer mixture 10 minutes, stirring occasionally.

CHEESE LAYER

Place tofu in food processor and blend until smooth. Add remaining sauce ingredients and blend until smooth.

ASSEMBLY

Preheat oven to 350.° On a large pizza pan, place a generous layer of corn chips. Top with TVP layer. Add bean layer over TVP. Arrange avocado slices attractively over top layer. Pour cheese sauce over all.

Bake 20 minutes or until heated through and sauce is bubbly. Scoop onto individual plates.

•69•

NUTRITION ANALYSIS
(PER SERVING)

Protein 22 gm., Carbohydrate 40 gm., Fiber 10 gm., Fat 5 gm.,
Cholesterol 0, Calcium 34 mg., Sodium 583 mg.

Calories 224
From protein: 30%; From carbohydrate: 55%; From fat: 15%

Soups, Stews, and Salads

I n this chapter we will prepare flavorful, well-seasoned soups and stews which offer exceptional nutritional value utilizing versatile soyfoods. There's a special warmth about the inviting aroma of a steaming bowl of soup or a robust stew, especially at the end of a tiring day. These savory soups and stews served with a hearty bread and crisp salad combine to make a meal that is satisfying and complete.

Classically elegant Vichyssoise, hearty Basque Stew, and creamy Mushroom Miso Soup are just a few of the irresistible recipes in this collection, which get a nutritional boost from the mighty soybean. Miso is a savory, high-protein seasoning that is used to add unparalleled nutrition and flavor to recipes throughout this book. Long touted for its health giving properties, some Japanese doctors and scientists believe that the amino acids in miso can provide protection against air pollution and other toxins like tobacco smoke.

Salads have always appealed to the health conscious and those concerned with physical fitness. Contemporary salads have become more than just a plate of crisp greens, tomatoes, and snipped herbs. Often they are artful compositions with colorful ingredients like radicchio, arugula, endive, and enoki mushrooms. However, the natural goodness of fresh, raw vegetables is often eclipsed by high-fat dressings which accompany them. Here is a perfect opportunity to replace the heavy ingredients found in traditional dressings with—you guessed it—*soyfoods*. Dressings like Garlic Basil, "Honey" Mustard Dill, and Raspberry Walnut are some of the tasty dressings featured here that are incredibly low in fat and calories. ◆

Salad Greens

Salads no longer have to be monochromatic bowls of chopped iceberg lettuce with sliced tomatoes. Salad making now presents an opportunity to create a colorful array of salad greens from a much broader spectrum than was once available.

When shopping for any kind of lettuce, choose those which are crisp and free of blemishes. Salad greens should always be washed thoroughly and drained, and then either blotted with paper towels or dried in a salad spinner. Never allow the greens to soak, as this will cause the leaves to soften and lose their treasured crunch. One exception is spinach, which, after rinsing, may be soaked briefly in a series of bowls of cold water to remove grit. The following is a list of salad greens that are readily available in supermarkets across the country.

ARUGULA

Sometimes called rocket lettuce, arugula is a tender salad green with a spicy mustard flavor and small, elongated leaves that sometimes have serrated edges.

BELGIAN ENDIVE
(or *Witloof Chicory*)

This endive is pleasantly bitter, with firm, slender, creamy white leaves edged in pale yellow.

BUTTER LETTUCE

The delicately ruffled leaves of this green have a buttery flavor.

CHINESE CABBAGE

This cabbage has mildly flavored pale green leaves on a long, tight head.

CURLY ENDIVE OR CHICORY

Another green with a pleasantly bitter flavor, curly endive has crisp, dark green leaves with curly edges.

ESCAROLE

This broad-leaf variety of endive has a mildly bitter flavor.

GREEN LEAF LETTUCE

This is a popular variety of loose-leaf lettuce with a delicate flavor.

ICEBERG LETTUCE

The crisp texture and very mild flavor of iceberg lettuce make it the best selling of all types of salad greens.

RADICCHIO

Sometimes called Italian Chicory, this colorful salad component has purplish-red to burgundy leaves with white ribs, shaped around a small round head. Hardy and flavorful, with a taste similar to escarole, this is a fine choice for a gourmet salad mix.

RED CABBAGE

This tastes much like green cabbage, but its bright reddish-purple leaves add a colorful contrast when shredded into a salad.

◆ 73 ◆

RED LEAF LETTUCE

This popular variety's tender, dark, red-tinged leaves are a mild and colorful addition to any salad.

ROMAINE

This favorite has dark green outer leaves which lighten toward the center. It has a particularly succulent midrib and a crisp and crunchy texture.

SPINACH

The earthy, lemony, slightly bitter taste of raw spinach is prized in salads. Fresh spinach is available year-round and should be thoroughly rinsed because it is usually very gritty.

WATERCRESS

A member of the mustard family, watercress has small, crisp, deep green leaves and a slightly bitter, peppery flavor. It can be used as an interesting addition to salads or as a garnish.

Basque Stew

This aromatic stew is bursting with the flavors of potatoes, tomatoes, robust herbs, and sausage.* This hearty entrée is extraordinary with Saffron Couscous (page 179).

◆ 1 2 S E R V I N G S ◆

1 Tbsp. olive oil

1/4 tsp. crushed red pepper

14-oz. pkg. Gimme Lean, sausage flavor (see Soyfoods Pantry)

4 cups unpeeled potatoes, cut into 2-inch wedges

2 cups baby carrots, cut into thirds

4 medium to large leeks, well rinsed (see Techniques)

8 cloves garlic, minced

1/3 cup chopped orange bell pepper

1 cup white wine

3 cups beef-flavored vegetable broth, boiling

4 1/2 cups chunky tomato sauce

1 large bay leaf

5 to 6 large basil leaves, snipped

2 Tbsp. drained capers

2 tsp. dried thyme

2 Tbsp. cornstarch

2 Tbsp. cold water

1 tsp. dried parsley

Preheat oven to 350.° Heat the crushed pepper in oil in a large stovetop- and oven-proof casserole over medium-high heat. Add Gimme Lean, breaking apart while stirring frequently, about 3 to 5 minutes. Add the next 5 ingredients. Sauté 8 minutes or until vegetables are crisp tender, stirring frequently. Add wine, and cook 3 minutes. Add broth, tomato sauce, and the next four ingredients. Cover stew, and place in oven. Bake 45 minutes. Remove casserole from oven. Make a paste of the cornstarch and water in a small bowl. Add to the stew along with parsley. Cover, and return to the oven for 15 minutes or until ready to serve.

*I use Gimme Lean for a healthy alternative to the sausage that is a traditional ingredient in Basque cuisine.

NUTRITION ANALYSIS
(PER SERVING)

Protein 10 gm., Carbohydrate 43 gm., Fiber 5 gm., Fat 1 gm., Cholesterol 0, Calcium 49 mg., Sodium 394 mg.

Calories 225
From protein: 17%; From carbohydrate: 77%; From fat: 6%

TVP Beef Stew

*This homey favorite has tender chunks of TVP and
colorful vegetables in a flavorful gravy.*

◆ 8 SERVINGS ◆

2 cups beef-flavored vegetable broth,
  boiling

1 1/2 cups TVP steak strips

1 1/2 tsp. olive oil

1/4 tsp. crushed red pepper

1 cup chopped red onion

4 cloves garlic, minced

2 cups sliced baby carrots,
  1-inch chunks

4 cups cubed, unpeeled potato

3 cups zucchini, cut into slices, then
  quartered

2 cups sliced mushrooms

1 cup white wine

4 cups beef-flavored vegetable broth

2 Tbsp. tamari

1 tsp. granulated garlic

1/4 cup beef-flavored vegetable
  broth, cold

3 Tbsp. cornstarch

1 tsp. dried thyme

1 tsp. dried marjoram

◆ *75* ◆

Combine broth and TVP in a medium glass bowl; steep for 5 minutes. Microwave
for 3 minutes; set aside. Sauté oil and crushed pepper in a medium saucepan over
medium-high heat for 2 minutes. Add onion and garlic; sauté 3 minutes. Add the
next 4 ingredients, and sauté 5 minutes, stirring occasionally. Add wine, and cook
5 minutes. Add reconstituted TVP, 4 cups broth, tamari, and granulated garlic. Lower
heat, and simmer 20 minutes, stirring occasionally. Blend cold broth with cornstarch in
a small bowl; add to stew. Add thyme and marjoram. Simmer 10 minutes or until
ready to serve.

NUTRITION ANALYSIS
(PER SERVING)

Protein 12 gm., Carbohydrate 38 gm., Fiber 6 gm., Fat 1 gm.,
Cholesterol 0, Calcium 39 mg., Sodium 323 mg.

Calories 211
From protein: 23%; From carbohydrate: 72%; From fat: 6%

Italian Sausage Stew

You will savor this delightful stew with its succulent chunks of Italian sausage (vegetarian, of course) in a richly flavored sauce laced with vermouth.

◆ 8 SERVINGS ◆

1 Tbsp. olive oil

1/4 tsp. crushed red pepper

1 small onion, chopped, about 1 cup

5 cloves garlic, minced

1/2 cup chopped red bell pepper

11.2-oz. pkg. Lean Links Italian, cut in 1/2-inch pieces

2 cups baby carrots, halved crosswise

4 cups diced, peeled potatoes

1 small zucchini, sliced and cut in half (about 1 1/2 cups)

1/3 cup vermouth

2 cups boiling beef-flavored vegetable broth

1 bay leaf

3 cups chunky tomato sauce

Heat oil and crushed red pepper in a 4- to 5-quart saucepan over medium-high heat for 2 minutes. Add the next 3 ingredients, and sauté for 2 minutes. Add sausage, and sauté about 8 minutes. Add the next 3 ingredients, and cook mixture 10 minutes, stirring frequently. Stir in vermouth, and cook for 2 minutes. Lower heat to simmer and add remaining ingredients. Simmer for 25 minutes or until ready to serve, stirring occasionally. Serve accompanied by a rice or couscous dish.

◆ *76* ◆

NUTRITION ANALYSIS
(PER SERVING)

Protein 10 gm., Carbohydrate 48 gm., Fiber 4 gm., Fat 4 gm., Cholesterol 0, Calcium 28 mg., Sodium 375 mg.

Calories 270
From protein: 15%; From carbohydrate: 72%; From fat: 13%

Creamy Tomato Orzo Soup

*This soup is so delicious, you'll want to make it often. Try adding
a few drops of hot pepper sauce at the table for an extra zing!*

◆ ABOUT 4 1/2 QUARTS ◆

1 piece kombu

2 quarts water

1 medium onion, chopped

4 cloves garlic, minced

1/3 cup chopped green bell pepper

1 Tbsp. grated fresh gingerroot

1 cup sliced carrots

2 cups beef-flavored vegetable
broth, boiling

14.5-oz. can Italian-style
stewed tomatoes

1 tsp. granulated garlic

1 tsp. dried basil

1 Tbsp. tamari

3/4 cup orzo (uncooked)

1/3 cup mellow white miso

1/2 cup white wine

Place kombu and water in a 5-quart pot. Soak kombu overnight or for at least
15 minutes. Add the next 5 ingredients, and bring to a boil. Reduce heat, and simmer
15 minutes, stirring occasionally. Remove kombu,* then add hot broth, tomatoes, and
seasonings. Bring to a boil again, and add orzo. Simmer 15 minutes, stirring occasionally. Place miso in a small bowl and cream with wine. When smooth, add to soup;
simmer 5 minutes or until ready to serve. Do not boil.

◆ 77 ◆

*Cooked kombu can be a delicious addition to a vegetable dish. You may store in refrig-
erator for future use or discard.

NUTRITION ANALYSIS
(PER 2-CUP SERVING)

Protein 2 gm., Carbohydrate 24 gm., Fiber 3 gm., Fat 1 gm.,
Cholesterol 0, Calcium 57 mg., Sodium 405 mg.

Calories 128
From protein: 7%; From carbohydrate: 76%; From fat: 5%

Golden Split Pea Curry

This aromatic stew has a lovely golden hue and rich flavor.
Serve this hearty stew with brown rice for a satisfying meal.

◆ 8   S E R V I N G S ◆

2 cups yellow split peas, sorted and rinsed

6 cups chicken-flavored vegetable broth

1 1/2 tsp. olive oil

1 tsp. black mustard seeds

1 cup chopped red onion

4 cloves garlic, minced

2 ribs celery, sliced

2 cups sliced carrots

2 cups peeled and cubed potatoes

1 Tbsp. grated gingerroot

1/2 tsp. turmeric

1 tsp. ground coriander

1 cup white wine

1/2 cup plus 2 Tbsp. lite silken tofu (extra firm), drained

1/2 cup soymilk lite

1/4 tsp. asafetida

◆ 78 ◆   Combine split peas with broth in a 5-quart saucepan; bring to a boil. Reduce heat and simmer 20 minutes, skimming foam from surface, and stirring occasionally. Heat oil over medium high heat in a 10" frying pan. Stir in mustard seeds, and cook until they begin to pop, about 2 minutes. Add the next 5 ingredients, stirring after each addition. Sauté for 5 minutes. Stir in the next 3 ingredients and continue to cook 5 minutes longer. Add the wine; reduce heat to medium low. Cover and cook until vegetables are soft, stirring occasionally.

Place the tofu in food processor, and blend. Add soymilk and asafetida, and blend until smooth, about 1 minute. Stir tofu mixture into frying pan, and simmer a few minutes. Add the vegetable tofu mixture to the peas, mixing thoroughly. Simmer until ready to serve.

NUTRITION ANALYSIS
(PER 1 1/2-CUP SERVING)

Protein 16 gm., Carbohydrate 52 gm., Fiber 7 gm., Fat 2 gm.,
Cholesterol 0, Calcium 66 mg., Sodium 220 mg.

Calories 303
From protein: 22%; From carbohydrate: 72%; From fat: 7%

Golden Vegetable Dill Soup

This soup is simply "dill-ightful."

◆ A B O U T   4   Q U A R T S ◆

1 1/2 tsp. olive oil

1 large onion, chopped (about 2 cups)

4 large cloves garlic, minced

1 large rib celery, sliced

2 cups sliced baby carrots

2 cups sliced summer squash

8 cups beef-flavored vegetable broth (hot)

1 1/2 cups frozen corn, thawed

1 1/4 cups lite silken tofu, drained

1 cup nutritional yeast

3 Tbsp. tapioca flour or arrowroot

1/4 cup soymilk lite

1 Tbsp. Bragg liquid aminos

1 Tbsp. tamari

1/2 cup chopped fresh dill

1 tsp. granulated garlic

1 tsp. dried tarragon

1 tsp. ground coriander

Heat oil in a 5-quart saucepan over medium-high heat for 1 minute. Add the next 4 ingredients; sauté 3 minutes. Add squash; sauté 2 minutes. Add broth and corn, then lower heat to simmer. Cover and cook until vegetables soften, about 20 minutes.

Blend tofu in food processor until smooth. Add nutritional yeast, and blend again. Scoop out 1 1/2 cups of soup vegetables with a slotted spoon, and purée with tofu. Add purée to soup pot gradually, stirring with a wire whisk. Blend flour with soymilk in a small bowl; stir into soup. Season with remaining ingredients. Simmer for 15 minutes or until ready to serve.

◆*79*◆

NUTRITION ANALYSIS
(PER 2-CUP SERVING)

Protein 16 gm., Carbohydrate 68 gm., Fiber 3 gm., Fat 2 gm.,
Cholesterol 0, Calcium 44 mg., Sodium 291 mg.

Calories 200
From protein: 18%; From carbohydrate: 76%; From fat: 6%

Italian Vegetable Soup

This is a delicious way to use the overflow of zucchini from your garden.

◆ A B O U T 4 1 / 2 Q U A R T S ◆

1 1/2 tsp. olive oil
1 large red onion, chopped
6 cloves garlic, minced
4 cups sliced zucchini, cut in half
2 cups sliced baby carrots,
   1/2-inch slices
1 rib celery, including top, sliced
1 cup dry vermouth
6 cups chicken-flavored
   vegetable broth

2 14.5-oz. cans Italian-flavored
   tomatoes, peeled and diced
10 large fresh basil leaves, snipped
1/2 cup dry TVP, ground poultry
   style
2 tsp. chicken-flavored vegetable
   bouillon powder
1 Tbsp. Bragg Liquid Aminos

Heat oil over medium-high heat in a 5-quart saucepan. Add the onion and garlic, and sauté 3 minutes. Add the next 3 ingredients and sauté until crisp tender, about 5 minutes. Add vermouth, and cook 3 minutes. Add broth, tomatoes, and basil; lower heat. Simmer 30 minutes.

Add TVP granules and remaining ingredients. Simmer an additional 20 minutes or until ready to serve.

◆ *80* ◆

NUTRITION ANALYSIS
(PER 2 1/4-CUP SERVING)

Protein 6 gm., Carbohydrate 57 gm., Fiber 4 gm., Fat 1 gm.,
Cholesterol 0, Calcium 70 mg., Sodium 490 mg.

Calories 134
From protein: 9%; From carbohydrate: 87%; From fat: 5%

Mushroom Miso Soup

*A delectable soup with a velvety smooth texture, this nutritious,
flavorful, dairy-free cream of mushroom soup is wonderful.*

◆ 8   S E R V I N G S ◆

1 1/2 tsp. olive oil

1 1/2 cups chopped sweet onion
(Vidalia, Maui, or red)

6 cloves garlic, minced

1/2 cup chopped green pepper

6 oz. cremini mushrooms, sliced

1 cup white wine

4 cups beef-flavored
vegetable broth, hot

2 medium red potatoes, parboiled,
quartered, and peeled

1 1/2 Tbsp. olive oil

3 Tbsp. whole wheat flour

1 cup soymilk lite

1/3 cup country barley miso

1/3 cup nutritional yeast

1 rounded Tbsp. dehydrated
mushroom powder

Sauté onion, garlic, and pepper in olive oil in a 5-quart saucepan over medium-high heat for 3 minutes. Add sliced mushrooms, and sauté about 5 minutes. Add wine, and cook 3 minutes. Add hot vegetable broth. Lower heat, then add potatoes and simmer 45 minutes.

Heat 1 1/2 tablespoons oil in a small saucepan over medium-high heat. Stir in flour to form a roux. Whisk in soymilk. Lower heat to simmer; stir until white sauce thickens. Set aside.

Remove potatoes and two-thirds of the vegetables to food processor, and blend until smooth. Add miso to processor, and blend again. Scrape mixture into soup, and stir until blended. Whisk white sauce into soup, and mix thoroughly. Whisk yeast and mushroom powder into soup. Heat *just* until it comes to a boil. Remove from heat. Serve.

◆*81*◆

N U T R I T I O N   A N A L Y S I S
(P E R   1   1 / 2 - C U P   S E R V I N G)

Protein 7 gm., Carbohydrate 23 gm., Fiber 2 gm., Fat 4 gm.,
Cholesterol 0, Calcium 20 mg., Sodium 290 mg.

Calories 175
From protein: 16%; From carbohydrate: 54%; From fat: 18%

Good Morning Miso Soup

Considered a nutritional keystone, miso soup is an integral part of the traditional Japanese breakfast. It's delicious any time of the day or evening.

◆ A B O U T   3   Q U A R T S ◆

1 piece of kombu
2 quarts water
3/4 cup chopped onion
3 cloves garlic, minced
1 large tomato, chopped
1/3 cup chopped green bell pepper
2 Tbsp. grated fresh gingerroot

2 cups chicken-flavored
  vegetable broth
1 tsp. granulated garlic
1/2 tsp. ground ginger
1/2 cup lite silken tofu (optional)
1/3 cup mellow white miso
1/4 cup country barley miso

Place kombu in water in a 4-quart saucepan. Let it soak while chopping vegetables (you may also soak the kombu overnight). Add the next 5 ingredients, and bring mixture to a boil. Simmer 15 minutes; remove kombu. Use a wire strainer with a handle to remove solids. Continue to simmer broth as you press the solids firmly against the strainer with the back of a large spoon, squeezing the juices back into the soup; discard solids. Add the vegetable broth, garlic, and ginger to the simmering broth.

Cut tofu into a 1/2-inch slice for each serving. Cut each slice into small cubes, and place the cubes in the bottom of soup bowls. Combine both varieties of miso in a small bowl. Gradually add a cup of the broth, blending with a small whisk or fork, until the mixture is creamed. Add the mixture back to the soup, and simmer gently 2 minutes. Serve immediately.

When reheating the soup, heat gently, just until the first bubbles appear.

NUTRITION ANALYSIS
(PER 1 1/2-CUP SERVING)

Protein 2 gm., Carbohydrate 7 gm., Fiber 1 gm., Fat 0,
Cholesterol 0, Calcium 12 mg., Sodium 306 mg.

Calories 41
From protein: 21%; From carbohydrate: 69%; From fat: 10%

Morning Miso II

The predominant flavor in this richly-flavored, savory soup is hatcho miso. Most of the vegetables are left in this version of miso soup, giving it a chunkier texture.

◆ A B O U T   3   Q U A R T S ◆

1 piece kombu
2 quarts water
1 medium tomato, diced
1 cup chopped onion
4 cloves garlic, minced
1/2 cup chopped green bell pepper
1 Tbsp. grated gingerroot
1 cup diced zucchini

2 cups chicken-flavored vegetable broth, hot
1 tsp. granulated garlic
1/2 tsp. ground ginger
1/4 cup hatcho miso
1/4 cup mellow white miso
2 Tbsp. mellow barley miso
1/2 cup plus 2 Tbsp. lite silken tofu (optional), drained

Soak kombu at least 15 minutes or overnight in water. Add the next 6 ingredients, bring to a boil, then simmer 15 minutes. Remove the kombu. Remove a third of the vegetables from the broth, and press against a strainer with the back of a spoon, squeezing the juices back into the soup; discard solids. Add the hot broth, garlic, and ginger, and continue to simmer. Place the miso varieties in a small bowl, and gradually blend in about a cup of the hot broth. Cream the miso with the broth until smooth. Add the creamed miso to the soup, and simmer gently. *Do not allow to boil!*

Slice the tofu into 1/4-inch slices. Cut each slice into small cubes, and place the cubes in each soup bowl. Ladle soup over the tofu. Serve hot.

◆*83*◆

NUTRITION ANALYSIS
(PER 1/2-CUP SERVING)

Protein 3 gm., Carbohydrate 9 gm., Fiber 1 gm., Fat 1 gm.,
Cholesterol 0, Calcium 17 mg., Sodium 360 mg.

Calories 53
From protein: 20%; From carbohydrate: 70%; From fat: 10%

Soybeans Polynesian

Soybeans are at the heart of this luscious stew. It takes its Hawaiian character from the sweet Maui onions and pineapple chunks that blend so well with the cinnamon-spiced sauce.

◆ 10 SERVINGS ◆

1 cup dried soybeans

6 cups water

1 1/2 tsp. olive oil

1/4 tsp. crushed red pepper

1 medium Maui onion, chopped (or other sweet onion)

6 cloves garlic, minced

2 Tbsp. grated gingerroot

1 medium gold bell pepper, chopped

2 medium Yukon Gold potatoes, unpeeled, diced

2 cups sliced baby carrots

1/2 pound. mushrooms, sliced

3 large fresh tomatoes, diced

20-oz. can pineapple chunks in juice, drained, reserve juice

1 bay leaf

1/4 cup mirin or dry sherry

1 cinnamon stick

1 Tbsp. Bragg Liquid Aminos

1/2 tsp. ground ginger

8 large fresh basil leaves

◆*84*◆

Precook soybeans (see Techniques). Heat oil with crushed pepper in a 6-quart saucepan over medium-high heat. Add the next 4 ingredients, and sauté 2 minutes. Add potatoes and carrots; sauté 5 minutes, stirring frequently. Add mushrooms, tomatoes, pineapple chunks, and bay leaf. Cook 5 minutes over medium heat, stirring occasionally. Add mirin, 1/4 cup of reserved pineapple juice, and cinnamon stick. Add cooked soybeans and remaining ingredients. Lower heat, and simmer for an hour, stirring occasionally, or until ready to serve. Serve with Pungent Basmati Rice (see page 142).

NUTRITION ANALYSIS
(PER 2-CUP SERVING)

Protein 11 gm., Carbohydrate 67 gm., Fiber 6 gm., Fat 5 gm.,
Cholesterol 0, Calcium 84 mg., Sodium 101 mg.

Calories 219
From protein: 12%; From carbohydrate: 76%; From fat: 13%

Split Pea Soup With Ham

This split pea soup is hearty and flavorful. Chunky vegetables and vegetarian bacon make this authentic-tasting remake quite remarkable.

◆ ABOUT 4 QUARTS ◆

1-pound. pkg. dry split peas, rinsed and sorted

7 cups chicken-flavored vegetable broth

1 1/2 tsp. olive oil

1/4 tsp. crushed red pepper

6 cloves garlic, minced

1 large red onion, chopped (about 3 cups)

2 cups sliced baby carrots

2 cups zucchini cut into julienne strips

6-oz. pkg. veggie Canadian bacon, diced

1 cup white wine

2 bay leaves

1/2 tsp. dried thyme

2 Tbsp. dried parsley

1 Tbsp. Bragg Liquid Aminos

Combine the peas with the broth in a 5-quart saucepan. Bring to a boil, then lower to simmer, covered. Heat olive oil and crushed red pepper in a 10" frying pan for 1 minute. Add the next 4 ingredients, and sauté over medium-high heat 10 minutes or until vegetables soften and the juices are rendered. Using a slotted spoon, remove the veggies and place in soup pot, leaving juices in frying pan. Add the diced bacon to the frying pan, and cook 5 minutes. Add bacon to soup pot, and deglaze the frying pan with wine, stirring up any browned bits that remain at the bottom. Add to pot. Add the remaining ingredients, and simmer, stirring occasionally, until the peas are tender (from 30 to 45 minutes) or until ready to serve.

◆ *85* ◆

NUTRITION ANALYSIS
(PER 1/2-CUP SERVING)

Protein 17 gm., Carbohydrate 68 gm., Fiber 6 gm., Fat 1 gm., Cholesterol 0, Calcium 61 mg., Sodium 323 mg.

Calories 242
From protein: 20%; From carbohydrate: 77%; From fat: 4%

Tempting Tomato Vegetable Soup

The wonderful flavors of leeks, mushrooms, zucchini, and carrots, along with a broth enriched with miso, combine to make this soup especially delicious.

◆ A B O U T   5   Q U A R T S ◆

1 Tbsp. olive oil
1/4 tsp. crushed red pepper
2 leeks, cleaned and cut into
   1/4-inch slices (see Techniques)
6 cloves garlic, minced
1 1/4 cups green beans, cut into
   1 1/2-inch pieces
1 1/2 cups baby carrots, halved
   crosswise
2 medium Yukon gold potatoes,
   unpeeled, cut into 1-inch chunks
2 cups zucchini, cut into
   julienne strips

2 cups sliced mushrooms, stems
   intact
1 1/4 cups white wine
14.5-oz. can Italian-flavored
   tomatoes, peeled and diced
10 cups beef-flavored vegetable broth
1/4 cup mellow white miso
1 tsp. Bragg Liquid Aminos
1 tsp. dried basil
1 tsp. dried marjoram

Heat oil and crushed pepper in a 6-quart saucepan. Add the leeks and garlic; sauté 3 minutes. Add the next 3 ingredients. Sauté 7 minutes, stirring frequently. Add zucchini and mushrooms; cook over medium-high heat 5 minutes. Stir in wine, and cook mixture 3 minutes. Add tomatoes and broth. Lower heat, and simmer 30 to 45 minutes. Place miso in a small bowl. Gradually stir in 1/2 cup of hot soup broth. Add creamed miso to soup along with remaining ingredients. Simmer 3 minutes—do not allow to boil. Serve immediately.

NUTRITION ANALYSIS
(PER 2 1/2-CUP SERVING)

Protein 5 gm., Carbohydrate 81 gm., Fiber 4 gm., Fat 2 gm.,
Cholesterol 0, Calcium 60 mg., Sodium 315 mg.

Calories 180
From protein: 5%; From carbohydrate: 90%; From fat: 5%

Vichyssoise

The irresistible yet subtle flavor of leeks is at the heart of this classic soup. Generally served chilled, this soup is also good hot.

◆ A B O U T   3   1 / 2   Q U A R T S ◆

1 Tbsp. olive oil

4 medium leeks, cleaned and cut into 1/4-inch slices (see Techniques)

3 cloves garlic, minced

1 cup chopped red onion

5 Yukon Gold potatoes, peeled and cubed (about 6 cups)

1/3 cup chopped gold bell pepper

4 cups chicken-flavored vegetable broth

1 1/4 cups lite silken tofu (firm), drained

3/4 cup soymilk lite

2 Tbsp. lemon juice

1 Tbsp. nutritional yeast

2 tsp. Bragg Liquid Aminos

1/4 tsp. white pepper

fresh parsley for garnish

Heat oil in a 5-quart saucepan over medium-high heat. Sauté the leeks, garlic, onion, potatoes, and bell pepper until vegetables are crisp tender, about 10 minutes. Add broth. Lower heat, and simmer 25 minutes or until vegetables are tender. Using a slotted spoon, place vegetables in food processor; purée. Set puréed vegetables aside in a large bowl. Blend tofu in food processor. Add the soymilk and the liquid from the soup, and blend. Add the remaining ingredients (except parsley) to the tofu, and blend. Combine the tofu mixture with the puréed vegetables.

If you're serving hot vichyssoise, return the mixture to the soup pot to heat until hot. Garnish with chopped fresh parsley. For the traditional cold vichyssoise, chill until ready to serve. You may want to adjust the seasonings or add more soymilk to thin before serving. The texture should be velvety smooth.

◆87◆

NUTRITION ANALYSIS
(PER 1 2/3-CUP SERVING)

Protein 8 gm., Carbohydrate 71 gm., Fiber 3 gm., Fat 3 gm.,
Cholesterol 0, Calcium 47 mg., Sodium 190 mg.

Calories 236
From protein: 9%; From carbohydrate: 83%; From fat: 7%

Chunky Chick-Pea Salad

This high-protein, low-fat salad is a wonderful lunchbox stuffer.
Try it on hearty whole wheat bread with lettuce, sprouts, and tomato.
Now that's a sandwich that will see you through the day.

◆ 8　SERVINGS ◆

4 15-oz. cans garbanzo beans, drained

1 stalk celery, chopped

2 scallions, sliced

1/2 cup chopped red onion

1/3 cup chopped green bell pepper

1/2 tsp. salt

1 1/4 cups lite silken tofu (firm), drained

1/4 cup lemon juice

3 Tbsp. cider vinegar

1 Tbsp. liquid Fruitsource or honey

2 Tbsp. Dijon mustard

2 Tbsp. capers, drained

◆88◆ Place garbanzo beans in a large bowl. Mash with a potato masher or fork. Add the next 5 ingredients. Place the tofu in food processor, and blend. Add the next 4 ingredients, and process until smooth. Add the tofu mixture to the garbanzo mixture; add capers. Mix well, and chill 4 hours or until ready to serve.

NUTRITION ANALYSIS
(PER 1 1/4-CUP SERVING)

Protein 15 gm., Carbohydrate 36 gm., Fiber 8 gm., Fat 3 gm.,
Cholesterol 0, Calcium 8 mg., Sodium 220 mg.

Calories 236
From protein: 25%; From carbohydrate: 62%; From fat: 13%

Couscous Salad

I like to serve this delicious salad at room temperature, but it can also be served chilled, scooped onto a bed of fresh greens.

◆ 8 SERVINGS ◆

1 1/2 cups chicken-flavored
vegetable broth

1 cup couscous

2 cups broccoli florets, sliced into
1/4-inch cuts

1/2 cup lite silken tofu (firm),
drained

1/4 cup tofu mayonnaise (see
Soyfoods Pantry)

1 clove garlic, peeled

2 Tbsp. lemon juice

1/2 tsp. dried cilantro

1/2 tsp. ground cumin

1/2 tsp. ground coriander

14.5-oz. can peeled and diced
tomatoes, well drained

1/3 cup sliced scallions

1/4 cup chopped red bell pepper

dried mint for garnish

Place broth and couscous in a medium saucepan. Cover and bring to a boil; stir, and remove from heat. Set aside. Blanch broccoli florets very briefly, no more than a minute. Remove to a bowl of ice water to stop cooking, then drain in a colander. Blend tofu in food processor. Add mayonnaise and garlic; blend until smooth. Add lemon juice, cilantro, cumin, and coriander, and blend thoroughly. Place cooked couscous in a large bowl, and fluff with a fork. Add drained tomatoes, scallions, and bell pepper. Mix well. Fold in tofu mixture, and mix thoroughly. Sprinkle with mint, and serve, or chill before serving.

◆89◆

NUTRITION ANALYSIS
(PER 1-CUP SERVING)

Protein 6 gm., Carbohydrate 24 gm., Fiber 3 gm., Fat 2 gm.,
Cholesterol 0, Calcium 44 mg., Sodium 88 mg.

Calories 137
From protein: 18%; From carbohydrate: 68%; From fat: 14%

Creamy Herbed Potato "Chill"

Chilled red potato slices nestle in a delectably creamy herb sauce for an intriguing alternative to the all-too-familiar potato salad.

◆ 1 0 S E R V I N G S ◆

5 medium new red potatoes, unpeeled (about 2 1/2 pound.)

2 Tbsp. olive oil

1 1/4 cups chopped red onion

2 large cloves garlic, minced

1/2 cup chopped orange or yellow bell pepper

1 rib celery, sliced

1/4 cup whole wheat flour

1/4 cup dry vermouth

1 cup soymilk lite

1 1/4 cups lite silken tofu (extra firm), drained

2 Tbsp. mellow white miso

2 Tbsp. dry vermouth

1 Tbsp. lemon juice

2 Tbsp. nutritional yeast

6 large basil leaves, snipped

1 tsp. dried marjoram

1/2 tsp. dried tarragon

1/2 tsp. dried thyme

1 cup frozen peas, cooked

◆ *90* ◆

Place whole, unpeeled potatoes in a large saucepan. Add water to cover. Bring to a boil; cook 45 minutes or until fork tender to the center. Set aside to cool in a colander. Cut into 1/4-inch slices (unpeeled). Chill.

Heat oil over medium-high heat in a medium saucepan. Add the next 4 ingredients, and sauté until tender, about 5 minutes. Add flour, and stir to coat vegetables, about 3 minutes. Add vermouth, and stir to a paste, about 2 minutes. Lower heat to simmer. Add soymilk 1/4 cup at a time. Stir frequently until thickened. Place tofu in a food processor; blend. Blend miso with vermouth in a small bowl. Add to tofu along with lemon juice and nutritional yeast; blend. Stir tofu mixture gently into white sauce, then add herbs and peas. Fold vegetables and herbed cream into chilled potato slices. Chill 1 hour or until ready to serve.

NUTRITION ANALYSIS
(PER SERVING)

Protein 8 gm., Carbohydrate 37 gm., Fiber 3 gm., Fat 4 gm., Cholesterol 0, Calcium 18 mg., Sodium 94 mg.

Calories 213
From protein: 15%; From carbohydrate: 70%; From fat: 16%

Curried Tofu & Basmati Rice Salad

*Savory baked tofu and delicate basmati rice in a creamy curry dressing
are especially appealing when served on a bed of colorful red leaf lettuce.
Garnished with starfruit, this dish makes an impressive presentation.*

◆ 6 SERVINGS ◆

DRESSING:

1 1/4 cups lite silken tofu (extra
  firm), drained

2 large shallots, peeled and quartered

1/4 cup soymilk lite

1 Tbsp. grated fresh gingerroot

1/2 tsp. ground cumin

1/2 tsp. ground coriander

1/4 tsp. turmeric

2 1/2 Tbsp. lemon juice

1 Tbsp. Dijon mustard

1 tsp. tamari

3 Tbsp. chopped fresh cilantro

2 Tbsp. nutritional yeast

1 1/2 cups chicken-flavored
  vegetable broth

1/2 cup basmati rice, rinsed

1/4 tsp. turmeric

1/4 tsp. granulated garlic

3 6-oz. pkgs. savory baked tofu

2 ripe carambola (starfruit)

salad greens

fresh cilantro

•91•

Place tofu in food processor; blend until smooth. Add the next 6 ingredients, and
process to blend. Add remaining dressing ingredients, and blend until smooth.
Refrigerate, covered.

Bring broth to a boil. Add basmati rice, then bring to a second boil; add seasonings.
Reduce heat and simmer 15 minutes or until tender and liquid is absorbed. Set rice
aside to cool. Slice the tofu lengthwise, dividing the width. Slice crosswise into julienne
strips. Toss with dressing, then add cooled rice, and toss again. Chill the salad several
hours or overnight (if allowed to sit overnight, the tofu will develop an even meatier
consistency). Place torn salad greens on individual serving plates. Scoop salad onto
greens, and garnish with thin slices of starfruit and sprigs of fresh cilantro.

NUTRITION ANALYSIS
(PER SERVING)

Protein 26 gm., Carbohydrate 31 gm., Fiber 3 gm., Fat 3 gm.,
Cholesterol 0, Calcium 29 mg., Sodium 620 mg.

Calories 253
From protein: 41%; From carbohydrate: 49%; From fat: 10%

Ravishing Rice Salad

*Plump and creamy Great Northern beans join vegetarian
Canadian bacon and brown rice in this delicious salad.*

◆ 8 SERVINGS ◆

3 cups cooked brown rice, cooled

2/3 cup sliced scallions

2 cloves garlic, minced

1/2 cup chopped green bell pepper

4.25-oz. can chopped black olives, drained

6-oz. pkg. veggie Canadian bacon, diced

15-oz. can Great Northern beans, drained

DRESSING:

1/2 cup plus 2 Tbsp. lite silken tofu (extra firm), drained

2 Tbsp. Dijon mustard

1 Tbsp. liquid Fruitsource or honey

1 1/2 Tbsp. mellow white miso

1/2 tsp. dried thyme

1/4 tsp. ground coriander

1/4 tsp. Tabasco sauce

◆*92*◆   Place cooked rice in a medium bowl. Add the next 6 ingredients, and mix thoroughly. Set aside.

Place tofu in food processor, and blend until smooth. Add the remaining dressing ingredients; pulse to mix, then blend until smooth. Fold dressing into rice mixture. Cover and refrigerate for at least an hour. Serve chilled.

NUTRITION ANALYSIS
(PER SERVING)

Protein 13 gm., Carbohydrate 30 gm., Fiber 5 gm., Fat 3 gm.,
Cholesterol 0, Calcium 28 mg., Sodium 596 mg.

Calories 183
From protein: 26%; From carbohydrate: 62%; From fat: 12%

Colorful Garden Mix

This is a beautiful salad—a study in contrasts—especially when
accented with delectable Raspberry Walnut Dressing (page 96).

◆ 8 SERVINGS ◆

1 head red leaf lettuce, torn

1 pound. fresh spinach, well rinsed
and torn

1 medium red onion, thinly sliced

1/2 ripe avocado, peeled, pitted,
thinly sliced, and drizzled with
lime juice

1/2 cup chopped red bell pepper

1/2 cup chopped orange bell pepper

6 large Calimyrna figs, sliced

2 Tbsp. chopped fresh parsley

Mix the lettuce and spinach in a large salad bowl, then layer the remaining ingredients in the order listed. Pass the dressing to guests at the table.

NUTRITION ANALYSIS
(PER SERVING)

◆93◆

Protein 4 gm., Carbohydrate 15 gm., Fiber 5 gm., Fat 2 gm.,
Cholesterol 0, Calcium 107 mg., Sodium 54 mg.

Calories 87
From protein: 15%; From carbohydrate: 63%; From fat: 22%

Shredded Tofu and Artichoke Salad

Hearty and colorful, this salad is delicious!

◆ 6 SERVINGS ◆

2 1/2 cups lite silken tofu (extra firm), frozen, defrosted, and shredded

1/2 cup sliced scallions

1/3 cup chopped green pepper

2 cups chopped fresh spinach

15-oz. can garbanzo beans, drained

13 3/4-oz. can quartered artichoke hearts, drained and sliced

DRESSING:

1 1/4 cups lite silken tofu, firm

2 cloves garlic, peeled

1 cup soymilk lite

1 Tbsp. cider vinegar

1 Tbsp. Bragg Liquid Aminos

1/4 cup nutritional yeast

1/2 tsp. dried thyme

1/2 tsp. dried marjoram

1/2 tsp. ground coriander

1/4 tsp. turmeric

1/2 tsp. granulated garlic

dash cayenne, to taste

◆94◆

Place shredded tofu (see Techniques) in a medium bowl and mix with the next 5 ingredients. Set aside.

Place 1 1/4 cups drained tofu in food processor and blend until smooth. Add the next 9 ingredients and blend until smooth. Fold dressing into the shredded tofu mixture; mix thoroughly. Add granulated garlic and cayenne, and mix well. Cover and chill 4 hours or overnight.

NUTRITION ANALYSIS
(PER SERVING)

Protein 20 gm., Carbohydrate 73 gm., Fiber 5 gm., Fat 3 gm.,
Cholesterol 0, Calcium 72 mg., Sodium 440 mg.

Calories 202
From protein: 20%; From carbohydrate: 73%; From fat: 7%

Tofu 'n Rice Salad

*An appealing salad garnished with fresh tomato wedges
and sprinkled with fragrant basil and thyme.*

◆ 8 SERVINGS ◆

3 cups chicken-flavored vegetable
   broth, boiling

1 cup short grain brown rice

2 1/2 cups frozen lite silken tofu,
   (extra firm) defrosted

1/3 cup sliced scallions

1/3 cup chopped green pepper

6 large mushrooms, slice caps and
   chop stems (about 1 1/4 cups)

DRESSING:

1 1/4 cups lite silken tofu (firm),
   drained

2 cloves garlic, peeled

2 Tbsp. mellow white miso

1 cup soymilk lite

1 Tbsp. Dijon mustard

1 Tbsp. tamari

2 1/2 Tbsp. lemon juice

8-oz. can sliced water chestnuts,
   drained

1 medium tomato, sliced into thin
   wedges

dried basil and dried thyme

◆95◆

Place brown rice in boiling broth and bring to a second boil. Cover saucepan, and simmer for 40 minutes, or until all liquid is absorbed. Shred defrosted tofu (see Techniques). Mix shredded tofu in a medium bowl with the next 3 ingredients; set aside. Place 1 1/4 cups drained tofu in food processor and blend until smooth. Add the next 6 ingredients and blend until smooth. Add the water chestnuts and pulse to mix, leaving the mixture chunky. Fold the dressing into the shredded tofu mixture. Arrange the tomato wedges around the edge of the bowl and sprinkle with basil and thyme. Cover and chill 4 hours or overnight.

NUTRITION ANALYSIS
(PER SERVING)

Protein 11 gm., Carbohydrate 29 gm., Fiber 2 gm., Fat 2 gm.,
Cholesterol 0, Calcium 53 mg., Sodium 315 mg.

Calories 177
From protein: 25%; From carbohydrate: 63%; From fat: 12%

Raspberry Walnut Dressing

Delightfully flavorful, the secret ingredient in this creamy dressing is dried cherries, which add a special zing. Try this tangy dressing on the Colorful Garden Mix (page 93).

◆ 3 C U P S ◆

1/2 cup plus 2 Tbsp. lite silken tofu (extra firm), drained

1/2 cup soymilk lite

1 Tbsp. olive oil

3 Tbsp. raspberry vinegar

1 clove garlic, peeled

2 scallions, minced

2 Tbsp. dried cherries

2 Tbsp. walnut pieces

1 Tbsp. liquid Fruitsource or honey

2 Tbsp. mellow white miso

1 tsp. dried parsley

In food processor, blend tofu until smooth. Add the next 5 ingredients, and process. Add the next 5 ingredients, and first pulse, then blend. Chill at least one hour. Dressing should be smooth with bits of fruit and parsley.

◆ *96* ◆

NUTRITION ANALYSIS
(PER 2-TABLESPOON SERVING)

Protein 1 gm., Carbohydrate 3 gm., Fiber 0, Fat 2 gm., Cholesterol 0, Calcium 3 mg., Sodium 36 mg.

Calories 32
From protein: 18%; From carbohydrate: 35%; From fat: 47%
(The percentage of calories from fat seems high because the calories are so low.)

Garlic Basil Dressing

This creamy, rich-tasting dressing will complement a salad of
your favorite greens with tomatoes and colorful bell peppers.

◆ A B O U T   2   C U P S ◆

1/2 cup plus 2 Tbsp. lite silken tofu
  (extra firm), drained
1/2 cup soymilk lite
1 clove garlic, peeled
2 Tbsp. mellow white miso

2 Tbsp. cider vinegar
1 Tbsp. olive oil
1 Tbsp. liquid Fruitsource or honey
1 tsp. dried basil
1 tsp. Bragg Liquid Aminos

Place drained tofu in food processor, and blend. Add the soymilk and garlic, and pulse to mix. Add the remaining ingredients, and process to mix thoroughly. Dressing should be creamy-smooth with bits of basil. Refrigerate for at least an hour to allow the flavors to blend.

◆*97*◆

NUTRITION ANALYSIS
(PER 2-TABLESPOON SERVING)

Protein 1 gm., Carbohydrate 11 gm., Fiber 0, Fat 1 gm.,
Cholesterol 0, Calcium 4 mg., Sodium 63 mg.

Calories 27
From protein: 8%; From carbohydrate: 71%; From fat: 21%

"Honey" Mustard Dill Dressing

This delightful dressing is excellent, whether livening up a tossed salad or a grilled vegetable sandwich on a whole wheat bun.

◆ ABOUT 2 CUPS ◆

1/2 cup plus 2 Tbsp. lite silken tofu (firm), drained

1/2 cup soymilk lite

1 clove garlic, peeled

1/4 cup Dijon mustard

3 Tbsp. liquid Fruitsource or honey

1 1/2 tsp. olive oil

1 Tbsp. cider vinegar

1 Tbsp. lemon juice

2 Tbsp. mellow white miso

1/4 cup sliced scallions

1 Tbsp. dried dillweed

Place drained tofu in food processor, and blend. Add the next 6 ingredients, and pulse to mix. Add the remaining ingredients, and process to mix thoroughly. Dressing should be creamy-smooth with bits of dill. Refrigerate for at least an hour to allow the flavors to blend.

NUTRITION ANALYSIS
(PER 2-TABLESPOON SERVING)

Protein 1 gm., Carbohydrate 4 gm., Fiber 0, Fat 1 gm.,
Cholesterol 0, Calcium 10 mg., Sodium 89 mg.

Calories 28
From protein: 17%; From carbohydrate: 55%; From fat: 28%

Lemon Poppy Seed Dressing

Try this delicious dressing on a salad of
baby greens topped with thinly sliced red onion.

◆ A B O U T   2   C U P S ◆

1 1/2 Tbsp. poppy seeds

1/2 cup plus 2 Tbsp. lite silken tofu
  (extra firm), drained

1/2 cup soymilk lite

1/4 cup lemon juice

1 Tbsp. liquid Fruitsource or honey

1 Tbsp. olive oil

2 scallions, sliced

1 large shallot, quartered

1 clove garlic, peeled

2 Tbsp. mellow white miso

Place poppy seeds in a small frying pan, and toast lightly about 3 minutes over medium heat, shaking pan gently. Set aside. Place tofu in food processor, and blend until smooth. Add soymilk, and blend. Add remaining ingredients and process to mix. Add poppy seeds. Blend. Chill until ready to serve.

◆*99*◆

NUTRITION ANALYSIS
(PER 2-TABLESPOON SERVING)

Protein 1 gm., Carbohydrate 3 gm., Fiber 0, Fat 1 gm.,
Cholesterol 0, Calcium 14 mg., Sodium 34 mg.

Calories 23
From protein: 19%; From carbohydrate: 45%; From fat: 37%
(The percentage of calories from fat seems high because the calories are so low.)

◆*100*◆

Bountiful Breads

Nothing compares with the tantalizing aroma or the taste of home-baked bread. Alas, how many of us have the luxury of time to guide yeast bread through the hours of preparation required to produce a fine loaf of homemade bread? In this chapter you will find recipes for baking delightful yeast breads that are a cinch, using your bread machine. Bread machines present a terrific contemporary approach to bread baking. All you need do is combine the ingredients according to the machine manufacturer's directions, set the controls, and press "start." As so many of us are discovering bread machine magic these days, I wanted to share my favorite recipes.

In my approach to soy-centered cuisine, making bread offers the splendid opportunity to enhance the nutritive value of this ever present staple. Not only can you avoid unhealthful ingredients, you can impart the wholesome goodness of soy into every slice. Together with soy these wonderful breads are made with whole grains. My favorite, White Wheat Bread, is very light in color and has a bouncy, airy texture not usually found in whole wheat bread.

There are also quick breads which use leavening agents like baking soda and baking powder. Tea breads, snack bars, and muffins are also included in this chapter. Whole Wheat Dinner Muffins, delightful Blueberry Tea Bread, and Peanut Butter Banana Squares are just a few of the easy to assemble quick breads included here. All are made using soy products, and contain no added fat, eggs, or dairy products. These easy-to-make, wholesome baked goods contribute healthful soy protein with each delicious bite! ◆

Apple Raisin Muffins

These muffins are great right out of the oven or split and toasted for breakfast.

◆ 18 MUFFINS ◆

Vegetable oil cooking spray
1 cup soymilk lite
2 Tbsp. lemon juice
1 2/3 cups whole wheat pastry flour
1/3 cup soy flour
1/4 cup soy grits
1 tsp. baking soda
1 tsp. baking powder
1/2 tsp. salt
1 tsp. cinnamon
1/4 cup unsweetened applesauce

1/3 cup Florida Crystals or sugar
1 Tbsp. egg replacer powder
1/4 cup water
1 tsp. vanilla extract
1 medium Pippin or Granny Smith
  apple, peeled, diced, and drizzled
  with lemon juice
1/2 cup golden raisins
cinnamon
ground nutmeg

Preheat oven to 375°. Spray muffin pans with cooking spray. Place soymilk in a small glass measuring cup; add lemon juice. Set aside. Mix together the next 7 ingredients (dry ingredients) in a medium bowl. Set aside.

Place applesauce in a large bowl, and cream with Florida Crystals. In a small bowl, whisk egg replacer powder with water until foamy. Add to creamed applesauce. Add soymilk and vanilla to liquid ingredients, and mix thoroughly. Fold wet ingredients into dry, and combine just until mixed. Fold in apples and raisins. Do not overmix. Spoon into muffin cups, filling the empty cups 1/3 with water. Sprinkle with cinnamon and nutmeg. Bake 15 minutes or until lightly browned and a toothpick inserted in the center comes out clean.

NUTRITION ANALYSIS
(PER MUFFIN)

Protein 4 gm., Carbohydrate 18 gm., Fiber 2 gm., Fat 1 gm.,
Cholesterol 0, Calcium 31 mg., Sodium 158 mg.

Calories 90
From protein: 16%; From carbohydrate: 78%; From fat: 7%

Blueberry Muffins

Dried blueberries and a touch of cornmeal give these muffins a special sweetness and crunch. They're delicious fresh from the oven or toasted under the broiler!

♦ 18 MUFFINS ♦

Vegetable oil cooking spray
1 1/2 cups whole wheat pastry flour
1/2 cup yellow cornmeal
1/3 cup soy grits
1 tsp. baking soda
1 tsp. baking powder
1/4 tsp. salt
1 tsp. ground cinnamon
1/2 cup unsweetened applesauce

1/3 cup Florida Crystals or sugar
1 Tbsp. egg replacer powder
1/4 cup water
1 cup soymilk lite
1 tsp. vanilla extract
1/4 cup walnut pieces
2 Tbsp. soy grits
1 cup dried blueberries

Preheat oven to 350.° Coat 18 muffin cups with cooking spray. Mix whole wheat flour with the next 6 ingredients (dry ingredients) in a medium bowl. Set aside. Cream applesauce and Florida Crystals in a large bowl. Whisk egg replacer with water in a small bowl until foamy; whisk into creamed applesauce. Add soymilk and vanilla, and mix thoroughly. Fold the wet ingredients into the dry ingredients just until mixed. Mix walnut pieces with soy grits, and add to batter along with blueberries. Do not overbeat. Spoon batter into muffin cups, filling empty cups 1/3 full with water. Bake 15 minutes or until toothpick inserted in the center comes out clean.

♦ *103* ♦

NUTRITION ANALYSIS
(PER MUFFIN)

Protein 5 gm., Carbohydrate 24 gm., Fiber 2 gm., Fat 1 gm.,
Cholesterol 0, Calcium 27 mg., Sodium 129 mg.

Calories 126
From protein: 14%; From carbohydrate: 76%; From fat: 10%

Blueberry Tea Bread

Sweet blueberries and buttery cashews make a superb combination!

◆ 1 2   S E R V I N G S ◆

Vegetable oil cooking spray
3/4 cup soymilk lite
2 Tbsp. lemon juice
1 1/2 cups whole wheat pastry flour
3/4 cup rolled oats
1/4 cup soy flour
1 tsp. baking soda
1 tsp. baking powder
1/4 tsp. salt
1/2 cup unsweetened applesauce

1 1/4 cups Florida Crystals or sugar
1 Tbsp. egg replacer powder
1/4 cup water,
1 tsp. vanilla extract
1 tsp. grated lemon rind
1/3 cup cashew pieces
1/3 cup soy grits
1 1/2 cups fresh or thawed
   frozen blueberries

◆ *104* ◆

Preheat oven to 350°. Spray a 9" x 5" loaf pan with cooking spray. Place soymilk in a small glass measuring cup; add lemon juice. Set aside. Mix together the next 6 ingredients (dry ingredients) in a medium bowl. Set aside. Cream the applesauce and Florida Crystals together in a large bowl. In a small bowl, whisk egg replacer powder with water until foamy. Whisk into creamed applesauce along with vanilla and lemon rind. Add soymilk mixture to liquid ingredients; mix thoroughly. Fold wet ingredients into dry ingredients, just until mixed. Mix cashew pieces with soy grits, and add to batter along with blueberries. Do not overmix. Pour into prepared loaf pan, and bake for 50 to 60 minutes or until toothpick inserted in center comes out clean.

NUTRITION ANALYSIS
(PER SLICE)

Protein 7 gm., Carbohydrate 35 gm., Fiber 3 gm., Fat 3 gm.,
Cholesterol 0, Calcium 44 mg., Sodium 192 mg.

Calories 186
From protein: 14%; From carbohydrate: 72%; From fat: 14%;

Buttermilk Wheat Bread

This bread machine recipe makes a terrific bread for sandwiches or toast.

SMALL LOAF (1 LB.)	LARGE LOAF (1 1/2 LB.)
3/4 cup soymilk lite	1 1/2 cups soymilk lite
1 1/2 tsp. cider vinegar	1 Tbsp. cider vinegar
1 Tbsp. unsweetened applesauce	2 Tbsp. unsweetened applesauce
2 Tbsp. Sucanat or brown sugar	1/4 cup Sucanat or brown sugar
1/4 tsp. salt	1/2 tsp. salt
1/4 tsp. baking soda	1/2 tsp. baking soda
1 Tbsp. vital wheat gluten	2 Tbsp. vital wheat gluten
2 cups whole wheat flour	4 cups whole wheat flour
1 tsp. yeast	2 tsp. yeast

Place soymilk in small measuring cup, and add vinegar. Set aside for 5 minutes. Place the ingredients in the bread machine pan in the order recommended by the machine's manufacturer. Set the controls, close the lid, and press "start."

NUTRITION ANALYSIS
(PER 1-OZ. SLICE)

Protein 3 gm., Carbohydrate 14 gm., Fiber 2 gm., Fat 0,
Cholesterol 0, Calcium 7 mg., Sodium 65 mg.

Calories 67
From protein: 16%; From carbohydrate: 79%; From fat: 5%

Cranberry Tea Bread

Dusted with powdered sugar and served with tea or coffee,
Cranberry Tea Bread hits the spot!

◆ 12 SERVINGS ◆

Vegetable oil cooking spray
2/3 cup soymilk lite
1 Tbsp. lemon juice
2 cups whole wheat pastry flour
1/4 cup yellow cornmeal
1/4 cup soy flour
1 tsp. baking soda
1 tsp. baking powder
1/4 tsp. salt
1 tsp. cinnamon

1/2 cup unsweetened applesauce
1 1/4 cups Florida Crystals or sugar
1 Tbsp. egg replacer powder
1/4 cup water
1 tsp. vanilla extract
1 cup fresh or thawed frozen
  cranberries
1/4 cup walnut pieces
1/4 cup soy grits

◆ *106* ◆

Preheat oven to 350°. Coat a loaf pan lightly with cooking spray. Place the soymilk in a small measuring cup, and add lemon juice. Set aside. Mix together the next 7 ingredients (dry ingredients) in a medium bowl; set aside. Cream the applesauce and the Florida Crystals in a large bowl. Whisk the egg replacer powder and water in a small bowl until foamy. Add to applesauce mixture along with the vanilla; mix thoroughly. Fold the dry ingredients into the applesauce mixture alternately with soymilk. Mix walnut pieces with soy grits. Fold into the batter with cranberries; do not overmix. Bake 55 minutes or until toothpick inserted in center comes out clean.

NUTRITION ANALYSIS
(PER SLICE)

Protein 6 gm., Carbohydrate 34 gm., Fiber 3 gm., Fat 2 gm.,
Cholesterol 0, Calcium 46 mg., Sodium 191 mg.

Calories 177
From protein: 13%; From carbohydrate: 74%; From fat: 12%

"Honey" Wheat Bread

This high-rising bread machine bread uses no fat-replacer
other than the Fruitsource, which is a source of pectins.

SMALL LOAF (1 LB.)

3/4 cup soymilk lite
1/4 cup liquid Fruitsource or honey
1/4 tsp. salt
1 Tbsp. vital wheat gluten
2 cups whole wheat flour
1 1/4 tsp. yeast

LARGE LOAF (1 1/2 LB.)

1 1/2 cups soymilk lite
1/2 cup liquid Fruitsource or honey
1/2 tsp. salt
2 Tbsp. vital wheat gluten
4 cups whole wheat flour
2 1/2 tsp. yeast

Place the ingredients in the bread machine pan in the order recommended by the machine's manufacturer. Set the controls, close the lid, and press "start."

NUTRITION ANALYSIS
(PER 1-OZ. SLICE)

Protein 3 gm., Carbohydrate 16 gm., Fiber 2 gm., Fat 0,
Cholesterol 0, Calcium 6 mg., Sodium 41 mg.

Calories 74
From protein: 14%; From carbohydrate: 81%; From fat: 5%

◆ *107* ◆

Jam-in-the-Middle Muffins

These muffins have a great taste and texture
with a dollop of apricot jam baked into the center.

◆ 1 2   M U F F I N S ◆

Vegetable oil cooking spray	1/4 cup Sucanat or brown sugar
3/4 cup soymilk lite	1 tsp. cinnamon
1 Tbsp. lemon juice	1/2 cup prune purée
1 1/2 cups whole wheat pastry flour	1/3 cup liquid Fruitsource or honey
1/2 cup yellow cornmeal	1 Tbsp. egg replacer powder
1/3 cup soy grits	1/4 cup water
1 tsp. baking powder	1 tsp. vanilla extract
1 tsp. baking soda	1/3 cup fruit-sweetened apricot jam

Preheat oven to 350°. Spray a muffin pan with cooking spray. Place soymilk in a small glass measuring cup, and add lemon juice. Set aside. Mix together the next 7 ingredients (dry ingredients) in a medium bowl. Set aside. Place prune purée in a large bowl. Add Fruitsource, and mix well. Whisk egg replacer powder with water in a small bowl until foamy; whisk into creamed prune mixture. Add soymilk and vanilla; mix thoroughly. Fold dry ingredients into liquid ingredients just until mixed. Spoon half of the batter into muffin cups. Drop 1 1/2 teaspoons jam in center of each cup. Top with remaining batter. Bake 12 minutes or until toothpick inserted in the center comes out clean.

NUTRITION ANALYSIS
(PER MUFFIN)

Protein 4 gm., Carbohydrate 36 gm., Fiber 3 gm., Fat 1 gm.,
Cholesterol 0, Calcium 41 mg., Sodium 162 mg.

Calories 165
From protein: 9%; From carbohydrate: 84%; From fat: 7%

Light 'n Lovely Whole Wheat Bread

Equal parts whole wheat flour and unbleached flour
give this bread machine recipe a lighter texture.

SMALL LOAF (1 LB.)

3/4 cup soymilk lite

1 Tbsp. unsweetened applesauce

1 Tbsp. mellow white miso

1 1/2 tsp. egg replacer powder

2 Tbsp. water

1 1/2 Tbsp. liquid Fruitsource
or honey

1 Tbsp. vital wheat gluten

3 Tbsp. soy grits

1 cup unbleached flour

1 cup whole wheat flour

1 1/4 tsp. yeast

LARGE LOAF (1 1/2 LB.)

1 1/2 cups soymilk lite

2 Tbsp. unsweetened applesauce

2 Tbsp. mellow white miso

1 Tbsp. egg replacer powder

1/4 cup water

3 Tbsp. liquid Fruitsource or honey

2 Tbsp. vital wheat gluten

1/3 cup soy grits

2 cups unbleached flour

2 cups whole wheat flour

2 1/2 tsp. yeast

♦ *109* ♦

Place ingredients in bread machine pan in the order recommended by the machine's manufacturer. Set the controls, close the lid, and press "start."

NUTRITION ANALYSIS
(PER 1-OZ. SLICE)

Protein 3 gm., Carbohydrate 12 gm., Fiber 1 gm., Fat 0,
Cholesterol 0, Calcium 4 mg., Sodium 14 mg.

Calories 62
From protein: 16%; From carbohydrate: 77%; From fat: 7%

Maple Wheat Bread

This delicious bread machine loaf rises nicely and slices well for sandwiches.

SMALL LOAF (1 LB.)

3/4 cup soymilk lite

1 Tbsp. unsweetened applesauce

2 Tbsp. maple syrup

2 Tbsp. liquid Fruitsource or honey

1/4 tsp. salt

1 Tbsp. vital wheat gluten

2 cups whole wheat flour

1 tsp. yeast

LARGE LOAF (1 1/2 LBS.)

1 1/2 cups soymilk lite

2 Tbsp. unsweetened applesauce

1/4 cup maple syrup

1/4 cup liquid Fruitsource or honey

1/2 tsp. salt

2 Tbsp. vital wheat gluten

4 cups whole wheat flour

2 tsp. yeast

Place ingredients in bread machine pan in the order recommended by the machine's manufacturer. Set the controls, close the lid, and press "start."

NUTRITION ANALYSIS
(PER 1-OZ. SLICE)

Protein 3 gm., Carbohydrate 16 gm., Fiber 2 gm., Fat 0,
Cholesterol 0, Calcium 7 mg., Sodium 42 mg.

Calories 75
From protein: 14%; From carbohydrate: 81%; From fat: 5%

Nutty Oat Bread

*Thanks to my neighbor Rosemary Campagna and her garden, I have
a constant supply of zucchini in the summer. The zucchini contributes
to the moist texture of this delightful bread.*

SMALL LOAF (1 LB.)	LARGE LOAF (1 1/2 LB.)
1/2 cup soymilk lite	1 cup soymilk lite
6 Tbsp. shredded zucchini	3/4 cup shredded zucchini
2 Tbsp. prune purée	1/4 cup prune purée
2 Tbsp. liquid Fruitsource or honey	1/4 cup liquid Fruitsource or honey
1/4 tsp. salt	1/2 tsp. salt
1/2 tsp. cinnamon	1 tsp. cinnamon
1/8 tsp. ground nutmeg	1/4 tsp. ground nutmeg
6 Tbsp. rolled oats	3/4 cup rolled oats
2 Tbsp. oat bran	1/4 cup oat bran
1 Tbsp. vital wheat gluten	2 Tbsp. vital wheat gluten
1 1/2 cups whole wheat flour	3 cups whole wheat flour
1 1/4 tsp. yeast	2 1/2 tsp. yeast

• 111 •

Place ingredients in bread machine pan in the order recommended by the machine's
manufacturer. Set the controls, close the lid, and press "start."

NUTRITION ANALYSIS
(PER 1-OZ. SLICE)

Protein 3 gm., Carbohydrate 14 gm., Fiber 2 gm., Fat 0,
Cholesterol 0, Calcium 7 mg., Sodium 40 mg.

Calories 66
From protein: 15%; From carbohydrate: 79%; From fat: 6%

Oat Bran Raisin Muffins

This sweet bran muffin contributes to a tasty breakfast.

◆ 18 MUFFINS ◆

Vegetable oil cooking spray
3/4 cup soymilk lite
1 Tbsp. lemon juice
1 1/3 cups whole wheat pastry flour
1/2 cup oat bran
1/4 cup yellow cornmeal
1/4 cup soy grits
1/4 cup Sucanat or brown sugar
1 tsp. baking powder
1 tsp. baking soda

1/4 tsp. salt
1 tsp. cinnamon
1/2 cup prune purée
1/4 cup liquid Fruitsource or honey
1 Tbsp. egg replacer powder
1/4 cup water
1 Tbsp. grated lemon zest
1 tsp. vanilla extract
1 cup golden raisins, tossed with
   1 tsp. flour

◆ *112* ◆

Preheat oven to 350°. Spray 18 muffin cups with cooking spray. Place soymilk and lemon juice in a small measuring cup. Set aside. Mix the next 9 ingredients (dry ingredients) in a medium bowl. Set aside. Combine prune purée and Fruitsource in a large bowl; mix well. Whisk egg replacer powder with water in a small bowl until foamy. Add to prune mixture, and whisk together. Add lemon zest, vanilla, and soymilk. Mix well. Fold the dry ingredients into the wet ingredients just until mixed. Add raisins. Spoon into muffin cups, filling empty cups 1/3 full with water. Bake 10 minutes or until toothpick inserted in center comes out clean.

NUTRITION ANALYSIS
(PER MUFFIN)

Protein 3 gm., Carbohydrate 27 gm., Fiber 3 gm., Fat 1 gm.,
Cholesterol 0, Calcium 33 mg., Sodium 137 mg.

Calories 118
From protein: 9%; From carbohydrate: 85%; From fat: 6%

Oat Wheat Bread

This light and flavorful bread has just a hint of oats.
It rises nicely and is perfect for sandwiches.

SMALL LOAF (1 LB.)

3/4 cup soymilk lite

3 Tbsp. liquid Fruitsource or honey

1 Tbsp. mellow white miso

1 Tbsp. vital wheat gluten

1/2 cup rolled oats

3 Tbsp. soy flour

1 1/3 cups white wheat flour

1 1/4 tsp. yeast

LARGE LOAF (1 1/2 LBS.)

1 1/2 cups soymilk lite

1/3 cup liquid Fruitsource or honey

2 Tbsp. mellow white miso

2 Tbsp. vital wheat gluten

1 cup rolled oats

1/3 cup soy flour

2 2/3 cups white wheat flour

2 1/2 tsp. yeast

Place ingredients in bread machine pan in the order recommended by the machine's manufacturer. Set the controls, close the lid, and press "start."

♦ *113* ♦

NUTRITION ANALYSIS
(PER 1-OZ. SLICE)

Protein 2 gm., Carbohydrate 13 gm., Fiber 2 gm., Fat 1 gm.,
Cholesterol 0, Calcium 3 mg., Sodium 17 mg.

Calories 66
From protein: 14%; From carbohydrate: 77%; From fat: 9%

Perfect Pumpernickel

*In my quest for a great pumpernickel bread, I hit upon this
bread machine recipe after many tries. Look for a medium rise,
firm crust, and soft interior in this fragrant bread.*

SMALL LOAF (1 LB.)	LARGE LOAF (1 1/2 LB.)
3/4 cup soymilk lite	1 1/2 cups soymilk lite
1 Tbsp. prune purée	2 Tbsp. prune purée
1 Tbsp. mellow white miso	2 Tbsp. mellow white miso
2 Tbsp. mild molasses	1/4 cup mild molasses
1 Tbsp. unsweetened cocoa powder	2 Tbsp. unsweetened cocoa powder
1 Tbsp. vital wheat gluten	2 Tbsp. vital wheat gluten
1/2 cup oat flour	1 cup oat flour
1/2 cup rye flour	1 cup rye flour
1 1/4 cups whole wheat flour	2 1/2 cups whole wheat flour
1 1/4 tsp. yeast	2 1/2 tsp. yeast

♦ *114* ♦

Place ingredients in bread machine pan in the order recommended by the machine's
manufacturer. Set the controls, close the lid, and press "start."

NUTRITION ANALYSIS
(PER SLICE)

Protein 2 gm., Carbohydrate 13 gm., Fiber 2 gm., Fat 0,
Cholesterol 0, Calcium 25 mg., Sodium 20 mg.

Calories 64
From protein: 14%; From carbohydrate: 79%; From fat: 7%

Peanut Butter Banana Squares

Low in fat and high in carbohydrates,
these squares could be called "energy bars."

◆ 2 5   S Q U A R E S ◆

Vegetable oil cooking spray
3/4 cup soymilk lite
1 Tbsp. lemon juice
2 1/2 cups whole wheat pastry flour
1/2 cup soy grits
1 1/2 tsp. baking soda
1 1/2 tsp. baking powder
1/4 tsp. salt
1 tsp. cinnamon

1/3 cup crunchy peanut butter
1/3 cup prune purée
1 cup mashed banana (2 medium)
1/2 cup liquid Fruitsource or honey
1 Tbsp. egg replacer powder
1/4 cup water
1/2 cup date nuggets (see page 24)
cinnamon
nutmeg

Preheat oven to 350.° Spray a 9" x 13" pan with cooking spray. Place soymilk and lemon juice in a small measuring cup; set aside. Mix together the next 6 ingredients in a large bowl; set aside. Blend peanut butter, prune purée, and banana in a medium bowl. Add Fruitsource, and blend well. Place egg replacer and water in a small bowl. Whisk until frothy, and add to peanut butter mixture. Fold liquid ingredients into the dry ingredients alternately with soymilk. Pour batter into prepared pan. Sprinkle generously with cinnamon and nutmeg. Bake 35 to 40 minutes or until toothpick inserted in center comes out clean.

◆*115*◆

NUTRITION ANALYSIS
(PER SQUARE)

Protein 5 gm., Carbohydrate 22 gm., Fiber 2 gm., Fat 2 gm.,
Cholesterol 0, Calcium 30 mg., Sodium 127 mg.

Calories 116
From protein: 15%; From carbohydrate: 70%; From fat: 15%

Spiced Carrot Muffins

Fragrant with fresh ginger, cinnamon, and other spices, these muffins are a treat!

◆ 1 2 MUFFINS ◆

Vegetable oil cooking spray
1/2 cup cup soymilk lite
1 Tbsp. lemon juice
1 1/2 cups whole wheat pastry flour
1 tsp. baking powder
1 tsp. baking soda
1 tsp. cinnamon
1/2 tsp. ground nutmeg
1/2 tsp. ground ginger

1/8 tsp. ground cloves
1/4 tsp. salt
1 1/2 cups Sucanat or brown sugar
1/2 cup prune purée
2 Tbsp. egg replacer powder
1/2 cup cold water
1 Tbsp. grated fresh gingerroot
1 1/2 cups grated carrots
1/2 cup golden raisins or currants

Preheat oven to 375.° Spray muffin pan with cooking spray. Place soymilk in a measuring cup. Add lemon juice; set aside. In a medium bowl, stir together flour with next 8 ingredients. Set aside. Measure prune purée into a large bowl. Whisk egg replacer powder with water in a small bowl. Whisk into prune purée. Add grated gingerroot and soymilk. Mix thoroughly. Add liquid ingredients to dry, mixing just until blended. Fold in grated carrots and raisins. Spoon into muffin cups. Bake for 12 minutes or until a toothpick inserted in the center comes out clean.

NUTRITION ANALYSIS
(PER MUFFIN)

Protein 3 gm., Carbohydrate 44 gm., Fiber 3 gm., Fat 0,
Cholesterol 0, Calcium 63 mg., Sodium 245 mg.

Calories 184
From protein: 6%; From carbohydrate: 92%; From fat: 2%

Josh's Banana Bread

I made this streusel-filled banana bread
for Susie Boch on the day her son was born.

◆ 12 SERVINGS ◆

Vegetable oil cooking spray
3/4 cup soymilk lite
1 Tbsp. lemon juice
2 cups whole wheat pastry flour
1/4 cup soy flour
1 tsp. baking soda
1 tsp. baking powder
1/4 tsp. salt
1 tsp. cinnamon
1/3 cup prune purée
1 cup mashed bananas
  (2 to 3 bananas)

3/4 cup Florida Crystals or sugar
1 Tbsp. egg replacer powder
1/4 cup water
1 tsp. vanilla extract
  STREUSEL:
1/3 cup walnut pieces
2 Tbsp. soy grits
2 Tbsp. brown sugar
1/2 tsp. cinnamon
1/4 tsp. ground nutmeg

◆ *117* ◆

Preheat oven to 350.° Coat a 9" x 5" loaf pan with cooking spray. Place soymilk in a small glass measuring cup, and add lemon juice. Set aside. Mix together the next 6 ingredients. Set aside. Place prune purée in a large bowl. Add mashed bananas and Florida Crystals. Whisk together egg replacer powder and water in a small bowl until foamy. Add egg replacer and vanilla to the prune/banana combination. Mix thoroughly. Fold liquid ingredients into dry ingredients alternately with soymilk. Mix together streusel ingredients. Pour half the batter into the prepared pan. Top with streusel, then add remainder of the batter. Sprinkle generously with cinnamon and nutmeg. Bake 50 to 55 minutes or until toothpick inserted in center comes out clean.

NUTRITION ANALYSIS
(PER SLICE)

Protein 5 gm., Carbohydrate 35 gm., Fiber 4 gm., Fat 3 gm.,
Cholesterol 0, Calcium 49 mg., Sodium 196 mg.

Calories 180
From protein: 10%; From carbohydrate: 74%; From fat: 16%

White Wheat Bread

Whole grain white wheat flour is naturally light in color. This high-rising bread machine bread has a fine crumbed, creamy interior, unlike the hearty, whole grain density one expects from whole wheat bread.

SMALL LOAF (1 LB.)

3/4 cup soymilk lite

2 Tbsp. liquid Fruitsource or honey

1 Tbsp. mellow white miso

1 1/2 tsp. egg replacer powder

2 Tbsp. water

1 Tbsp. vital wheat gluten

2 Tbsp. soy flour or soy grits

2 cups white wheat flour

1 1/4 tsp. yeast

LARGE LOAF (1 1/2 LBS.)

1 1/2 cups soymilk lite

1/4 cup liquid Fruitsource or honey

2 Tbsp. mellow white miso

1 Tbsp. egg replacer powder

1/4 cup water

2 Tbsp. vital wheat gluten

1/4 cup soy flour or soy grits

3 3/4 cups white wheat flour

2 1/2 tsp. yeast

◆ 118 ◆

Place the first 3 ingredients in the bread machine pan. Place egg replacer powder in a small bowl, and whisk in water until foamy. Add to pan, then add the remaining ingredients in the order listed unless the manufacturer of your bread machine recommends a different order. Close the lid, set the controls, and press "start."

NUTRITION ANALYSIS
(PER 1-OZ. SLICE)

Protein 2 gm., Carbohydrate 13 gm., Fiber 2 gm., Fat 0,
Cholesterol 0, Calcium 1 mg., Sodium 15 mg.

Calories 60
From protein: 14%; From carbohydrate: 79%; From fat: 7%

Whole Wheat Dinner Muffins

Simple to prepare and bursting with flavor, these tasty muffins are perfect with dinner. If you have any left over, just split and pop under the broiler, top with your favorite jam, and enjoy at breakfast.

◆ 1 2 M U F F I N S ◆

Vegetable oil cooking spray
1 cup soymilk lite
1 tsp. cider vinegar
2 cups whole wheat pastry flour
1/4 cup soy grits
1 tsp. baking soda
1 tsp. baking powder

1/2 tsp. salt
1/4 cup unsweetened applesauce
1/4 cup Florida Crystals or sugar
1 Tbsp. egg replacer powder
1/4 cup water
3/4 cup wheat germ

Preheat oven to 375.° Spray muffin pan with cooking spray. Place soymilk in a small measuring cup; add vinegar. Set aside. Stir together the next 5 ingredients in a large bowl. Set aside. Place applesauce in a medium bowl. Stir in Florida Crystals. Whisk egg replacer with water in a small bowl until foamy. Add to applesauce mixture. Make a well in the dry ingredients, and pour liquid in all at once. Fold quickly together, just until blended but still lumpy. Do not overbeat. Spoon into prepared muffin cups. Sprinkle with wheat germ. Bake for 15 to 20 minutes or until lightly browned.

◆ *119* ◆

NUTRITION ANALYSIS
(PER MUFFIN)

Protein 5 gm., Carbohydrate 20 gm., Fiber 3 gm., Fat 1 gm.,
Cholesterol 0, Calcium 37 mg., Sodium 236 mg.

Calories 105
From protein: 19%; From carbohydrate: 76%; From fat: 5%

Exceptional Entrées

Soyfoods are at the heart of the entrées in this irresistible collection. Hearty, richly flavored meals, needn't be heavy with fat and cholesterol. Rich-tasting cream sauces and delicate quiche are a snap when you know how to make the most of products like lite silken tofu and soymilk lite. The recipes offered in this section use the nutritional powerhouse of soyfoods to mimic a variety of dairy products and to create familiar fare using some new and ingenious products made from soybeans.

Healthful entrées that are flavorful and satisfying are highlighted in this chapter, using a wide variety of the new lower fat soyfoods. Textured vegetable protein, veggie Canadian bacon, tempeh, Ready Ground Tofu, and Gimme Lean are just some of the intriguing products that are used to make delectable dishes your family will love. You will also be introduced to some innovative techniques that change the texture of tofu to a chewier substance that will readily absorb well-seasoned marinades.

Traditional meals that were once made with high-fat, low-fiber, cholesterol-laden ingredients are just as delicious when made with these wholesome alternatives. Fiesta Scramblers, Savory Stuffed Peppers, and Oven-Baked Tempeh are just a few of the delightful dishes in this collection that demonstrate the undeniable versatility of the remarkable soybean. Highly authentic flavor and texture coupled with impressive nutritional content are the signature here. These exceptional entrées were created for the discriminating palate, and here you will learn to make delectable meals that are wholesome, satisfying, and delicious. ◆

Broiled Tofu Cutlets With Brown Rice

Firm Nigari tofu is used in this delightful entrée or first course.

◆ 4 SERVINGS ◆

3 cups cooked brown rice
1 cup frozen peas, cooked
1 tsp. dried thyme
1 tsp. dried basil
1 tsp. Bragg liquid aminos
2 8-oz. pkg. Nigari tofu (firm),
   drained

MARINADE:
1/4 cup hatcho miso
1/3 cup burgundy wine
1 cup beef-flavored vegetable broth
2 Tbsp. balsamic vinegar
2 Tbsp. tomato paste
1 tsp. granulated garlic
1/2 tsp. dried thyme
1/2 tsp. dried Mexican oregano

Slice each block of tofu along the width into three 1/4-inch cutlets. Blend marinade ingredients in a blender (a hand-held blender works fine). Pour marinade over tofu cutlets. Cover, and refrigerate overnight.

The next day, toss brown rice with peas, herbs, and aminos; keep warm. Spoon extra marinade over the tofu cutlets. Place in preheated broiler. Cook 3 to 4 minutes, then turn cutlets over and spoon additional marinade over cutlets. Cook an additional 3 to 4 minutes. Serve with rice dish.

◆ *122* ◆

NUTRITION ANALYSIS
(PER SERVING)

Protein 21 gm., Carbohydrate 77 gm., Fiber 9 gm., Fat 5 gm.,
Cholesterol 0, Calcium 52 mg., Sodium 310 mg.

Calories 349
From protein: 19%; From carbohydrate: 71%; From fat: 10%

Bubbling Potato Casserole

*This aromatic, hearty dish is wonderful
with whole grain bread and a crisp salad.*

◆ 8 SERVINGS ◆

1 Tbsp. olive oil

1 cup chopped onion

4 cloves garlic, minced

14-oz. pkg. Gimme Lean,
sausage flavor

6-oz. pkg. Yves veggie Canadian
bacon, chopped

5 medium unpeeled russet potatoes,
quartered and cut into 1/4-inch
slices

2 cups zucchini cut into 1/2-inch-
wide julienne strips

1/2 cup white wine

1 cup beef-flavored vegetable broth,
boiling

25-oz. jar fat-free tomato sauce

1 cup frozen peas, thawed

1 large bay leaf

Preheat oven to 350°. Heat oil in a large oven- and stovetop-safe casserole dish.
Add the onions and garlic; sauté 2 minutes. Stir in the Gimme Lean, breaking it apart
with a wooden spoon as it cooks. Add the veggie bacon, and sauté the mixture 5
minutes. Add the potatoes and zucchini. Continue to cook over medium-high heat,
stirring frequently, until the vegetables soften, about 8 minutes. Add wine, and stir 2
minutes. Add boiling broth; reduce heat to low. Cook 5 minutes, stirring occasionally.
Add remaining ingredients. Cook 5 minutes longer. Cover the dish. Bake 1 hour or
until ready to serve.

◆ *123* ◆

NUTRITION ANALYSIS
(PER SERVING)

Protein 20 gm., Carbohydrate 55 gm., Fiber 5 gm., Fat 2 gm.,
Cholesterol 0, Calcium 21 mg., Sodium 651 mg.

Calories 318
From protein: 25%; From carbohydrate: 69%; From fat: 6%

Creamed Chicken (TVP) and Corn

Tender chunks of chicken TVP in a delectable sake-laced sauce make a lovely presentation when served with basmati rice.

◆ 6 SERVINGS ◆

2 cups TVP chicken chunks

1 3/4 cups chicken-flavored vegetable broth, boiling

1 1/2 tsp. olive oil

1/4 cup scallions, sliced thin

3 cloves garlic, minced

1/4 cup chopped green pepper

1/4 cup sake

1 Tbsp. tamari

2 cups corn

1/2 tsp. granulated garlic

1 tsp. dried marjoram

1 cup nutritional yeast

2/3 cup soymilk lite

dash cayenne

dash lemon pepper

◆ *124* ◆

Place TVP in a medium bowl. Cover with boiling broth; set aside. Heat oil in a 4-quart saucepan over medium-high heat for 1 minute. Add scallions, garlic, and green pepper. Sauté 3 minutes. Add reconstituted TVP and any remaining liquid. Cook over medium heat 5 minutes, stirring frequently. Add sake and tamari, and continue cooking 5 minutes. Stir in corn and granulated garlic. Cook for 5 minutes. Gradually add remaining ingredients, stirring to blend. Lower heat and simmer 10 minutes, stirring occasionally.

NUTRITION ANALYSIS
(PER SERVING)

Protein 30 gm., Carbohydrate 34 gm., Fiber 6 gm., Fat 3 gm., Cholesterol 0, Calcium 9 mg., Sodium 226 mg.

Calories 268
From protein: 42%; From carbohydrate: 48%; From fat: 10%

Fiesta Scrambler

Serve this tequila-laced entrée with black beans and rice
for a quick and easy Mexican fiesta!

◆ 4 SERVINGS ◆

2 1/2 cups lite silken tofu (firm or
    extra firm), drained
1 1/2 tsp. olive oil
1/8 tsp. crushed red pepper
3 scallions, sliced
3 large cloves garlic, minced
1/3 cup chopped green bell pepper

1/4 tsp. turmeric
1 Tbsp. tamari
3/4 cup chunky medium-hot salsa,
    drained
3 to 4 Tbsp. tequila
1 Tbsp. lime juice
1/4 cup chopped fresh cilantro

Drain tofu, and pat dry. Place tofu in a microwave-safe medium bowl, and use potato masher to mash tofu. Microwave on high for 2 1/2 minutes. Place tofu in a fine mesh colander. Heat olive oil and crushed pepper in a 10″ frying pan over medium-high heat. Add scallions, garlic, and bell pepper. Sauté for 3 minutes or until crisp tender. Add drained tofu, and continue to cook for 5 minutes, stirring frequently. Stir in remaining ingredients. Reduce heat, and simmer 5 minutes or until ready to serve. Serve with warm whole wheat tortillas and extra salsa.

◆ *125* ◆

NUTRITION ANALYSIS
(PER SERVING)

Protein 12 gm., Carbohydrate 7 gm., Fiber 2 gm., Fat 4 gm.,
Cholesterol 0, Calcium 20 mg., Sodium 396 mg.

Calories 126
From protein: 39%; From carbohydrate: 21%; From fat: 26%

Gourmet Soyburgers

A cast of exceptional ingredients joins soybeans in this tasty burger.

◆ 10 BURGERS ◆

1 cup dried soybeans

6 cups water

Vegetable oil cooking spray 3/4 cup roasted chestnuts, peeled

6-oz. pkg. portobello mushrooms, cubed

1/2 cup chopped red bell pepper

2 cups fresh spinach leaves, firmly packed

8 cloves garlic, peeled

2/3 cup sliced scallions

3 Tbsp. egg replacer powder

2/3 cup water

1 cup cooked basmati rice

2 Tbsp. Dijon mustard

1/4 cup whole wheat bread crumbs

1/4 cup nutritional yeast

Rinse and sort soybeans. Soak in 4 cups of water overnight in the refrigerator. Discard soaking water. Bring beans to boil in 6 cups of water. Reduce heat, and simmer for 3 hours, stirring occasionally; drain.

Preheat oven to 375°. Spray baking pans with cooking spray. Place chestnuts and next 5 ingredients in food processor; pulse just to mix. Whisk egg replacer powder with 2/3 cup water in a small bowl until foamy. Add to processor along with soybeans, and pulse just to mix; do not purée. Scrape mixture into a large bowl, and add basmati rice. Mix well. Add mustard, bread crumbs, and yeast; mix thoroughly. Form mixture into burgers. Place burgers on baking pans; bake 25 minutes. Spray top of burgers lightly with cooking spray, then brown under the broiler. You may also panfry these burgers using cooking spray along with olive oil, with very good results.

NUTRITION ANALYSIS
(PER BURGER)

Protein 12 gm., Carbohydrate 28 gm., Fiber 4 gm., Fat 4 gm.,
Cholesterol 0, Calcium 83 mg., Sodium 25 mg.

Calories 175
From protein: 25%; From carbohydrate: 56%; From fat: 19%

Basque Stew ♦ *page 74*
Saffron Couscous ♦ *page 179*

Sauced Five-Spice Tofu With Sun-Dried Tomatoes & Cauliflower ♦ *page 141*
Pungent Basmati Rice ♦ *page 142*

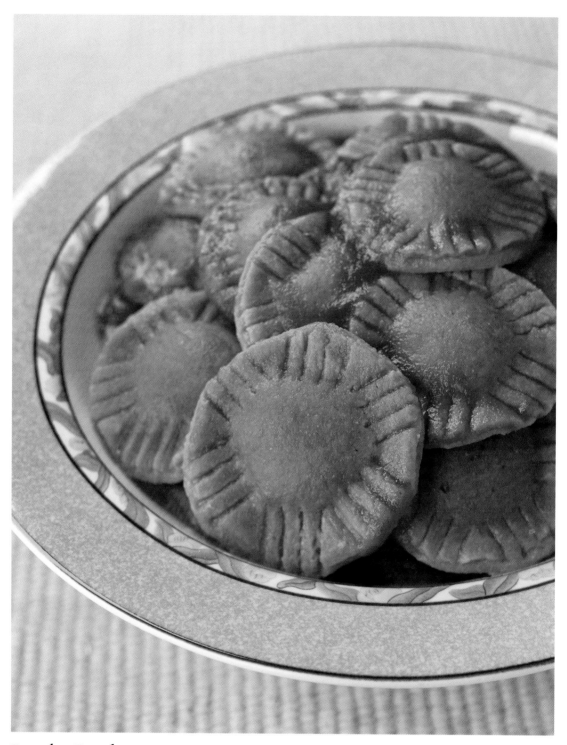

Pumpkin Ravioli ◆ *page 197*

Tempeh Shish Kebobs ♦ *page 152*
Minted Orzo—"Mimi" ♦ *page 177*

Spicy Pizza Abbondanza ◆ *page 194*

Savory Stuffed Peppers ◆ *page 145*

Lime 'n Ginger Chicken ◆ *page 132*

Brussels Sprouts and Chestnuts in a Savory Sauce ◆ *page 164*

Split Pea Soup With Ham ◆ *page 85*

Curried Tofu & Basmati Rice Salad ◆ *page 91*

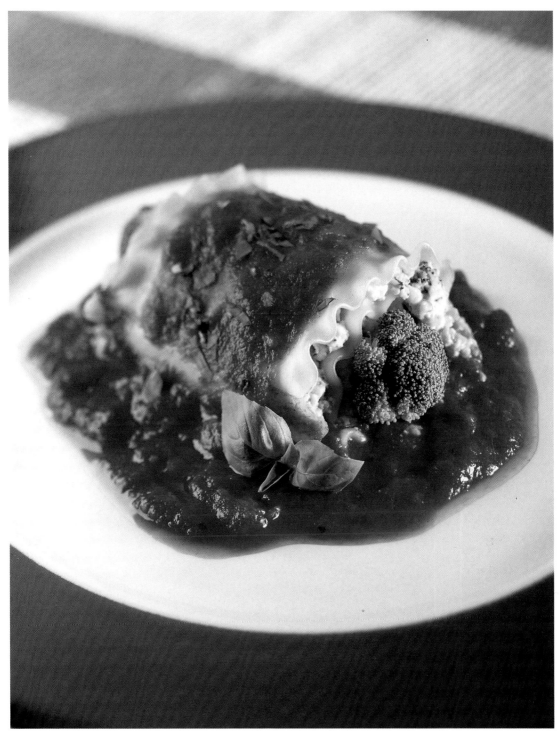

Broccoli Lasagna Rolls ◆ *page 185*

White Wheat Bread ◆ *page 118*

Whole Wheat Dinner Muffins ◆ *page 110*

Lemon Blueberry Delite ◆ *page 234*

Glazed Apple Custard Pie ♦ *page 230*

Pumpkin Fudge Brownies ◆ *page 241*

Fudgy Chocolate Walnut Ring ◆ *page 227*

Hearty Shepherd's Pie

The Ready Ground Tofu adds a nice texture to this peasant dish, and the portobello mushrooms and sliced baby carrots elevate it to new heights.

◆ 8 SERVINGS ◆

1 1/2 tsp. olive oil
1/4 tsp. crushed red pepper
1 cup chopped red onion
2 cups sliced baby carrots
4 cloves garlic, minced
6 oz. portobello mushrooms, cut to 1-inch cubes (about 2 1/4 cups)
3 Tbsp. whole wheat flour
2 1/2 cups beef-flavored vegetable broth, hot (separated)
2 10-oz. pkg. savory garlic Ready Ground Tofu, drained

1 cup frozen peas, thawed
1/4 cup nutritional yeast
1 Tbsp. dehydrated ground mushrooms
1 Tbsp. tamari
MASHED POTATO TOPPING:
2 1/4 cups water
1 cup soymilk lite
1/2 tsp. salt
2 1/4 cups mashed potato flakes
1/4 tsp. lemon pepper
paprika

◆*127*◆

Preheat oven to 350.° Heat oil and crushed pepper over medium-high heat 2 minutes in a 3- or 4-quart ovenproof and stovetop-safe casserole. Add onion, carrots, and garlic. Sauté 5 minutes, stirring frequently. Add mushrooms; cover and sauté another 3 minutes. Stir in flour. Add 1 1/2 cups hot broth, and stir until thickened, about 3 minutes. Lower heat; add ground tofu and peas. Add remaining broth, nutritional yeast, dehydrated mushrooms, and tamari.

Bring water to a boil in a medium pan. Turn off heat, and add soymilk. Stir in potato flakes and salt, stirring until smooth. Add lemon pepper. Arrange mashed potatoes over top of stew. Sprinkle with paprika. Bake for 15 minutes, then place under broiler for 3 minutes to brown.

NUTRITION ANALYSIS
(PER SERVING)

Protein 14 gm., Carbohydrate 34 gm., Fiber 4 gm., Fat 5 gm., Cholesterol 0, Calcium 29 mg., Sodium 326 mg.

Calories 214
From protein: 23%; From carbohydrate: 58%; From fat: 19%

Homestyle Veggie Loaf

This delicious baked loaf is easy to prepare and goes well with pasta and a salad.

◆ 8 SERVINGS ◆

Vegetable oil cooking spray
1 1/2 cups beef-flavored vegetable broth
1 cup soy grits
4 cloves garlic, minced
2/3 cup chopped onion
1 cup whole wheat bread crumbs
1 cup grated carrots
1 1/2 cups grated zucchini
1 1/4 cups frozen corn, thawed

1/4 cup nutritional yeast
2 Tbsp. Dijon mustard
2 Tbsp. tamari
2 Tbsp. egg replacer powder
1/2 cup water
1 tsp. dried thyme
1 tsp. dried basil
1 tsp. dried marjoram

◆ 128 ◆

Preheat oven to 350.° Lightly coat a 9" x 5" loaf pan with cooking spray. Place broth and soy grits in a medium saucepan, and bring to a boil. Reduce heat, cover, and simmer, stirring occasionally, 10 to 15 minutes or until liquid is absorbed. Cool slightly. Place cooked grits in a large bowl, and add the next 9 ingredients, mixing well after each addition. Whisk egg replacer with water in a small bowl until foamy. Add to vegetable mixture; mix. Add the herbs, and mix thoroughly. Turn into the prepared pan. Sprinkle with additional thyme, basil, and marjoram. Bake for 45 minutes.

NUTRITION ANALYSIS
(PER SERVING)

Protein 17 gm., Carbohydrate 46 gm., Fiber 5 gm., Fat 3 gm.,
Cholesterol 0, Calcium 27 mg., Sodium 218 mg.

Calories 173
From protein: 24%; From carbohydrate: 65%; From fat: 10%

Jasmine Chicken TVP

TVP chicken chunks in a vermouth-laced tomato sauce form the basis for this delicious mélange of vegetables and fragrant jasmine rice.

◆ 6 SERVINGS ◆

1 1/4 cups chicken-flavored
  vegetable broth, boiling
2 cups chunk chicken-style TVP
1 1/2 tsp. olive oil
1/8 tsp. crushed red pepper
1 1/2 cups chopped sweet onion
  (like Vidalia or Maui)
4 cloves garlic, minced

3 large mushroom caps, sliced
3 cups sliced yellow squash
1/3 cup dry vermouth
25-oz. jar fat-free tomato sauce
1 bay leaf
1 tsp. dried marjoram
1 1/2 cups cooked jasmine rice

Combine boiling broth and TVP; set aside. Heat oil and crushed pepper in a 5-quart saucepan over medium-high heat for 1 minute. Add onion and garlic; sauté 2 minutes. Add mushrooms and squash; cook 5 minutes. Add reconstituted TVP, and cook 3 minutes. Add vermouth, tomato sauce, bay leaf, and marjoram. Reduce heat to simmer. Gently stir in cooked rice, and simmer 10 minutes or until ready to serve.

◆129◆

NUTRITION ANALYSIS
(PER SERVING)

Protein 19 gm., Carbohydrate 43 gm., Fiber 9 gm., Fat 2 gm.,
Cholesterol 0, Calcium 37 mg., Sodium 232 mg.

Calories 248
From protein: 28%; From carbohydrate: 66%; From fat: 6%

Jungle Curry

This Thai classic loses nothing in the translation. Highly saturated coconut milk has been replaced with a clever blend of wholesome ingredients.

◆ 8 S E R V I N G S ◆

1 1/2 tsp. olive oil

1 medium red onion, quartered and cut into thin slices

6 cloves garlic, minced

1 green bell pepper, cut into thin strips

2 cups sliced mushrooms

1 medium zucchini, thinly sliced

2 cups green beans, cut into 2-inch pieces

1 1/2 cups shredded cabbage

15 large fresh basil leaves

1/2 cup white wine

15-oz. can peeled and diced tomatoes

3 Tbsp. fresh lime juice (juice of 1 lime)

1 Tbsp. grated lemon zest

1/2 cup plus 2 Tbsp. lite silken tofu (firm), drained

1/2 cup soymilk lite

1 tsp. coconut extract

1 jalapeño pepper

1 Tbsp. tamari

Heat oil in a 5-quart saucepan over medium-high heat. Add the next 3 ingredients, and sauté 3 minutes. Add the next 4 ingredients, and cook 5 minutes. Add basil leaves, white wine, tomatoes, lime juice, and lemon zest. Reduce heat to medium, and cover, stirring occasionally. Place tofu in food processor; blend. Add soymilk and coconut extract. Working with rubber-gloved hands, remove stem from jalapeño pepper, and quarter. Add pepper, along with seeds, to food processor (to reduce heat, omit seeds). Pulse to blend. Fold tofu mixture into pot, and reduce to simmer. Add tamari. Serve with jasmine rice.

NUTRITION ANALYSIS
(PER SERVING)

Protein 5 gm., Carbohydrate 14 gm., Fiber 3 gm., Fat 2 gm.,
Cholesterol 0, Calcium 55 mg., Sodium 207 mg.

Calories 89
From protein: 21%; From carbohydrate: 62%; From fat: 17%

Lentils 'n Sausage

This high-protein dish is delicious served with pasta.

◆ 8   SERVINGS ◆

2 cups brown lentils

4 cups water

1 1/2 tsp. olive oil

1/8 tsp. crushed red pepper

3/4 cup chopped onion

6 cloves garlic, minced

2 cups sliced baby carrots

14 oz. pkg. Gimme Lean Sausage

1/4 cup dry sherry

14.5 oz. can Mexican-style
stewed tomatoes

Rinse and sort lentils, and place them in a 4-quart saucepan with the water. Bring to a boil, stir, and reduce heat. Simmer 20 minutes or until liquid is absorbed. In a 10" frying pan, heat oil and crushed pepper over medium-high heat 2 minutes. Add onion and garlic, and sauté 2 minutes. Add carrots and cook 5 minutes or until vegetables are crisp tender. Add the vegetarian sausage and cook mixture 10 to 12 minutes, stirring often and breaking up sausage. Add sausage mixture to cooked lentils. Add sherry, then stir in tomatoes. Simmer 10 minutes, stirring often.

◆ *131* ◆

NUTRITION ANALYSIS
(PER SERVING)

Protein 23 gm., Carbohydrate 44 gm., Fiber 10 gm.,
Cholesterol 0, Calcium 64 mg., Sodium 296 mg.

Calories 276
From protein: 32%; From carbohydrate: 63%; From fat: 5%

Lime 'n Ginger Chicken

*Hearty chunks of TVP chicken, carrots, sweet peas, and zesty
seasonings combine in this lively, Caribbean-inspired dish.*

◆ 8 SERVINGS ◆

3 cups TVP chicken chunks
2 cups chicken-flavored vegetable
  broth, boiling, separated
1 1/2 tsp. olive oil
6 cloves garlic, minced
2 Tbsp. grated fresh gingerroot
1 jalapeño pepper, chopped,
  with seeds*
1 1/2 cups chopped red onion

1 rib celery, sliced
2 cups sliced baby carrots
juice of 1 lime (about 3 to 4 Tbsp.)
3/4 cup white wine
1/3 cup mango chutney, chopped
1 cup frozen peas, thawed
1 tsp. dried thyme
2 Tbsp. Bragg liquid aminos

Immerse TVP in 1 1/2 cups boiling broth, reserving 1/2 cup. Heat oil in a 5-quart saucepan over medium-high heat for 1 minute. Add the next 5 ingredients, and sauté 3 minutes. Add the carrots, and cook 3 minutes. Add reconstituted TVP. Cook 5 minutes, stirring frequently. Add the lime juice and white wine; cook 3 minutes. Add the remaining ingredients plus the reserved 1/2 cup of broth; lower heat. Simmer 12 to 15 minutes, stirring occasionally, or until the vegetables and TVP are tender.

*Always wear rubber gloves when working with jalapeño peppers. The addition of seeds will increase the heat of the dish; you may omit.

NUTRITION ANALYSIS
(PER SERVING)

Protein 18 gm., Carbohydrate 102 gm., Fiber 9 gm., Fat 1 gm.,
Cholesterol 0, Calcium 41 mg., Sodium 318 mg.

Calories 182
From protein: 15%; From carbohydrate: 83%; From fat: 3%

Moussaka

This popular Greek casserole can be served warm or at room temperature.

◆ 8 SERVINGS ◆

vegetable oil cooking spray

5 medium russet potatoes

1 2/3 cups beef-flavored vegetable broth, boiling

3 cups TVP, ground beef style

1 1/2 tsp. olive oil

1 cup chopped red onion

6 cloves garlic, minced

28-oz. can peeled and diced tomatoes

1 tsp. dried basil

1/4 tsp. lemon pepper

cayenne to taste

1/3 cup whole wheat bread crumbs (reserve 3 Tbsp.)

WHITE SAUCE:

1 Tbsp. olive oil

2 large shallots, chopped (1/4 cup)

3 Tbsp. whole wheat flour

1/2 cup white wine

1 1/2 cups soymilk lite

1 cup nutritional yeast

2 Tbsp. cornstarch

3 Tbsp. water

1/8 tsp. ground nutmeg

◆ *133* ◆

Preheat oven to 350.° Spray a 9" x 13" baking pan with cooking spray. Cut unpeeled potatoes in 1/4-inch slices, and parboil for 10 minutes. Set aside. Pour boiling broth over TVP in a medium bowl. Set aside. Heat olive oil in a 5-quart saucepan over medium-high heat. Add onion and garlic; sauté for 3 minutes. Stir in reconstituted TVP, and cook mixture 3 minutes. Add tomatoes and seasonings. Reduce heat to simmer, stirring occasionally. Heat olive oil in a medium saucepan. Add shallots, and sauté 3 minutes. Stir in flour to form a paste. Add wine; stir until smooth. Gradually add soymilk, then whisk in yeast 1/3 cup at a time. Blend cornstarch with water, and add to sauce. Simmer until thickened. Sprinkle half of the bread crumbs along the bottom and sides of the prepared pan. Layer the potato slices along the bottom of the pan, overlapping slightly. Top with the TVP mixture. Pour the sauce over all, then sprinkle with nutmeg and reserved bread crumbs. Bake for 30 minutes, then cool 20 minutes before serving.

NUTRITION ANALYSIS
(PER SERVING)

Protein 33 gm., Carbohydrate 60 gm., Fiber 7 gm., Fat 5 gm.,
Cholesterol 0, Calcium 22 mg., Sodium 242 mg.

Calories 345
From protein: 32%; From carbohydrate: 58%; From fat: 10%

Outrageous Oatmeal

*The soymilk in this oatmeal recipe makes it so very creamy, and the sweet
dried fruit, cinnamon, and nutmeg start your day with a smile.*

◆ 3 SERVINGS ◆

1 3/4 cups soymilk lite
1 cup rolled oats (5-minute variety)
1/8 tsp. salt
vanilla soy milk or rice milk to taste
1/4 cup snipped dried apricots

2 Tbsp. dried fruit, such as golden
   raisins, blueberries, or cranberries
1 mashed banana
3 large fresh strawberries, sliced
pure maple syrup to taste
cinnamon and nutmeg to taste

Place soymilk in medium saucepan. Heat over medium heat 2 minutes. Stir in
rolled oats, and reduce heat to low. Cook 3 minutes, stirring occasionally. When mixture
begins to thicken, add fruit of your choice, cinnamon, and nutmeg. Continue to cook,
stirring occasionally, 2 to 3 minutes or until liquid is absorbed and oatmeal is thick and
creamy. Spoon into bowls. Serve with syrup and extra milk.

◆ *134* ◆

NUTRITION ANALYSIS
(PER 8-OZ. SERVING)

Protein 7 gm., Carbohydrate 59 gm., Fiber 4 gm., Fat 3 gm.,
Cholesterol 0, Calcium 40 mg., Sodium 156 mg.

Calories 285
From protein: 10%; From carbohydrate: 80%; From fat: 10%

Oven-Baked Tempeh

This dish has a flavor reminiscent of baked chicken and vegetables.

◆ 6 SERVINGS ◆

1 1/2 tsp. olive oil

1/8 tsp. crushed red pepper

1 leek, well rinsed, and cut into
   1/8-inch slices (see Techniques)

1/3 cup sliced shallots

1/2 cup chopped red bell pepper

4 cloves garlic

2 cups baby carrots, halved

1 cup diced zucchini

8-oz. pkg. tempeh, seasoned
   (see Soyfoods Pantry)

1/2 cup dry sherry

1 medium tomato, diced

1 Tbsp. tamari

Preheat oven to 350°. Place oil and crushed pepper in a stovetop-safe and oven-proof casserole dish. Sauté over medium-high heat 1 minute. Add the next 4 ingredients, and sauté 3 minutes. Add carrot chunks and zucchini. Sauté, stirring frequently, 5 minutes. Add tempeh, and sauté 5 minutes. Add sherry, diced tomato, and tamari; cook mixture 5 minutes. Cover casserole, and bake 30 minutes.

◆ *135* ◆

NUTRITION ANALYSIS
(PER SERVING)

Protein 11 gm., Carbohydrate 16 gm., Fiber 3 gm., Fat 3 gm.,
Cholesterol 0, Calcium 39 mg., Sodium 288 mg.

Calories 144
From protein: 31%; From carbohydrate: 47%; From fat: 23%

Pasta de Patate

This is a delightful dish loosely based on an Italian potato pie. This version features light phyllo pastry, marinated mushrooms, and a delectable layered filling. Don't be discouraged by the individual preparation of the separate layers. It all comes together quite easily and results in an exceptional entrée.

◆ 1 2 S E R V I N G S ◆

MUSHROOM MARINADE:

2 6-oz. pkgs. sliced portobello mushrooms

1 cup white wine

3 Tbsp. tamari

2 Tbsp. Dijon mustard

1 tsp. granulated garlic

1 Tbsp. cider vinegar

1 Tbsp. mild molasses

2 Tbsp. vegetarian Worcestershire sauce

3 large russet potatoes, unpeeled, cut into 1/4-inch slices

3 oz. sun-dried tomatoes, snipped

1 cup boiling water

"CHEEZY" WINE SAUCE:

2 Tbsp. olive oil

1/4 cup whole wheat flour

1 cup white wine

1 cup soymilk lite

1/2 cup nutritional yeast

1 tsp. dried marjoram

1/2 tsp. granulated garlic

2 1/2 cups lite silken tofu (extra firm), drained

1/3 cup sliced scallions

1 tsp. granulated garlic

2 cups frozen corn, thawed

vegetable oil cooking spray

1/2 pound. phyllo pastry

6-oz. pkg. Yves veggie Canadian bacon, cut to 1/4-inch julienne strips

Clean mushrooms, and place in a large ziplock bag. Whisk together marinade ingredients, and pour over mushrooms. Set aside, turning a few times during marinating. Parboil the potatoes 10 minutes in 1 quart of boiling salted water. Set aside in colander. Steep sun-dried tomatoes in boiling water; set aside.

Heat olive oil in a medium saucepan over medium heat. Whisk in flour. Stir 3 minutes. Whisk in wine, then when mixture starts to thicken, add soymilk. Lower heat, and simmer 3 minutes. Whisk in remaining wine sauce ingredients. Simmer 3 minutes, then set aside.

Place the tofu in a large bowl. Mash with a potato masher. Add scallions, garlic, corn, and sun-dried tomatoes (reserving liquid). Set aside.

Spray a 10" frying pan with cooking spray. Using a slotted spoon, remove mushrooms from the marinade, and sauté 10 minutes, over medium-high heat, until browned on both sides and and remaining marinade is re-absorbed. Set aside.

Preheat oven to 350°. Spray a 9" x 13" baking pan with cooking spray. Prepare phyllo pastry (see Techniques). Spray 8 phyllo leaves with cooking spray, then place them in the 9" x 13" pan. Place a single layer of potato slices on the phyllo leaves. Top with a layer of veggie bacon. Spread with tofu mixture, then top with a layer of the remaining potatoes. Pour the reserved sun-dried tomato soaking water over the potato layer. Pour the wine sauce over all. Top with 8 leaves of phyllo pastry, spraying each with cooking spray, as in the bottom crust. Spray the top of the pastry with cooking spray, and tuck the top leaves under the bottom into the sides of the pan. Score the top layers with a diamond pattern, being careful not to cut through to the filling. Bake 35 to 40 minutes, or until lightly browned. Serve with a rice dish.

♦ *137* ♦

NUTRITION ANALYSIS
(PER SERVING)

Protein 14 gm., Carbohydrate 44 gm., Fiber 3 gm., Fat 3 gm.,
Cholesterol 0, Calcium 14 mg., Sodium 383 mg.

Calories 293
From protein: 20%; From carbohydrate: 61%; From fat: 10%

Quiche Lorraine

This outstanding rendition of a classic is both egg- and dairy-free.

◆ 8 SERVINGS ◆

CRUST

1 cup rolled oats
1 cup whole wheat flour
1/4 tsp. salt
1/3 cup lite silken tofu (firm),
  drained

1 Tbsp. canola oil
1 Tbsp. liquid Fruitsource or honey
1/4 cup ice water

Place oats, wheat flour, and salt in food processor; blend to mix. Add tofu, and process. Add oil and Fruitsource; pulse to blend. Slowly add ice water, with the machine running, until the dough begins to form a ball. Knead the dough a few times, and shape into a ball. Chill in a plastic bag in the refrigerator. Remove from the refrigerator an hour or so before needed.

FILLING

1 1/2 tsp. olive oil
1/3 cup sliced scallions
2 large cloves garlic, minced
1/4 cup chopped green pepper
6-oz. pkg. Yves veggie Canadian
  bacon, diced
2 1/2 cups lite silken tofu (extra
  firm), drained
1/4 cup mirin or dry sherry

2 Tbsp. mellow white miso
1/3 cup mashed potato flakes (see
  Quick Guide to Ingredients)
1/3 cup nutritional yeast
1/4 tsp. ground nutmeg
1/4 tsp. turmeric
1/2 cup soymilk lite
1 Tbsp. lemon juice

Preheat oven to 400.° Heat oil in a 10" frying pan. Add scallions, garlic, and green pepper. Sauté 3 minutes. Add bacon, and sauté 2 minutes, or until the vegetables are crisp tender. Blend tofu in the food processor. Place the mirin and miso in a small bowl, and blend. Add with the next 4 ingredients to the food processor; process. Add soymilk and lemon juice, and blend until smooth. Fold into the vegetables and bacon.

Roll out dough 1/4-inch thick on a cutting board sprinkled with flour. Press the dough into a pie pan. Fill with tofu mixture. Bake in the center of the oven 25 to 30 minutes. Serve at room temperature.

NUTRITION ANALYSIS
(PER SERVING)

Protein 20 gm., Carbohydrate 29 gm., Fiber 3 gm., Fat 5 gm.,
Cholesterol 0, Calcium 17 mg., Sodium 401 mg.

Calories 232
From protein: 33%; From carbohydrate: 48%; From fat: 18%

Roghan Josh

This version of a popular, spicy curried East Indian dish is as aromatic and delicious as can be.

◆ 8 SERVINGS ◆

1 1/2 cups beef-flavored vegetable broth, boiling
3 cups TVP steak strips
1 Tbsp. olive oil
1/4 tsp. crushed red pepper
2 bay leaves
2 cinnamon sticks
1 rounded Tbsp. grated gingerroot
2 cups chopped red onion
2 ribs celery, sliced
1 1/2 cups sliced baby carrots
2 cups cubed zucchini
1 tsp. granulated garlic
1/8 tsp. asafetida
1/2 tsp. ground coriander

1/2 tsp. ground cardamom
1/2 tsp. ground cumin
1/2 tsp. ground ginger
1 1/2 tsp. dried cilantro
6 cherry tomatoes, halved
1 1/4 cups lite silken tofu (firm), drained
2 Tbsp. lemon juice
1 clove garlic, peeled
1/2 cup soymilk lite
1 1/2 Tbsp. country barley miso
1/4 cup white wine (Chablis is nice)
2 Tbsp. Brinjal Pickle (spicy eggplant relish)

Place TVP in boiling broth, and set aside. Heat the oil with crushed red pepper in a 5-quart saucepan for 1 minute. Add the next 7 ingredients; sauté 5 minutes. Then add garlic and the following 7 ingredients; simmer. Place tofu in food processor, and blend until smooth. Add the next 3 ingredients; blend. Blend miso with wine in a small bowl. Add to tofu mixture. Fold tofu mixture into vegetable/TVP mixture in saucepan. Stir in eggplant relish. Serve.

NUTRITION ANALYSIS
(PER SERVING)

Protein 20 gm., Carbohydrate 22 gm., Fiber 8 gm., Fat 3 gm.,
Cholesterol 0, Calcium 43 mg., Sodium 217 mg.

Calories 176
From protein: 41%; From carbohydrate: 45%; From fat: 14%

Sauced Five-Spice Tofu With Sun-Dried Tomatoes & Cauliflower

This tempting dish is easy to assemble and very delicious.
Serve it with Pungent Basmati Rice (recipe follows).

◆ 6 SERVINGS ◆

1 cup halved sun-dried tomatoes
1 1/3 cups boiling water
1 1/2 tsp. olive oil
1/4 tsp. crushed red pepper
1 cup chopped onion
6 cloves garlic, minced
1 Tbsp. grated gingerroot
1/2 cup chopped red bell pepper
6-oz. pkg. Five-Spice Baked Tofu,
  drained, cut into 1/4-inch slices

1 medium head cauliflower, broken
  into florets
1/4 cup mirin or dry sherry
6 large basil leaves, snipped
1 Tbsp. Bragg liquid aminos
1 Tbsp. cornstarch
2 Tbsp. water

◆ *141* ◆

Steep sun-dried tomatoes in boiling water; set aside. Heat olive oil and crushed pepper in a medium saucepan over medium-high heat for 1 minute. Add the next 4 ingredients, and sauté 3 minutes. Add tofu, and sauté 3 minutes, stirring frequently. Add cauliflower, and sauté 3 minutes. Add mirin, basil, and liquid aminos. Lower heat, and simmer 10 minutes, stirring frequently. Blend cornstarch and water in a small bowl. Add to saucepan, and simmer 5 minutes or until ready to serve, stirring occasionally.

NUTRITION ANALYSIS
(PER SERVING)

Protein 16 gm., Carbohydrate 86 gm., Fiber 11 gm., Fat 1 gm.,
Cholesterol 0, Calcium 35 mg., Sodium 341 mg.

Calories 203
From protein: 16%; From carbohydrate: 82%; From fat: 2%

Pungent Basmati Rice

*This delightful rice variety is enhanced by Indian
spices in this quick and easy treatment.*

◆ 6 SERVINGS ◆

1 cup basmati rice, rinsed thoroughly
2 1/2 cups chicken-flavored
  broth, boiling

1/4 tsp. turmeric
1/2 tsp. ground coriander

Place rinsed rice in the boiling broth; stir and bring to a second boil. Stir, add
remaining ingredients, and reduce heat. Cover and simmer, undisturbed, for 20 minutes.
Liquid should be absorbed. Serve.

NUTRITION ANALYSIS
(PER 1/2-CUP SERVING)

Protein 3 gm., Carbohydrate 24 gm., Fiber 0, Fat 0,
Cholesterol 0, Calcium 3 mg., Sodium 3 mg.

Calories 114
From protein: 10%; From carbohydrate: 90%; From fat: 0%

Sausage Scrambler

Fragrant and delicious, this great Sunday brunch dish owes its abundant flavor to savory vegetarian sausage. Serve with pita pockets and a dollop of salsa.

◆ 6 SERVINGS ◆

2 1/2 cups lite silken tofu (extra firm), drained

1 1/2 tsp. olive oil

1/8 tsp. crushed red pepper

5 cloves garlic, minced

1/2 cup sliced scallions

1/2 cup chopped green pepper

14-oz. pkg. Gimme Lean, sausage style

1/4 tsp. turmeric

1/2 tsp. dried thyme

2 Tbsp. dry sherry

1 Tbsp. tamari

14.5-oz. can Mexican-style stewed tomatoes, well drained

Drain and pat dry the tofu. Place in a microwave-safe, medium bowl. Using a potato masher, press tofu into curds. Cover and heat in the microwave 3 minutes. Pour tofu curds in a colander to drain. Set aside. Heat oil and crushed pepper in a 4-quart saucepan 1 minute over medium-high heat. Add garlic, scallions, and pepper; sauté 2 minutes. Add Gimme Lean. Sauté, stirring and breaking sausage apart. Cook 5 minutes or until sausage is brown. Add drained tofu. Stir in spices, sherry, and tamari. Cook mixture 2 minutes. Add drained tomatoes; lower heat, and simmer 5 minutes.

◆ *143* ◆

NUTRITION ANALYSIS
(PER SERVING)

Protein 19 gm., Carbohydrate 17 gm., Fiber 3 gm., Fat 2 gm., Cholesterol 0, Calcium 38 mg., Sodium 560 mg.

Calories 167
From protein: 45%; From carbohydrate: 41%; From fat: 13%

Savory Sausage Patties

These delicious vegetarian patties are very low in fat and contain no cholesterol.

◆ 8 PATTIES ◆

vegetable oil cooking spray

14-oz. pkg. Gimme Lean, sausage
  style

2 cloves garlic, minced

1/4 cup whole wheat bread crumbs

1/4 cup soy grits

1 Tbsp. country Dijon mustard

1 Tbsp. egg replacer powder

1/4 cup water

Preheat oven to 400.° Spray a baking sheet with cooking spray. Place Gimme Lean in a large bowl. Add the next 4 ingredients; mix well. Whisk egg replacer with water in a small bowl. Add to sausage mixture, and mix thoroughly. Form into 8 patties, and place on baking sheet. Bake 15 to 20 minutes, turning over after 8 minutes to brown second side.

◆ 144 ◆

NUTRITION ANALYSIS
(PER PATTY)

Protein 11 gm., Carbohydrate 16 gm., Fiber 2 gm., Fat 1 gm.,
Cholesterol 0, Calcium 3 mg., Sodium 256 mg.

Calories 92
From protein: 39%; From carbohydrate: 56%; From fat: 6%

Savory Stuffed Peppers

This colorful dish is tasty and satisfying.

◆ 8 SERVINGS ◆

2 quarts boiling water

4 bell peppers (2 green and 2 gold or orange), halved lengthwise and seeded

1 1/2 tsp. olive oil

1 medium red onion, chopped

5 cloves garlic, minced

14-oz. pkg. Gimme Lean, sausage flavor

2 cups cooked brown rice

2 tsp. dried thyme

4 fresh basil leaves, snipped

1/2 cup white wine

25-oz. jar fat-free tomato sauce

14.5-oz. can Italian-style stewed tomatoes

1 bay leaf

4 fresh basil leaves, snipped

1 tsp. granulated garlic

Preheat oven to 375.° Place halved peppers in boiling water, and blanch 5 minutes. Remove to colander, and rinse with cold water; set aside. Heat oil in a 10" frying pan over medium-high heat for 1 minute. Add onions and garlic; sauté 3 minutes. Add Gimme Lean. Cook for 5 minutes, using a large spoon to break it apart as it cooks. Add the next 3 ingredients, and cook 3 minutes. Add wine, and simmer 5 minutes or until ready to stuff peppers.

In a medium saucepan, heat the tomato sauce with the remaining ingredients for 10 minutes. Spread about half the sauce on the bottom of a 9" x 13" baking pan. Spoon filling into each pepper half and place in pan. Top with remaining sauce. Cover with foil. Bake 30 minutes. Remove foil, and continue to bake an additional 10 to 15 minutes.

◆ *145* ◆

NUTRITION ANALYSIS
(PER SERVING)

Protein 13 gm., Carbohydrate 42 gm., Fiber 7 gm., Fat 2 gm.,
Cholesterol 0, Calcium 55 mg., Sodium 409 mg.

Calories 232
From protein: 22%; From carbohydrate: 72%; From fat: 6%

Savory Tofu Bake

Savory tofu is baked with fresh vegetables to create this flavorful mélange.

◆ 8 SERVINGS ◆

1 1/2 tsp. olive oil
1/8 tsp. crushed red pepper
6 cloves garlic, minced
1/2 cup sliced scallions
1/3 cup chopped shallots
2 1/2 cups sliced carrots
2 pounds green beans, cut into
   2-inch pieces

6 oz. cremini mushrooms, sliced
12 cherry tomatoes, halved
   lengthwise
2 6-oz. pkgs. savory baked tofu,
   cut into julienne strips
1/4 cup very dry sherry
1 Tbsp. tamari
6 large basil leaves, snipped

Preheat oven to 350°. Heat oil and crushed pepper in a large stovetop- and oven-safe casserole over medium-high heat for 1 minute. Add the next 3 ingredients, and sauté 2 minutes. Add carrots and green beans, and cook 5 minutes. Add mushrooms, tomatoes, and tofu, and cook 5 minutes. Add sherry and remaining ingredients; stir and cook 2 minutes. Cover, and bake 30 minutes. Serve with a rice or noodle dish.

◆ *146* ◆

NUTRITION ANALYSIS
(PER SERVING)

Protein 13 gm., Carbohydrate 23 gm., Fiber 7 gm., Fat 2 gm.,
Cholesterol 0, Calcium 70 mg., Sodium 380 mg.

Calories 162
From protein: 31%; From carbohydrate: 56%; From fat: 12%

Scrumptious Stewed Tempeh

*This tasty combination of seasoned tempeh, fresh
green beans, and cremini mushrooms is a real treat!*

◆ 6 SERVINGS ◆

1 1/2 tsp. olive oil
1/8 tsp. crushed red pepper
1/2 cup chopped onions
6 cloves garlic, minced
1/3 cup chopped red bell pepper
1/3 cup chopped green bell pepper
8 oz. pkg. seasoned tempeh, cubed
(see page 148)
6 oz. cremini mushrooms
(caps only)

2 cups fresh green beans, cut into
1-inch pieces
1/3 cup dry sherry
14.5-oz. can Italian-style stewed
tomatoes
4 fresh basil leaves, snipped
1 Tbsp. cornstarch
1 Tbsp. water

Heat oil and crushed pepper in a 4-quart saucepan over medium-high heat for 1 minute. Add the next 4 ingredients, and sauté 2 minutes. Add the tempeh, and sauté 3 minutes. Add the mushroom caps and green beans. Cook 10 minutes, stirring frequently. Add sherry, and cook 3 minutes. Add the tomatoes and basil. Reduce heat, and simmer for 15 minutes. Blend cornstarch with water in a small bowl. Add to the sauce. Simmer 5 to 8 minutes, stirring frequently. Serve with Garlic Mashed Potatoes (page 175), a rice dish, or noodles.

NUTRITION ANALYSIS
(PER SERVING)

Protein 11 gm., Carbohydrate 16 gm., Fiber 4 gm., Fat 3 gm.,
Cholesterol 0, Calcium 49 mg., Sodium 144 mg.

Calories 141
From protein: 31%; From carbohydrate: 46%; From fat: 22%

Seasoned Tempeh

Some cooks like to steam tempeh before use, but I've found that seasoning tempeh before using it in a recipe enhances the flavor and texture. This recipe will provide enough tempeh for use in 2 to 4 recipes. It will keep for up to a week in the refrigerator.

◆ 8 SERVINGS ◆

2 8-oz. pkg. soy tempeh   2 Tbsp. tamari
3 1/2 cups water   1 piece of kombu, cut in two

Divide each 8-ounce block of tempeh into 2 or 4 pieces. Place in a medium saucepan with remaining ingredients. Bring to a boil; reduce heat. Simmer about 30 to 45 minutes or until tempeh is fragrant and liquid is almost absorbed. As it simmers, gently rotate tempeh from time to time so it's equally submerged. Cool slightly. Cover, and refrigerate. Seasoned tempeh can be used with any tempeh recipe.

◆ *148* ◆

NUTRITION ANALYSIS
(PER SERVING)

Protein 13 gm., Carbohydrate 5 gm., Fiber 1 gm., Fat 3 gm.,
Cholesterol 0, Calcium 2 mg., Sodium 196 mg.

Calories 98
From protein: 52%; From carbohydrate: 21%; From fat: 28%

South-of-the-Border Scrambler

This Mexican-spiced scrambler is colorful, flavorful, and filling.

◆ 6 SERVINGS ◆

2 1/2 cups lite silken tofu (extra firm), drained

1 1/2 tsp. olive oil

1/4 tsp. crushed red pepper

1 cup chopped onion

4 cloves garlic, minced

1/2 cup chopped green bell pepper

4 oz. seasoned tempeh, cubed (see page 148)

1/4 tsp. turmeric

1 Tbsp. tamari

14.5-oz. can diced tomatoes and jalapeños, drained

1 medium baked potato, unpeeled, cubed (Yukon Gold is a good choice)

Place drained tofu in microwave-safe bowl, and mash with potato masher. Cover, and cook 3 minutes. Place in colander to drain; set aside. Heat oil and crushed pepper in a 4-quart saucepan over medium-high heat for 1 minute. Add onion, garlic, and green pepper. Cook and stir 2 minutes. Crumble tempeh, add to mixture, and cook 3 minutes. Add drained tofu, turmeric, and tamari. Stir to mix. Add drained tomatoes and potato. Lower heat, and simmer 10 minutes, stirring occasionally, or until ready to serve.

◆ *149* ◆

NUTRITION ANALYSIS
(PER SERVING)

Protein 14 gm., Carbohydrate 18 gm., Fiber 1 gm., Fat 3 gm.,
Cholesterol 0, Calcium 13 mg., Sodium 448 mg.

Calories 151
From protein: 35%; From carbohydrate: 45%; From fat: 20%

Tempeh Burgers

Serve these hearty, flavorful burgers with french fries and a salad – very tasty!

◆ 6 BURGERS ◆

15-oz. can low-sodium garbanzo
beans, drained

8 ounces seasoned tempeh
(see page 148)

4 cloves garlic, minced

1/4 cup whole wheat bread crumbs

2 Tbsp. Dijon mustard

1 Tbsp. ketchup

2 Tbsp. tamari

1 Tbsp. egg replacer powder

1/4 cup water

vegetable oil cooking spray

1 Tbsp. olive oil

Place garbanzo beans in a large bowl, and mash with a fork. Crumble seasoned tempeh into the bowl; mix with mashed beans. Add the next 5 ingredients and mix well. Whisk egg replacer with water in a small bowl until foamy. Add to the tempeh mixture; mix thoroughly. (At this point, you may cover mixture and set aside in the refrigerator before proceeding.)

Spray a 10-inch frying pan with cooking spray. Add a tablespoon of olive oil. Form mixture into 6 burgers. Cook over medium heat until browned on both sides, about 15 minutes. If necessary, use additional cooking spray on the pan to keep the burgers from sticking.

◆ *150* ◆

NUTRITION ANALYSIS
(PER BURGER)

Protein 16 gm., Carbohydrate 26 gm., Fiber 3 gm., Fat 4 gm.,
Cholesterol 0, Calcium 6 mg., Sodium 402 mg.

Calories 191
From protein: 32%; From carbohydrate: 50%; From fat: 19%

Tempeh in Brown Gravy

Fresh shiitake mushrooms and colorful vegetables accent
succulent chunks of tempeh in a rich brown sauce.

◆ 6 SERVINGS ◆

1 Tbsp. olive oil

1 cup chopped red onion

6 cloves garlic, minced

1 rib celery, sliced

2 1/2 cups sliced carrots

8 ounces seasoned tempeh, cubed
(see page 148)

3 oz. fresh shiitake mushrooms,
sliced

3 Tbsp. whole wheat flour

1 1/3 cups beef-flavored vegetable
broth, hot

1/4 cup white wine

2 Tbsp. tamari

1 cup frozen peas, thawed

1/2 tsp. dried thyme

Heat olive oil in a 4-quart saucepan over medium-high heat. Add the next 3 ingredients; cook and stir 2 minutes. Add the carrots, and cook 3 minutes. Add the tempeh, and sauté 5 minutes. Add mushrooms, and continue to cook 3 minutes. Sprinkle with flour; stir to coat. Pour hot broth over the mixture, and stir until thickened. Stir in wine and remaining ingredients. Simmer 10 minutes or until ready to serve.

◆ *151* ◆

NUTRITION ANALYSIS
(PER SERVING)

Protein 13 gm., Carbohydrate 22 gm., Fiber 4 gm., Fat 5 gm.,
Cholesterol 0, Calcium 44 mg., Sodium 476 mg.

Calories 181
From protein: 28%; From carbohydrate: 48%; From fat: 24%

Tempeh Shish Kebobs

Chunks of succulent, marinated tempeh and vegetables are skewered and baked, then finished under the broiler. This dish makes an impressive presentation.

◆ 6 KEBOBS ◆

1/3 cup hot barbecue sauce
1/3 cup mild hickory barbecue sauce
1/4 cup ketchup
2 Tbsp. Dijon mustard
3 Tbsp. lemon juice
3 Tbsp. frozen apple juice concentrate
1 Tbsp. tamari
1 tsp. dried basil
1/2 tsp. granulated garlic
1/2 tsp. dried thyme

cayenne pepper to taste
8 ounces seasoned tempeh (see page 148)
1/4 pound. button mushrooms, stems intact
2 small zucchini, cut into 1/2-inch rounds
1 medium yellow onion, cut into 3/4-inch wedges
12 cherry tomatoes
6 bamboo skewers, soaked 20 minutes in hot water

◆ *152* ◆

Mix together the first 11 ingredients in a medium bowl. Set aside. Cut the tempeh into 24 cubes. Skewer the tempeh and vegetables in an alternating pattern, beginning and ending with a mushroom at each end. Place in a 9" x 13" baking pan. Spoon marinade over kebobs, turning to coat both sides. Cover pan with foil, and refrigerate for at least an hour. Preheat oven to 400.° Bake in covered pan for 20 minutes. Remove kebobs from pan and place on broiler rack. Spoon marinade over kebobs; place under broiler. Broil kebobs for 5 minutes, then turn them over and recoat with marinade. Broil for about 5 more minutes or until tempeh and vegetables are browned.

NUTRITION ANALYSIS
(PER SERVING)

Protein 13 gm., Carbohydrate 25 gm., Fiber 7 gm., Fat 2 gm.,
Cholesterol 0, Calcium 37 mg., Sodium 426 mg.

Calories 167
From protein: 30%; From carbohydrate: 57%; From fat: 13%

Tempeh Teriyaki

*This easy-to-assemble dish features succulent
chunks of tempeh in a tasty teriyaki sauce.*

◆ 8 SERVINGS ◆

1 1/2 tsp. olive oil

1/8 tsp. crushed red pepper

6 cloves garlic, minced

1/2 cup sliced scallions

1 Tbsp. grated fresh gingerroot

16 ounces seasoned tempeh, cubed
(see page 148)

2 medium tomatoes, diced

3 oz. fresh shiitake mushrooms,
cleaned, stemmed, and sliced (if
dried, soak before proceeding)

1/4 cup mirin or dry sherry

1 Tbsp. tamari

1 1/2 cups frozen peas, thawed

Heat oil and crushed pepper in large saucepan over medium-high heat for 1 minute.
Add the next 3 ingredients; stir for 2 minutes. Add tempeh to pan. Sauté mixture
5 minutes, stirring frequently. Add the next 4 ingredients. Cook 5 minutes. Add peas,
then lower heat. Simmer 5 minutes or until ready to serve.

◆ *153* ◆

NUTRITION ANALYSIS
(PER SERVING)

Protein 16 gm., Carbohydrate 22 gm., Fiber 4 gm., Fat 4 gm.,
Cholesterol 0, Calcium 19 mg., Sodium 327 mg.

Calories 183
From protein: 34%; From carbohydrate: 46%; From fat: 20%

Tempting Triple Layer Casserole

This hearty dish is very appealing and reheats well.

◆ 1 2   S E R V I N G S ◆

2 cups red lentils, rinsed

4 cups chicken-flavored
vegetable broth

1 3/4 cups beef-flavored
vegetable broth

1 cup soy grits

1 Tbsp. tamari

14.5-oz. can peeled and diced
tomatoes

1/2 tsp. granulated garlic

1 Tbsp. olive oil

1/4 tsp. crushed red pepper

1 cup chopped onion

4 cloves garlic, minced

5 medium unpeeled russet potatoes,
sliced thin

1/2 cup white wine

3/4 cup chicken-flavored vegetable
broth, boiling

1 Tbsp. dried basil

1 medium tomato, sliced into
1/4-inch wedges

◆ *154* ◆

Preheat oven to 350.° Place lentils and chicken-flavored broth in a 5-quart saucepan. Bring to a boil. Reduce heat, and simmer for 12 to 15 minutes, or until liquid is absorbed. Set aside. Place beef-flavored broth, soy grits, and tamari in a medium saucepan; bring to a boil. Reduce heat, and simmer until liquid is absorbed, about 10 minutes. Stir tomatoes and granulated garlic into the grits. Set aside.

Heat oil and crushed pepper in a large oven- and stovetop-safe casserole dish over medium-high heat for 1 minute. Add the onion and garlic; sauté 2 minutes. Add sliced potatoes, and sauté 5 minutes, stirring frequently, or until potatoes start to soften. Add wine, and cook for 2 minutes. Add broth. Cook 10 minutes over medium heat, allowing liquid to reduce by half. Spread the soy grits mixture over the potato mixture, and top with a layer of lentils. Arrange tomato wedges over top layer; sprinkle with basil. Cover casserole, and bake 1 hour. Let casserole stand 10 minutes before serving.

NUTRITION ANALYSIS
(PER SERVING)

Protein 19 gm., Carbohydrate 45 gm., Fiber 6 gm., Fat 2 gm.,
Cholesterol 0, Calcium 42 mg., Sodium 110 mg.

Calories 267
From protein: 28%; From carbohydrate: 67%; From fat: 6%

Tender Tofu With Mixed Vegetables

This dish has color, flavor, texture, and balance.

◆ 4 SERVINGS ◆

MARINADE:

1 1/4 cups beef-flavored vegetable broth, hot

1/2 cup dry sherry

2 Tbsp. tomato paste

1 Tbsp. tamari

2 Tbsp. liquid Fruitsource or honey

2 Tbsp. cider vinegar

2 Tbsp. fresh grated gingerroot

4 cloves garlic, minced

1 scallion, sliced

2 8-oz. pkgs. firm Nigari tofu, frozen, thawed, and cubed (see Techniques)

1 1/2 tsp. olive oil

2 cups sliced carrots

2 cups green beans, cut into 1-inch pieces

1/2 cup sliced scallions

4 large cloves garlic

3 oz. fresh shiitake mushrooms (if dried, soak before proceeding)

14.5-oz. can peeled and diced tomatoes

◆ *155* ◆

Using a wire whisk, blend together the marinade ingredients in the order listed. Immerse the prepared tofu in marinade for at least 3 hours or overnight, turning occasionally.

Warm oil over medium heat in a medium saucepan. Add carrots and green beans; sauté 3 minutes. Stir in scallions, garlic, and mushrooms. Sauté 5 minutes or until vegetables are crisp tender. Push vegetables to sides of pan and place tofu in center of pan with a slotted spoon. Cover, and cook 5 minutes or until tofu is browning. Turn tofu over and pour remaining marinade over tofu. Cook 5 minutes. Add tomatoes, and mix gently. Lower heat, and simmer 10 minutes or until ready to serve. Serve with brown rice and a crisp salad.

NUTRITION ANALYSIS
(PER SERVING)

Protein 19 gm., Carbohydrate 36 gm., Fiber 10 gm., Fat 5 gm.,
Cholesterol 0, Calcium 104 mg., Sodium 498 mg.

Calories 275
From protein: 28%; From carbohydrate: 54%; From fat: 18%

Tofu in Burgundy Sauce

In this delectable dish, marinated tofu is baked in a French-style burgundy sauce.

◆ 6 SERVINGS ◆

MARINADE:

1 3/4 cups burgundy

1/4 cup mellow white miso

1 Tbsp. tamari

3 Tbsp. balsamic vinegar

2 Tbsp. mirin or dry sherry

1/2 tsp. granulated garlic

3 6-oz. pkgs. Nigari tofu (firm),
  frozen, thawed, and cubed
  (see Techniques)

vegetable oil cooking spray

1/2 cup whole wheat flour

1/4 tsp. lemon pepper

1/8 tsp. salt

1/4 tsp. granulated garlic

dash cayenne

1 1/2 cups lightly steamed baby carrots

BURGUNDY SAUCE:

1 Tbsp. olive oil

6 cloves garlic, minced

3/4 cup thinly sliced shallots
  (3-oz. pkg.)

6-oz. pkg. cremini mushrooms,
  stemmed and sliced

3 Tbsp. whole wheat flour

1 1/4 cups reserved marinade

1/2 cup soymilk

◆ *156* ◆

Whisk together the marinade ingredients. Place the tofu in a single layer in a shallow glass pan. Pour marinade over tofu. Marinate for 30 minutes, turning occasionally. Preheat oven to 350°. Spray a 9" x 13" baking pan with cooking spray. In a small bowl, mix together the flour, lemon pepper, salt, granulated garlic, and cayenne. Gently squeeze some of the marinade from the tofu; reserve marinade. Spray a 10" frying pan with cooking spray. Lightly coat tofu chunks with flour mixture. Sauté tofu over medium-high heat, browning on all sides. Remove to 9" x 13" pan, and arrange with baby carrots; set aside.

Heat oil in a medium saucepan. Sauté garlic and shallots two minutes. Add mushrooms. Cook until mushrooms start to soften; stir in flour. Add reserved marinade. Lower heat, and simmer until sauce starts to thicken. Stir in soymilk; simmer 2 minutes. Pour over tofu and carrots, and cover with foil. Bake 25 to 30 minutes.

NUTRITION ANALYSIS (PER SERVING)

Protein 16 gm., Carbohydrate 30 gm., Fiber 6 gm., Fat 5 gm.,
Cholesterol 0, Calcium 38 mg., Sodium 296 mg.

Calories 267
From protein: 23%; From carbohydrate: 45%; From fat: 18%;

TVP Chicken Delight

This intensely flavorful dish is delightful served over brown rice.

◆ 6 SERVINGS ◆

1 cup chicken-flavored vegetable
  broth, boiling

2 cups TVP chicken chunks

1 cup sun-dried tomatoes

1 cup boiling water

1 1/2 tsp. olive oil

1/4 tsp. crushed red pepper

3 large cloves garlic, minced

1/2 cup chopped red bell peppers

3/4 cup sliced scallions

1 Tbsp. tamari

1/4 cup mirin or dry sherry

Combine broth and TVP in a medium bowl. Set aside. Cut dried tomatoes into thirds using a kitchen shears. Place in a small bowl, and cover with boiling water. Set aside. Sauté oil and crushed pepper in a large saucepan over medium-high heat for 2 minutes. Stir in the next 3 ingredients; sauté 3 minutes. Add reconstituted TVP. Cook 5 minutes. Add tomatoes and soaking water. Cover, and reduce heat to medium. Cook 10 minutes, stirring frequently. Add tamari and mirin; simmer for 10 minutes, stirring occasionally, or until ready to serve.

◆ *157* ◆

NUTRITION ANALYSIS
(PER SERVING)

Protein 16 gm., Carbohydrate 16 gm., Fiber 6 gm., Fat 2 gm.,
Cholesterol 0, Calcium 25 mg., Sodium 378 mg.

Calories 127
From protein: 44%; From carbohydrate: 45%; From fat: 11%

Vegetarian Beef Stroganoff

This version of a classic is easy to make and quite delicious.
Serve with rice or noodles.

◆ 8 SERVINGS ◆

vegetable oil cooking spray
1 Tbsp. cider vinegar
1 1/2 cups soymilk lite
2 14-oz. pkg. Gimme Lean, ground
  beef style
1/4 cup bread crumbs
1/3 cup ketchup
1 Tbsp. Dijon mustard
1/2 tsp. granulated garlic
2 Tbsp. olive oil

3/4 cup chopped sweet onion
  (Texas, Vidalia, Maui)
6 cloves garlic, minced
1/4 cup whole wheat flour
1/2 cup white wine
1/4 cup dry vermouth
1/2 tsp. ground nutmeg
2/3 cup nutritional yeast
6 large fresh basil leaves, snipped

◆ *158* ◆

Preheat oven to 400.° Spray a baking pan with cooking spray. Add vinegar to soymilk in a small glass measuring cup; set aside. Place the next 5 ingredients in a large bowl, and mix thoroughly. Form into 3-inch balls, and place on prepared pan. Spray "meatballs" lightly with cooking spray. Bake for 10 minutes, then broil to brown tops.

Meanwhile, heat oil in a 5-quart saucepan over medium heat for 1 minute. Add onions and garlic; sauté 3 minutes. Add flour and stir for 2 minutes; then add wine, vermouth, and nutmeg. Lower heat, and gradually add soymilk, stirring frequently as it simmers. Whisk in nutritional yeast, and add snipped basil. Add cooked "meatballs" to simmering sauce. Simmer 10 minutes or until ready to serve, stirring gently.

NUTRITION ANALYSIS
(PER SERVING)

Protein 26 gm., Carbohydrate 38 gm., Fiber 3 gm., Fat 4 gm.,
Cholesterol 0, Calcium 13 mg., Sodium 553 mg.

Calories 289
From protein: 35%; From carbohydrate: 51%; From fat: 14%

Western Scrambler

*Serve this delicious tofu scrambler with pita pockets for
a delightful brunch or light supper.*

◆ 6 SERVINGS ◆

2 1/2 cups lite silken tofu (extra
firm), drained

14.5-oz. can diced tomatoes
and jalapeños

1 1/2 tsp. olive oil

1/8 tsp. crushed red pepper

2/3 cup chopped onion

4 cloves garlic, minced

1/3 cup chopped green bell pepper

6-oz. pkg. Yves veggie Canadian
bacon, diced

1/2 tsp. turmeric

1 rounded Tbsp. mellow white miso

1 1/2 Tbsp. very dry sherry

1 tsp. dried cilantro

Place tofu in a large microwave-safe bowl, and mash with a potato masher. Cover
and microwave for 3 minutes. Transfer tofu to a colander to drain. Set aside. Place
tomatoes in a separate strainer, and set aside to drain. In a 4-quart saucepan, heat oil
and crushed pepper over medium-high heat. Add the next 3 ingredients, and sauté
2 minutes. Add diced veggie bacon. Sauté mixture an additional 5 minutes. Add well-
drained tofu and tomatoes along with turmeric. Simmer 5 minutes, stirring frequently.
Place miso in a small bowl. Add sherry, and blend until smooth. Stir miso into the
mixture; sprinkle with cilantro. Simmer gently 1 minute. Serve with pita pockets.

◆*159*◆

NUTRITION ANALYSIS
(PER SERVING)

Protein 16 gm., Carbohydrate 8 gm., Fiber 2 gm., Fat 2 gm.,
Cholesterol 0, Calcium 25 mg., Sodium 672 mg.

Calories 117
From protein: 54%; From carbohydrate: 28%; From fat: 19%

Soyful Sides

In this section you will find side dishes to complement any type of entrée, all of which bring the goodness of soy to the table. Dishes that accompany the main course needn't be an afterthought; a little advance planning will ensure balance of color, texture, and flavor. Of course, choosing a side dish with an abundance of soy protein will boost the nutritional value of any meal. Plan your meals with recipes from *Soy of Cooking* for each course and you will enjoy the benefits of a high-fiber, low-fat diet, an abundance of complex carbohydrates, and all those nifty little phytochemicals.

Side dishes are chosen to complement the main entrée, without clashing with, or overshadowing the overall presentation. If you were serving an entrée with a lusty tomato sauce, you wouldn't choose a side dish drenched in brown gravy. Likewise a heavy potato dish wouldn't be a good bet to accompany Pasta Primavera. In this section you can choose creamy Garlic Mashed Potatoes to accompany Tempeh Burgers or Homestyle Veggie Loaf. Dilly Broccoli Rice is a delightfully colorful dish that would complement Tofu in Burgundy Sauce or the Vegetarian Beef Stroganoff, equally. How about a wonderful, crusty gratin, like the Florentine Penne Gratin, or the Crusted Butternut Squash Casserole? One of the succulent tofu-based breads would surely round out the meal.

Whether it's an interesting side pasta you are looking for, a soysational Creamed Spinach, or an elegant treatment like Brussels Sprouts and Chestnuts in a Savory Sauce, you will find them here. Whatever you choose, you can be assured of the wholesomeness of the ingredients, and quality of flavor, texture, and style. ◆

Acorn Squash With Tofu & Vegetables

*A flavorful marinade, firm and chewy tofu, chick-peas, and
vegetables make a delicious filling for acorn squash.*

◆ 8 S E R V I N G S ◆

2 8-oz. pkg. firm Nigari tofu (frozen
in cutlet form), thawed

MARINADE:

1 Tbsp. mellow barley miso
1/2 cup white wine
3 Tbsp. tomato paste
2 Tbsp. balsamic vinegar
1 tsp. granulated garlic
2 Tbsp. Dijon mustard
1 Tbsp. mild molasses
1/3 cup sliced scallions
2 acorn squash, seeded and quartered
(about 2 lbs.)

Vegetable oil cooking spray
1/4 tsp. crushed red pepper
2 Tbsp. grated gingerroot
3/4 cup chopped onions
4 cloves garlic, minced
2 cups sliced baby carrots
2 cups sliced mushrooms
15-oz. can garbanzo beans, drained
1/4 cup mirin or dry sherry
1/3 cup nutritional yeast
1 Tbsp. Bragg liquid aminos

Thaw and squeeze tofu (see Techniques). Slice each tofu cutlet in fourths, and
place in a shallow pan. Place miso in a small bowl. Blend wine into miso. Add the rest
of the marinade ingredients, and blend well. Pour marinade over tofu. Cover and refrigerate at least an hour or overnight.

Preheat oven to 350.° Coat squash quarters lightly with cooking spray. Place
squash, cut side down, in shallow baking pan in 2 inches of water. Bake 45 minutes,
turning at 15-minute intervals. Spray a 4-quart stovetop- and ovensafe casserole dish
with cooking spray. Add red pepper, and heat 1 minute. Add the next 4 ingredients, and
sauté 5 minutes. Add mushrooms; cook 2 minutes. Add remaining ingredients; cook
3 minutes. Gently add marinated tofu, and lower heat. Simmer 5 minutes, gently
turning mixture with a slotted spoon. Cover casserole and bake 30 minutes while the
squash bakes. Place squash on dinner plates, cut side up, and top with filling.

NUTRITION ANALYSIS
(PER SERVING)

Protein 17 gm., Carbohydrate 80 gm., Fiber 10 gm., Fat 3 gm.,
Cholesterol 0, Calcium 80 mg., Sodium 193 mg.

Calories 266
From protein: 16%; From carbohydrate: 78%; From fat: 7%

Bonzo Rice Loaf

Serve this tasty and nutritious brown rice loaf with tomato sauce.

◆ 8 SERVINGS ◆

vegetable oil cooking spray
2 cups beef-flavored vegetable broth
1 cup brown rice
15-oz. can garbanzo beans, drained
1 cup soy grits
1/2 cup thinly sliced scallions
1/4 cup chopped red bell peppers

1 tsp. granulated garlic
2 Tbsp. Dijon mustard
1 Tbsp. Bragg liquid aminos
2 Tbsp. egg replacer powder
1/2 cup water
2 tsp. dried marjoram, separated
2 Tbsp. whole wheat bread crumbs

Preheat oven to 350°. Spray a loaf pan with cooking spray. Bring broth to a boil. Add rice, bring to a second boil, and simmer, covered, about 40 minutes. Set aside to cool. Place garbanzo beans in a large bowl. Partially mash the beans, leaving some whole. Add rice, and mix well. Add the next 6 ingredients, and mix well. Whisk egg replacer powder with water in a small bowl until foamy. Add egg replacer with 1 teaspoon marjoram to mixture; mix thoroughly. Spoon into prepared loaf pan. Top with remaining marjoram, and sprinkle with bread crumbs. Bake 30 to 40 minutes or until browned. Serve topped with tomato sauce.

◆ *163* ◆

NUTRITION ANALYSIS
(PER SERVING)

Protein 12 gm., Carbohydrate 76 gm., Fiber 6 gm., Fat 4 gm.,
Cholesterol 0, Calcium 16 mg., Sodium 139 mg.

Calories 230
From protein: 13%; From carbohydrate: 77%; From fat: 10%

Brussels Sprouts and Chestnuts in a Savory Sauce

This dish features the rich flavors and textures of chestnuts and pungent brussels sprouts in a luscious, creamy sauce.

◆ 6 SERVINGS ◆

2 cups shelled chestnuts, blanched and peeled

1 1/2 tsp. olive oil

1/8 tsp. crushed red pepper

1/2 cup sliced scallions

4 cloves garlic, minced

1 1/2 cups baby carrots, cut crosswise into thirds

1 1/2 pound. brussels sprouts, trimmed and halved vertically

1/4 cup mirin or dry sherry

1 Tbsp. Bragg liquid aminos

1 cup soymilk lite

1 tsp. dried parsley

1/2 tsp. granulated garlic

1/2 tsp. ground coriander

1/2 cup nutritional yeast

1 Tbsp. cornstarch

2 Tbsp. water

Prepare chestnuts (see Techniques) Cover and set aside. Heat oil and crushed pepper in a 4-quart saucepan over medium-high heat for 1 minute. Add scallions and garlic, and sauté 2 minutes. Add carrot chunks; sauté 2 minutes. Add brussels sprouts, and sauté 5 minutes or until crisp tender. Add mirin, and cook 2 minutes. Add chestnuts. Lower heat, and simmer 3 minutes. Add liquid aminos, soymilk, and next 3 ingredients; stir gently. Stir in nutritional yeast. Blend together cornstarch and water in a small bowl; stir into pan. Simmer gently 5 minutes or until ready to serve.

NUTRITION ANALYSIS
(PER SERVING)

Protein 14 gm., Carbohydrate 92 gm., Fiber 11 gm., Fat 3 gm., Cholesterol 0, Calcium 96 mg., Sodium 198 mg.

Calories 241
From protein: 12%; From carbohydrate: 81%; From fat: 6%

Cranberry Surprise

This is a lovely side dish, especially for Thanksgiving or Christmas dinner.

◆ 8 SERVINGS ◆

12-oz. pkg. fresh or frozen
  cranberries

1/2 cup white grape juice concentrate,
  thawed

1/2 cup Sucanat or brown sugar

1/2 tsp. almond extract

1 1/4 cups lite silken tofu
  (extra firm)

1/2 cup prune purée

1 1/2 cups canned pumpkin

1/2 tsp. ground allspice

1/2 tsp. cinnamon

1/2 cup Florida Crystals or sugar

1 tsp. vanilla extract

1 cup slivered apricots

1/4 cup apricot brandy

1/3 cup chopped pecans

nutmeg

Preheat oven to 350.° Place cranberries in a 2-quart stovetop- and oven-safe casserole over medium heat. Add juice concentrate, Sucanat, and almond extract. Cook 8 to 10 minutes, stirring frequently. Remove from heat when mixture thickens and berries begin to pop. Place tofu in food processor, and blend. Add prune and pumpkin purées. Blend until smooth. Add the next 4 ingredients, and blend until smooth. Spread pumpkin mixture evenly over cranberries. Place slivered apricots in a small saucepan with brandy. Simmer 5 minutes or until liquid is absorbed. Remove from heat, and mix with chopped pecans. Arrange apricot/pecan topping over pumpkin layer. Sprinkle with nutmeg. Bake 20 to 25 minutes or until bubbling and lightly browned.

◆ *165* ◆

NUTRITION ANALYSIS
(PER SERVING)

Protein 4 gm., Carbohydrate 56 gm., Fiber 4 gm., Fat 4 gm.,
Cholesterol 0, Calcium 36 mg., Sodium 85 mg.

Calories 244
From protein: 6%; From carbohydrate: 81%; From fat: 13%

Creamed Artichokes

Tender artichokes melt in your mouth, drenched in a luscious, creamy sauce.

◆ 4 S E R V I N G S ◆

1 Tbsp. olive oil

1/8 tsp. crushed red pepper

3/4 cup sliced scallions

3 cloves garlic, minced

3 Tbsp. whole wheat flour

1 1/2 cups soymilk lite

1/2 cup nutritional yeast

13 3/4-oz. can quartered artichokes

1 cup frozen white corn, thawed

1 Tbsp. dried marjoram

1 Tbsp. tamari

dash cayenne

Heat oil and crushed pepper in a medium saucepan over medium-high heat. Add scallions and garlic; sauté 3 minutes. Stir in flour and cook to a paste, 1 to 2 minutes. Add soymilk gradually, stirring over medium heat. Add nutritional yeast, stirring until smooth and thickened, about 2 minutes. Add remaining ingredients and lower heat. Simmer 8 minutes, or until ready to serve.

NUTRITION ANALYSIS
(PER SERVING)

Protein 17 gm., Carbohydrate 36 gm., Fiber 5 gm., Fat 5 gm.,
Cholesterol 0, Calcium 33 mg., Sodium 493 mg.

Calories 250
From protein: 26%; From carbohydrate: 56%; From fat: 18%

Creamed Peas and Pearl Onions

*This simple yet elegant side dish features delicate pearl onions
and sweet peas simmered in a dairy-free cream sauce.*

◆ 6 SERVINGS ◆

1 1/2 cups pearl onions, blanched
and peeled (see Techniques)
2 Tbsp. olive oil
1/4 cup whole wheat flour
1/4 cup dry vermouth
1 cup soymilk lite

16-oz. pkg. frozen peas, thawed
1 Tbsp. nutritional yeast
1 tsp. dried parsley
1/2 tsp. dried thyme
1 tsp. Bragg liquid aminos

Prepare onions, and set aside in a colander. Heat olive oil in a medium saucepan over medium heat. Add onions, and cook 10 minutes, stirring frequently. They will brown lightly. Add flour, and stir 2 minutes. Stir in vermouth, and then gradually add the soymilk. Add the remaining ingredients. Simmer for 10 minutes, stirring frequently. Keep warm until ready to serve.

◆*167*◆

NUTRITION ANALYSIS
(PER SERVING)

Protein 7 gm., Carbohydrate 38 gm., Fiber 6 gm., Fat 5 gm.,
Cholesterol 0, Calcium 37 mg., Sodium 232 mg.

Calories 166
From protein: 12%; From carbohydrate: 67%; From fat: 21%

Creamed Spinach

This flavorful side dish loses nothing in its translation to dairy freedom.

◆ 6 SERVINGS ◆

10-oz. pkg. frozen spinach, thawed
1 1/2 tsp. olive oil
1/2 cup sliced scallions
1 rib celery, sliced, including tops
1/3 cup dry vermouth

1 1/4 cups lite silken tofu (firm), drained
1 cup soymilk lite
3 Tbsp. nutritional yeast
1/4 tsp. ground nutmeg
1 tsp. Bragg liquid aminos

Place thawed spinach in a colander; press out moisture. Heat oil in a medium saucepan. Sauté the scallions and celery over medium-high heat for 3 minutes. Add spinach, and sauté 5 minutes, stirring to mix. Add vermouth, and lower heat. Simmer 5 minutes. Place tofu in food processor, and blend. Add soymilk, and blend. Add spinach mixture, and pulse to mix. Add remaining ingredients. Process, but do not purée. Return to pan, and simmer until ready to serve, stirring frequently.

NUTRITION ANALYSIS
(PER SERVING)

Protein 9 gm., Carbohydrate 26 gm., Fiber 2 gm., Fat 2 gm.,
Cholesterol 0, Calcium 80 mg., Sodium 150 mg.

Calories 103
From protein: 21%; From carbohydrate: 65%; From fat: 13%

Crusted Asparagus Bake

*This delightful mélange is baked in a creamed
tomato sauce under a crisp crumb topping.*

◆ 8 SERVINGS ◆

1 Tbsp. olive oil

1 leek, cleaned and cut into
  1/4-inch slices (see Techniques)

4 cloves garlic

2 cups baby carrots, cut into thirds

1 medium zucchini, sliced (about
  2 cups)

1 pound. asparagus, cut in 4-inch
  pieces

1/2 pound. mushrooms, sliced

1 cup white wine

2 cups chopped fresh tomatoes
  (about 1 large)

1 cup frozen peas, thawed

1/4 cup whole wheat flour

1 cup soymilk lite

TOPPING:

2 Tbsp. soy grits

2 Tbsp. whole wheat bread crumbs

1 Tbsp. nutritional yeast

1 tsp. dried basil

1 tsp. dried rosemary, crumbled

◆ *169* ◆

Preheat oven to 375.° Heat oil over medium-high heat in an oven- and stovetop-proof 3-quart casserole. Add the leeks and garlic, and sauté 3 minutes. Add carrots, and sauté 2 minutes. Add zucchini and asparagus; sauté 2 minutes. Add mushrooms, and cook 3 minutes or until vegetables are crisp-tender. Add wine, tomatoes, and peas. Lower heat to simmer, 3 minutes. Stir in flour, forming a paste. Gradually add soymilk, and stir until mixture starts to thicken.

Combine the topping ingredients in a small bowl. Sprinkle this topping over all, and place casserole in preheated oven. Bake 20 minutes or until topping is browned and casserole is bubbling.

NUTRITION ANALYSIS
(PER SERVING)

Protein 8 gm., Carbohydrate 23 gm., Fiber 4 gm., Fat 3 gm.,
Cholesterol 0, Calcium 54 mg., Sodium 51 mg.

Calories 145
From protein: 20%; From carbohydrate: 64%; From fat: 16%

Crusted Butternut Squash Casserole

This "gratin" is tasty, colorful, and simple to prepare.

◆ 6 SERVINGS ◆

1 Tbsp. olive oil

1/4 tsp. crushed red pepper

1 medium onion, cut into 1-inch
wedges

4 large cloves garlic, minced

1 large red bell pepper, cut into
1-inch strips

8 cups peeled, cubed butternut
squash* (about 3 lbs.)

1 1/2 cups halved cherry tomatoes

1/2 cup white wine

TOPPING:

1/4 cup whole wheat bread crumbs

1/4 cup soy grits

3 Tbsp. nutritional yeast

1 tsp. dried basil

1 tsp. dried rosemary, crumbled

◆ *170* ◆

Preheat oven to 350.° Heat olive oil and crushed pepper in a 4-quart stovetop-safe
and ovenproof casserole over medium-high heat for 1 minute. Add the next 3 ingredients, and sauté 3 minutes. Add the squash and cook mixture 5 minutes. Add tomatoes
and wine. Lower heat, and simmer 10 minutes. In a small bowl, mix together the topping
ingredients. Sprinkle the topping over all. Bake 30 minutes.

*The easiest way to peel a butternut squash is to make several crosswise cuts with a
sharp knife. Then place the squash cut side down on a cutting board, and slice the peel
away from you.

NUTRITION ANALYSIS
(PER SERVING)

Protein 13 gm., Carbohydrate 50 gm., Fiber 9 gm., Fat 3 gm.,
Cholesterol 0, Calcium 139 mg., Sodium 19 mg.

Calories 243
From protein: 18%; From carbohydrate: 72%; From fat: 10%

Dilly Broccoli Rice

This quick and easy dish is quite dill-icious!

◆ 6 SERVINGS ◆

1 1/2 tsp. olive oil

3 cloves garlic, minced

1/3 cup sliced scallions

3 cups cooked brown rice

10-oz. pkg. frozen chopped broccoli,
    thawed and drained

1 cup corn (if frozen, thawed)

3/4 cup soymilk lite

2/3 cup nutritional yeast

1 tsp. dried dillweed

In a medium saucepan, heat oil over medium heat. Add garlic and scallions; sauté 3 minutes. Add rice. Cook and stir 3 minutes. Add broccoli and corn. Lower heat, and simmer, stirring occasionally. Place soymilk in a small bowl. Add nutritional yeast, 1/3 cup at a time, blending with a whisk or fork. Stir dill into soymilk mixture; add to saucepan. Simmer 5 minutes or until ready to serve.

◆*171*◆

NUTRITION ANALYSIS
(PER SERVING)

Protein 15 gm., Carbohydrate 36 gm., Fiber 4 gm., Fat 3 gm.,
Cholesterol 0, Calcium 39 mg., Sodium 23 mg.

Calories 224
From protein: 25%; From carbohydrate: 63%; From fat: 12%

Dirty Rice

This hearty version of a Cajun specialty is made especially delicious with tofu and Cajun-spiced stewed tomatoes.

◆ 8 SERVINGS ◆

2 tsp. olive oil
3 cloves garlic, minced
3/4 cup chopped red onion
1/4 cup green bell pepper
1 cup white rice
3 1/2 cups beef-flavored vegetable broth, separated

14.5-oz. can Cajun- (or Mexican-) style stewed tomatoes
16-oz. pkg. Ready Ground Tofu, hot and spicy
1/2 tsp. ground cumin
1/2 tsp. ground coriander
1/3 cup snipped fresh cilantro

In a 10" frying pan, heat oil over medium-high heat. Add the next 3 ingredients, and sauté 3 minutes. Stir in the rice, and sauté 2 minutes. Add 2 cups of the broth. Bring mixture to a boil, then lower heat and simmer 12 minutes or until liquid is almost absorbed. Add tomatoes and tofu, and simmer 5 minutes longer. Add the reserved broth and remaining ingredients. Simmer until liquid is absorbed and rice is tender, about 10 minutes.

NUTRITION ANALYSIS
(PER SERVING)

Protein 5 gm., Carbohydrate 24 gm., Fiber 2 gm., Fat 3 gm.,
Cholesterol 0, Calcium 27 mg., Sodium 263 mg.

Calories 140
From protein: 15%; From carbohydrate: 66%; From fat: 19%

Fettuccine With Sun-Dried Tomato/Basil Cream Sauce

The luscious sauce clinging to thick ribbons of pasta is so flavorful and rich tasting, you won't believe it's dairy free.

◆ 6 SERVINGS ◆

1 cup soymilk lite

1 Tbsp. cider vinegar

1/2 cup snipped sun-dried tomatoes

2/3 cup boiling water

1 1/2 Tbsp. olive oil

1/2 cup chopped onion

4 large cloves garlic, minced

1/3 cup white wheat or unbleached flour

1/4 cup dry vermouth

1 1/2 cups chicken-flavored vegetable broth

1/4 cup loosely packed snipped fresh basil leaves

1 1/4 cups lite silken tofu (firm), drained

1 tsp. tamari

1 Tbsp. nutritional yeast

16-oz. pkg. egg-free fettuccine, cooked according to package directions

◆ *173* ◆

Place soymilk in a small glass measuring cup. Add vinegar, and set aside. Immerse sun-dried tomatoes in boiling water, and set aside. Heat olive oil in a large saucepan over medium-high heat. Add onions and garlic. Sauté 3 minutes or until crisp tender. Stir in flour, then add vermouth. Stir in broth with a wire whisk. Lower heat to simmer. Add sun-dried tomatoes, soaking water, and basil. Simmer, stirring frequently. Place tofu in food processor, and blend. Add soymilk, and blend until smooth. Whisk tofu mixture into the saucepan along with tamari and yeast. Continue to simmer, stirring frequently. Serve over pasta.

NUTRITION ANALYSIS
(PER SERVING)

Protein 11 gm., Carbohydrate 37 gm., Fiber 2 gm., Fat 5 gm.,
Cholesterol 0, Calcium 36 mg., Sodium 267 mg.

Calories 244
From protein: 18%; From carbohydrate: 62%; From fat: 20%

Florentine Penne Gratin

This delicious dish is dairy-free and true to its French roots.

◆ 6 SERVINGS ◆

1 cup snipped sun-dried tomatoes

1 cup boiling water

10-oz. pkg. frozen chopped spinach, thawed

1/2 pound. penne rigate*, cooked al dente, rinsed in cold water

1 tsp. dried basil

1/4 cup nutritional yeast

SAUCE:

1 Tbsp. olive oil

1/4 tsp. crushed red pepper

1/3 cup chopped shallots

4 cloves garlic, minced

6 oz. cremini mushrooms, sliced

3 Tbsp. whole wheat flour

2 cups soymilk lite, separated

3 Tbsp. tomato paste

TOPPING:

1/4 cup whole wheat bread crumbs

1/4 cup soy grits

3 Tbsp. nutritional yeast

1 tsp. dried basil

1 tsp. dried thyme

◆ *174* ◆

Preheat oven to 350°. In a small bowl, steep the snipped tomatoes in boiling water; set aside. Place spinach in a colander, and squeeze out liquid; set aside. While penne is cooking, make the sauce:

Heat oil and crushed pepper in a medium saucepan 1 minute. Stir in shallots and garlic; cook 2 minutes. Add mushrooms. Cook 3 to 4 minutes or until mushrooms are tender. Stir in flour, and cook mixture 2 minutes. Add 1/2 cup of the soymilk and the tomato paste; stir until blended. Add the remainder of the soymilk; reduce heat and simmer. Place the well-drained pasta in a shallow 3-quart baking dish. Toss with the tomatoes and soaking liquid, spinach, basil, and yeast. Add the sauce, and mix thoroughly. Combine the topping ingredients in a small bowl; sprinkle generously over all. Bake 20 minutes or until casserole is bubbly and topping is browned.

*You may use plain penne, but the ridges in rigate hold the sauce nicely.

NUTRITION ANALYSIS
(PER SERVING)

Protein 20 gm., Carbohydrate 48 gm., Fiber 4 gm., Fat 4 gm., Cholesterol 0, Calcium 111 mg., Sodium 333 mg.

Calories 274
From protein: 26%; From carbohydrate: 62%; From fat: 12%

Garlic Mashed Potatoes

This is a flavorful version of mashed potatoes.

◆ 8 SERVINGS ◆

6 medium russet potatoes, peeled
  and diced
4 cups salted water
1 Tbsp. olive oil

3 cloves garlic, minced
1/4 cup sliced scallions
2/3 cup hot soymilk lite
1/4 tsp. salt

Place diced potatoes in a medium saucepan with water. Bring to a boil, and reduce to medium-low heat. Cook potatoes (covered, with lid left slightly ajar) 20 minutes or until pierced easily with a fork, but not mushy. Drain thoroughly, and return to the saucepan. Use a potato masher to mash potatoes. When you've reached the desired consistency, set aside. Heat oil in a small frying pan over medium heat. Add garlic and scallions. Sauté 8 minutes, stirring frequently, or until cooked through and softened. Scrape scallion mixture and any remaining oil into potatoes. Add hot soymilk gradually, beating with a fork after each addition; add salt. Keep warm until ready to serve.

◆ *175* ◆

NUTRITION ANALYSIS
(PER SERVING)

Protein 4 gm., Carbohydrate 40 gm., Fiber 1 gm., Fat 2 gm.,
Cholesterol 0, Calcium 4 mg., Sodium 78 mg.

Calories 191
From protein: 8%; From carbohydrate: 82%; From fat: 9%

Indian-Spiced Potatoes and Spinach

*Aromatic Indian spices lend a complex flavor that transforms
potatoes and spinach into an exciting side dish.*

◆ 8 SERVINGS ◆

1 Tbsp. olive oil

1 tsp. black mustard seeds

2 bay leaves

2 sticks cinnamon

1/4 tsp. crushed red pepper

3 cups coarsely chopped red onion

4 medium unpeeled Yukon Gold
potatoes, cubed (about 4 cups)

1 tsp. granulated garlic

1/4 tsp. turmeric

1 tsp. ground cumin

1 tsp. ground coriander

10-oz. pkg. frozen spinach, thawed
and drained

2 tsp. Bragg liquid aminos

1 cup soymilk lite

Heat oil in a 5-quart saucepan. Add mustard seeds. Cook and stir over medium heat until the seeds begin to pop. Add the bay leaves, cinnamon sticks, and crushed pepper. Stir 1 minute. Add the onions and potatoes; cook 3 minutes. Add the garlic, turmeric, cumin, and coriander. Cook 5 minutes. Add the spinach and the remaining ingredients; reduce heat. Cook over low heat for 35 minutes or until the sauce is reduced and the potatoes are tender.

NUTRITION ANALYSIS
(PER SERVING)

Protein 5 gm., Carbohydrate 61 gm., Fiber 3 gm., Fat 2 gm.,
Cholesterol 0, Calcium 80 mg., Sodium 103 mg.

Calories 179
From protein: 7%; From carbohydrate: 85%; From fat: 8%

Minted Orzo—"Mimi"

*This is a delectably creamy dish reminiscent of Alfredo-type cream sauces.
I designed it for Mimi Clark, a talented culinary instructor.*

◆ 8   S E R V I N G S ◆

1 Tbsp. olive oil
1/3 cup chopped red onion
1 1/2 cups sliced baby carrots
1 medium zucchini, cut into
  julienne strips
4 large cloves garlic, minced
1 cup freshly shelled peas
1/2 cup white wine

1 1/4 cups lite silken tofu (firm),
  drained
3/4 cup soymilk lite
2 Tbsp. lemon juice
1 tsp. dried mint
1/4 cup nutritional yeast
1 cup orzo pasta
fresh mint leaves for garnish

Heat oil over medium-high heat in a 10" frying pan. Add onion, and sauté
1 minute. Add carrots. Cook covered, 5 minutes, stirring occasionally. Stir in zucchini,
garlic, and peas; cook 3 minutes. Add wine, and cover, stirring occasionally, for 5 to 8
minutes. In a food processor, blend tofu until smooth. Add soymilk, lemon juice, mint,
and yeast. Blend. Stir into pan. Reduce heat, and simmer until ready to serve.

In a small saucepan, boil 2 quarts water with a bit of salt and canola oil. Add orzo,
and boil uncovered, stirring frequently, for 8 minutes. Rinse with water, and set aside.
Pack cooked orzo into ramekins or custard cups. Overturn cup onto dinner plate and
pour sauce over top. Garnish with sprigs of mint.

◆ *177* ◆

NUTRITION ANALYSIS
(PER SERVING)

Protein 10 gm., Carbohydrate 25 gm., Fiber 3 gm., Fat 3 gm.,
Cholesterol 0, Calcium 31 mg., Sodium 68 mg.

Calories 172
From protein: 24%; From carbohydrate: 60%; From fat: 16%

Potatoes "Marie"

This easy stovetop potato dish works equally well at brunch
or dinner. The creamy, flavorful sauce is spectacular.

◆ 8 SERVINGS ◆

Vegetable oil cooking spray
1 Tbsp. olive oil
1/8 tsp. crushed red pepper
3 cloves garlic, minced
1/2 cup sliced scallions

6 cups unpeeled, thinly sliced Yukon
   Gold potatoes
1/4 cup mirin or dry sherry
1 cup soymilk lite
1 1/3 tsp. Bragg liquid aminos
1 Tbsp. nutritional yeast

Coat a 4-quart saucepan lightly with cooking spray. Heat oil and crushed pepper over medium-high heat for 1 minute. Add garlic and scallions; sauté 2 minutes. Add potatoes. Sauté 12 minutes, stirring frequently with a gentle lifting and turning technique so as not to break potato slices. Add mirin, and cook 5 minutes longer, stirring gently and frequently. Place soymilk in a small measuring cup. Stir in liquid aminos. Add soymilk to saucepan. Lower heat, and simmer 3 minutes. Sprinkle nutritional yeast over mixture; carefully stir to mix. Keep warm until ready to serve.

◆ *178* ◆

NUTRITION ANALYSIS
(PER SERVING)

Protein 44 gm., Carbohydrate 52 gm., Fiber 1 gm., Fat 2 gm.,
Cholesterol 0, Calcium 5 mg., Sodium 51 mg.

Calories 176
From protein: 7%; From carbohydrate: 85%; From fat: 8%

Saffron Couscous

*This unusual treatment for couscous is
the perfect accompaniment to hearty entrées.*

◆ 6 SERVINGS ◆

1/2 cup white wine
1/2 tsp. saffron threads
2 cups soymilk lite

2 cups couscous
2 tsp. Bragg liquid aminos
1 tsp. dried parsley

Place wine in a small bowl. Add saffron, and set aside for 15 minutes. In a medium saucepan, heat soymilk until almost boiling. Stir in wine mixture, and heat an additional 2 minutes. (It's OK if mixture separates.) Add couscous, aminos, and parsley. Stir to mix. Cover, and remove from heat for 5 minutes. Fluff with fork, then serve immediately.

NUTRITION ANALYSIS
(PER 3/4-CUP SERVING)

Protein 10 gm., Carbohydrate 86 gm., Fiber 0, Fat 1 gm.,
Cholesterol 0, Calcium 4 mg., Sodium 114 mg.

Calories 279
From protein: 10%; From carbohydrate: 88%; From fat: 2%

◆*179*◆

Savory Summer Medley

You will want to serve this colorful, flavorful side dish often.

◆ 6 SERVINGS ◆

1 Tbsp. olive oil

1/4 tsp. crushed red pepper

1 small sweet onion, chopped
  (about 1 cup)

5 cloves garlic, minced

1/3 cup chopped red bell pepper

1 large russet potato, unpeeled, cut
  into 1/4-inch slices

2 cups baby carrots, halved vertically

3 cups sliced yellow squash

1 cup dry vermouth, separated

1 bay leaf

1/4 cup mellow white miso

1 cup frozen baby peas, thawed

2 tsp. dried thyme

1 tsp. Bragg liquid aminos

1 Tbsp. nutritional yeast

◆ *180* ◆

Heat oil over medium-high heat in a 5-quart saucepan. Add crushed pepper and sauté 1 minute. Add the next 3 ingredients, and sauté 2 minutes. Add potatoes and carrots, and sauté 3 minutes. Add the squash, and continue to cook, stirring frequently, over medium-high heat until vegetables are crisp tender (about 10 minutes). Add 1/2 cup vermouth and bay leaf; cook 5 minutes. Blend the miso into the remaining 1/2 cup vermouth. Stir into the vegetables. Lower heat, then add peas. Simmer 2 minutes. Stir in remaining ingredients, and simmer 5 minutes or until ready to serve. Remove bay leaf before serving.

NUTRITION ANALYSIS
(PER 1 1/4-CUP SERVING)

Protein 6 gm., Carbohydrate 45 gm., Fiber 5 gm., Fat 3 gm.,
Cholesterol 0, Calcium 59 mg., Sodium 223 mg.

Calories 196
From protein: 9%; From carbohydrate: 79%; From fat: 12%

Yams 'n Cranberries

*The aroma of this casserole is delightful, and
the tart-sweet flavors complement a hearty meal.*

◆ 8   S E R V I N G S ◆

3 medium yams, peeled and cubed

12-oz. pkg. fresh or frozen
  cranberries

1/2 cup golden raisins

1 cup soymilk lite

1/4 cup liquid Fruitsource or honey

1 cinnamon stick

3 Tbsp. brown sugar

1 tsp. ground nutmeg

Preheat oven to 350.° Place the first three ingredients in a 3 1/2-quart ovenproof casserole. Heat soymilk, Fruitsource, and cinnamon stick in the microwave for 1 minute or in a saucepan for 3 minutes. Pour over yam mixture. Sprinkle with brown sugar and nutmeg. Cover, and bake 1 1/2 hours, stirring a few times during baking.

NUTRITION ANALYSIS
(PER SERVING)

◆ *181* ◆

Protein 3 gm., Carbohydrate 67 gm., Fiber 2 gm., Fat 1 gm.,
Cholesterol 0, Calcium 19 mg., Sodium 170 mg.

Calories 280
From protein: 5%; From carbohydrate: 93%; From fat: 2%

Pizza and Pasta

I s it possible to make eggless pasta and cheeseless pizza that are as delicious as they are nutritious? How can you replace eggs and cheese in classic cream sauces and ricotta-style fillings? The answer to these and other timely questions are quite simple. It's all in the bean! The soybean is incredibly versatile as it lends itself to many forms and functions. As lite silken tofu, it is chameleon-like, able to replace eggs and dairy products artfully. When used in fillings and doughs, this low-fat ingredient becomes an invaluable ally to the health conscious cook. When soy is processed into textured vegetable protein, or TVP, it allows even the novice to create delicious meals in a timely fashion. Soymilk lite can be used anywhere cow's milk is called for, and becomes soy buttermilk with the addition of lemon juice or cider vinegar.

Create fabulous homemade pasta dishes like Pumpkin or Spinach Ravioli and Gnocci Primavera, all delectable gourmet feasts! Pizza is everyone's favorite and there's really no need to drown it in mountains of gelatinous cheese. Try my Saucy Pizza Abbondanza or Hawaiian Pizza for a delightful change of pace. You will be surprised at how easy it is to make a gourmet pizza that is dairy-free and delicious.

This collection of marvelous meals utilizes the versatility of the soybean as it offers a taste of Italy with an American accent. If it's homemade pastas or creamy sauces you are looking for without harmful fat and cholesterol, this is the place to find them. Tasty pizzas and hearty calzones that invite creativity are easy to assemble and sure to please. It's all here, and so wholesome and delicious, all because of the incredible soybean. ◆

Angel Hair in Sausage/Tomato Sauce

This nutritious and tasty recipe features Jerusalem
artichoke pasta in a hearty and flavorful tomato sauce.

◆ 6 SERVINGS ◆

1 1/2 tsp. olive oil

1/8 tsp. crushed red pepper

1/2 cup chopped onion

5 cloves garlic, minced

1/3 cup chopped red bell pepper

1 cup baby carrots, cut into thirds

14-oz. pkg. Gimme Lean,
 sausage style

28-oz. can peeled and diced tomatoes

28-oz. can crushed tomatoes

2 6-oz. cans tomato paste

6 oz. burgundy wine (fill tomato
 paste can)

6 oz. water (fill tomato paste can)

1 tsp. dried basil

16-oz. pkg. Jerusalem artichoke angel
 hair pasta

Heat olive oil and crushed pepper in a large saucepan over medium-high heat for
1 minute. Add the next 4 ingredients. Saute 5 minutes or until crisp tender. Add
vegetarian sausage. Cook 5 minutes, breaking apart with a large spoon, until sausage is
browned. Add tomatoes, tomato paste, wine, and water. Lower heat, and simmer 20
minutes. Add basil during the last 5 minutes of cooking. Cook pasta according to
package directions. Drain, and serve with sauce.

◆ *184* ◆

NUTRITION ANALYSIS
(PER SERVING)

Protein 20 gm., Carbohydrate 69 gm., Fiber 6 gm., Fat 2 gm.,
Cholesterol 0, Calcium 84 mg., Sodium 619 mg.

Calories 379
From protein: 22%; From carbohydrate: 74%; From fat: 4%

Broccoli Lasagna Rolls

The unique presentation and exceptional flavor of this entrée add flair to an elegant buffet.

◆ 1 0 S E R V I N G S ◆

3/4 lb. broccoli crowns, cut into
   20 florets
25-oz. jar fat-free tomato sauce
28-oz. can whole plum tomatoes
14.5-oz. can Italian-style
   stewed tomatoes
6-oz. can tomato paste
6 oz. burgundy wine (fill tomato
   paste can)
4 fresh basil leaves, snipped, or 1 tsp.
   dried basil
1/2 tsp. granulated garlic

2 bay leaves
8-oz. pkg. lasagna noodles
3 3/4 cups lite silken tofu (extra
   firm), drained
1/3 cup sliced scallions
4 large cloves garlic, minced
10-oz. pkg. frozen chopped broccoli,
   thawed and well drained
1/2 cup nutritional yeast
1 tsp. dried thyme
1 Tbsp. Bragg liquid aminos
dried basil for garnish

Preheat oven to 350.° Bring a quart of water to a boil, and blanch broccoli for 30 seconds. Immediately plunge broccoli into ice water to stop cooking process. Set aside. Stir together the next 3 ingredients in 5-quart saucepan over low heat. Add the tomato paste and wine; stir. Add basil, garlic, and bay leaves. Simmer until ready to assemble casserole. Cook lasagna noodles according to package directions. Drain noodles and rinse in cold water.

Place drained tofu in a large bowl, and mash with potato masher. Add all remaining ingredients except basil, one at a time, stirring after each addition. Drain and rinse noodles. Cover bottom of a 9" x 13" pan with prepared sauce. Remove the bay leaves. Spread about 1/2 cup of filling along the center of a each noodle, then roll the noodles up. Tuck a broccoli floret in both open ends of each roll, and place in the pan, 2 across and 5 down. The rolls should lay side by side with the florets facing outward. Top with sauce, and sprinkle with dried basil. Cover loosely with foil. Bake 30 minutes, then remove foil and bake another 15 minutes.

◆ *185* ◆

NUTRITION ANALYSIS
(PER SERVING)

Protein 17 gm., Carbohydrate 62 gm., Fiber 5 gm., Fat 2 gm.,
Cholesterol 0, Calcium 66 mg., Sodium 440 mg.

Calories 181
From protein: 20%; From carbohydrate: 75%; From fat: 5%

Chunky-Sauced Pasta

Serve this hearty sauce over interesting pasta shapes like wagon wheels or tri-colored twists. The rich flavor will cling to every bite.

◆ 6 SERVINGS ◆

1 1/2 tsp. olive oil

1/8 tsp. crushed red pepper

5 cloves garlic, minced

1 cup chopped onions

1/4 cup chopped green bell pepper

2 cups coarsely grated zucchini

1 1/2 cups white wine

28-oz. can plum tomatoes

6-oz. can tomato paste

25-oz. jar fat-free tomato sauce

1 cup ground beef-style TVP granules, dry

1 Tbsp. beef-flavored vegetable powder

1 small can (2 1/4 oz. dry wt.) sliced black olives, drained

8 large basil leaves

1 lb. pasta, any variety, cooked according to package directions

◆ *186* ◆ Heat crushed pepper in oil in a medium saucepan over medium heat for 2 minutes. Add the next 4 ingredients, and sauté 5 minutes. Add wine, and cook 3 minutes. Add the next 3 ingredients, and reduce heat to simmer. Cook for 10 minutes, stirring occasionally. Stir in the TVP and remaining ingredients except pasta. Continue to simmer for 20 minutes or until ready to serve over cooked pasta.

NUTRITION ANALYSIS
(PER SERVING)

Protein 16 gm., Carbohydrate 55 gm., Fiber 8 gm., Fat 3 gm.,
Cholesterol 0, Calcium 48 mg., Sodium 597 mg.

Calories 300
From protein: 20%; From carbohydrate: 70%; From fat: 9%

Creamed Pasta With Vegetables

This colorful dish features a spicy cream sauce, delicate leeks,
fresh spinach, and green beans complemented with your pasta of choice.

◆ 6 S E R V I N G S ◆

1 Tbsp. olive oil

1/4 tsp. crushed red pepper

1 leek, well rinsed, cut into 1/4-inch slices (see Techniques)

5 cloves garlic, minced

1 lb. green beans, cut into 1-inch pieces (2 cups)

1 cup white wine

1 1/4 cups lite silken tofu (firm), drained

1 1/2 cups soymilk lite

1 Tbsp. Bragg liquid aminos

2 Tbsp. mellow white miso

3 Tbsp. nutritional yeast

2 Tbsp. whole wheat flour

1/2 lb. pasta (penne, large elbows, etc.)

1 bunch fresh spinach, well rinsed

◆ *187* ◆

Heat olive oil and crushed pepper in a large saucepan over medium-high heat for 1 minute. Add leeks, garlic, and green beans. Sauté 5 minutes. Add wine, and reduce heat; simmer 10 minutes. Place tofu in food processor, and blend. Add soymilk and next 4 ingredients. Pulse to mix, then blend until smooth. Fold into green bean mixture; simmer. Cook pasta according to package directions. Three minutes before pasta is finished, add spinach to the cooking water. Drain pasta and spinach in a colander. Remove green bean/cream sauce mixture from heat, and fold in pasta/spinach mixture. Serve immediately.

NUTRITION ANALYSIS
(PER SERVING)

Protein 14 gm., Carbohydrate 82 gm., Fiber 6 gm., Fat 4 gm.,
Cholesterol 0, Calcium 124 mg., Sodium 311 mg.

Calories 239
From protein: 13%; From carbohydrate: 78%; From fat: 9%

Curried Ragu

*This sumptuous dish features spinach pasta, zucchini,
and garbanzo beans in a heavenly, curry-laced cream sauce.*

◆ 6 SERVINGS ◆

1 1/2 tsp. olive oil
1/2 cup chopped shallots
1 jalapeño pepper, with seeds,
  chopped (remove seeds
  to reduce heat)
5 cloves garlic, minced
1 medium zucchini,
  cut in julienne strips
15-oz. can low-sodium garbanzo
  beans, drained
28-oz. can tomatoes, peeled and diced
1 1/4 cups lite silken tofu (firm),
  drained
1/3 cup white wine

1/4 cup soymilk lite
2 Tbsp. lemon juice
1 tsp. ground coriander
1 tsp. ground cumin
1/2 tsp. turmeric
2 Tbsp. Bragg liquid aminos
1/4 tsp. cinnamon
1/2 tsp. granulated garlic
Cayenne pepper to taste
1 Tbsp. cornstarch
2 Tbsp. cold water
1 lb. spinach penne (or other
  spinach pasta)

Heat oil over medium-high heat in a 5-quart saucepan. Add the next 3 ingredients, and sauté 3 minutes. Add zucchini and garbanzo beans, and cook for 5 minutes. Add tomatoes. Cover and cook over low heat for 5 minutes. Place tofu in food processor; blend. Add wine, soymilk, and lemon juice; blend. Add the next 7 ingredients, and blend until smooth. Remove saucepan from heat. Use a wire whisk to blend in tofu mixture gradually. Return saucepan to heat, and simmer. Blend cornstarch and water in a small bowl. Add to sauce. Simmer sauce, stirring frequently, while cooking pasta.

NUTRITION ANALYSIS
(PER SERVING)

Protein 17 gm., Carbohydrate 151 gm., Fiber 6 gm., Fat 3 gm.,
Cholesterol 0, Calcium 36 mg., Sodium 560 mg.

Calories 260
From protein: 9%; From carbohydrate: 87%; From fat: 3%

Hawaiian Pizza

Vegetarian Canadian bacon and pineapple rings
set the stage for this gourmet pizza.

◆ 16-INCH PIZZA ◆

vegetable oil cooking spray
1 recipe Prolific Pizza Dough
(see page 195)

TOPPING:
25-oz. jar fat-free tomato sauce

6-oz. pkg. Yves veggie Canadian
bacon, sliced in half
20-oz. can pineapple rings, drained
8 large fresh basil leaves, snipped

Preheat oven to 425°. Lightly spray a 16" heavy gauge pizza pan with cooking spray. Roll prepared pizza dough into a large circle 1/2-inch larger than pan. Place dough on pan, patting into place and folding overlap into a lip around the edge. Spread with tomato sauce. Arrange Canadian bacon and pineapple rings in an attractive pattern. Garnish with snipped basil. Set aside for 20 minutes, then place in preheated oven. Bake 20 minutes, or until topping and the crust are lightly browned.

◆ *189* ◆

NUTRITION ANALYSIS
(PER 2-SLICE SERVING)

Protein 14 gm., Carbohydrate 51 gm., Fiber 5 gm., Fat 1 gm.,
Cholesterol 0, Calcium 19 mg., Sodium 621 mg.

Calories 262
From protein: 21%; From carbohydrate: 75%; From fat: 4%

Hearty Elbow Macaroni Casserole

This homey casserole is easy and delicious.

◆ 12 SERVINGS ◆

vegetable oil cooking spray

1 1/2 cups beef-flavored vegetable broth, boiling

2 cups TVP, ground beef style

16-oz. pkg. large elbow macaroni

2 Tbsp. olive oil

1/2 cup chopped onion

1/4 cup whole wheat flour

2 cups soymilk lite

2/3 cup nutritional yeast

1 tsp. dried marjoram

1 tsp. tamari

1 tsp. granulated garlic

14.5-oz. can Italian-style tomatoes, peeled and diced

Preheat oven to 350.° Spray a 9" x 13" baking pan with cooking spray. Add boiling broth to TVP in a medium bowl. Stir, and set aside. Cook macaroni according to package directions. Rinse in cold water. Set aside, and rinse again in cold water from time to time. Heat oil in a medium saucepan over medium-high heat. Add onion, and sauté 3 minutes or until crisp tender. Stir in flour, and cook mixture 2 minutes over medium heat. Add soymilk gradually, stirring constantly. Whisk in yeast, 1/3 cup at a time. Add marjoram, tamari, and granulated garlic, then lower heat. Simmer 5 minutes, stirring occasionally. Add tomatoes to reconstituted TVP. Mix well. Place half the macaroni and all the TVP mixture in the prepared pan. Mix together using a large spoon. Top with remaining macaroni, and stir just to mix. Pour "cheese" sauce over all, and cover loosely with foil. Bake 30 minutes. Serve hot.

NUTRITION ANALYSIS
(PER SERVING)

Protein 17 gm., Carbohydrate 35 gm., Fiber 4 gm., Fat 4 gm., Cholesterol 0, Calcium 18 mg., Sodium 117 mg.

Calories 230
From protein: 27%; From carbohydrate: 59%; From fat: 14%

Mostaccioli in Creamy Mushroom Sauce

This rich-tasting dish is flavorful and satisfying.

◆ 6 SERVINGS ◆

1 1/2 Tbsp. olive oil

1/8 tsp. crushed red pepper

4 cloves garlic

1 cup sweet onion (Maui, Texas,
  or Vidalia)

1 cup chopped carrots

1/2 lb. mushroom caps, quartered

1/4 cup whole wheat flour

1/4 cup mirin or dry sherry

2 cups beef-flavored vegetable broth,
  boiling

1 1/4 cups lite silken tofu (firm),
  drained

1 cup soymilk lite

1 Tbsp. tamari

1/4 cup nutritional yeast

1 lb. mostaccioli, cooked according to
  package directions

In a large stovetop-safe serving dish, heat oil and crushed pepper over medium-high heat for 1 minute. Add the next 3 ingredients, and sauté 3 minutes. Add mushrooms, and sauté 5 minutes. Add flour, and stir 1 minute. Add mirin, and stir 2 minutes. Add hot broth; stir to blend. Reduce heat and simmer 5 minutes, stirring frequently. Place tofu in food processor, and blend. Add soymilk, tamari, and yeast; blend until smooth. Add tofu mixture to pan ingredients, using a whisk to blend smoothly. Simmer mixture while preparing pasta. Remove pan from heat, and add drained pasta to sauce. Toss to blend.

◆ *191* ◆

NUTRITION ANALYSIS
(PER SERVING)

Protein 14 gm., Carbohydrate 40 gm., Fiber 3 gm., Fat 5 gm.,
Cholesterol 0, Calcium 25 mg., Sodium 257 mg.

Calories 258
From protein: 21%; From carbohydrate: 60%; From fat: 18%

Mushroom Broccoli Calzones

*These delicious turnovers are hearty and colorful
with a delightful sherry-laced filling.*

◆ 6 CALZONES ◆

1 recipe Prolific Pizza Dough
 (see page 195)
1 1/2 tsp. olive oil
1/4 tsp. crushed red pepper
1 cup sliced scallions
4 cloves garlic, minced
1/4 cup chopped green bell pepper
6 oz. cremini mushrooms, sliced

4 cups broccoli florets
1/4 cup very dry sherry
1 Tbsp. tamari
1 tsp. dried thyme
1 Tbsp. cornstarch
2 Tbsp. water
vegetable oil cooking spray
cornmeal

While pizza dough is rising, make filling.

Heat oil and crushed pepper in a medium saucepan for 2 minutes. Add scallions, garlic, and green pepper; sauté 3 minutes. Add mushrooms, and cook 3 minutes. Add broccoli, and cook 3 minutes. Add sherry, tamari, and thyme. Blend cornstarch and water in a small bowl; stir into mixture.

Preheat oven to 400°. Spray a baking pan with cooking spray. Dust lightly with cornmeal. Divide dough into 6 equal portions. Work with one portion at a time; keep remaining dough covered with a clean towel. Roll each portion into a ball between palms of hands. Pat dough gently, and roll into a circle. Place filling on one side of the circle, then fold dough over the filling. Press the crescent closed with a fork. Place on prepared baking pan and bake 15 to 20 minutes, until lightly browned.

NUTRITION ANALYSIS
(PER SERVING)

Protein 12 gm., Carbohydrate 59 gm., Fiber 8 gm., Fat 3 gm.,
Cholesterol 0, Calcium 68 mg., Sodium 500 mg.

Calories 306
From protein: 15%; From carbohydrate: 75%; From fat: 10%

Penne Cacciatore

This delicious TVP variation on chicken cacciatore reheats well.

◆ 6 SERVINGS ◆

1 1/2 cups chicken-flavored vegetable broth, boiling (separated)

2 1/2 cups TVP, chicken chunk style

1 1/2 tsp. olive oil

1/4 tsp. crushed red pepper

3/4 cup chopped onion

6 cloves garlic, minced

1/2 cup chopped green pepper

1 cup sliced carrots

1 cup zucchini, cut into julienne strips

1/3 cup white wine

28-oz. can tomatoes, peeled and diced

28-oz. can crushed Italian-style tomatoes

6-oz. can tomato paste

1 bay leaf

6 large fresh basil leaves, snipped

1 lb. penne pasta, cooked according to package directions

◆ *193* ◆

Pour 1 cup of the boiling broth over TVP in a medium bowl. Set aside. Heat oil and crushed pepper in a 5-quart saucepan over medium-high heat. Add the next 3 ingredients, and sauté 2 minutes. Add the carrots and zucchini; sauté 3 minutes, stirring frequently. Add reconstituted TVP. Sauté 5 minutes, stirring frequently. Add wine; cook and stir for 1 minute. Add tomatoes and tomato paste. Add reserved 1/2 cup of broth along with bay leaves and basil. Lower heat, and simmer 20 to 30 minutes, stirring occasionally. Remove bay leaf. Ladle half of the sauce over the well-drained pasta. Toss, then top with remaining sauce. Garnish with fresh whole basil leaves.

NUTRITION ANALYSIS
(PER SERVING)

Protein 25 gm., Carbohydrate 56 gm., Fiber 13 gm., Fat 3 gm., Cholesterol 0, Calcium 111 mg., Sodium 342 mg.

Calories 316
From protein: 29%; From carbohydrate: 66%; From fat: 6%

Saucy Pizza Abbondanza

Abbondanza means "abundant" or "bountiful" in Italian. I think you will agree that this delightful pizza with the generous topping qualifies.

◆ 16-INCH PIZZA ◆

vegetable oil cooking spray
1 recipe Prolific Pizza Dough
(see page 195)
1 cup beef-flavored vegetable
broth, boiling
1 1/4 cups TVP, ground beef style

3 large cloves garlic, minced
25-oz. jar fat-free tomato sauce
3 cups broccoli florets
3 scallions, thinly sliced
6 large fresh basil leaves, snipped

Preheat oven to 425°. Lightly spray a 16" round pizza pan with cooking spray. Add broth to TVP, and set aside. Punch down dough, and knead briefly. Roll out on a floured surface into a circle 1/2-inch larger than the pan. Place dough on pizza pan. Fold the overlap, pinching to form a lip around the edge of the pan. Lightly spray dough with cooking spray. Sprinkle with minced garlic. Top with tomato sauce, TVP, broccoli, scallions, and basil. Bake 20 minutes or until crust is golden brown (check the bottom).

NUTRITION ANALYSIS
(PER 2-SLICE SERVING)

Protein 17 gm., Carbohydrate 54 gm., Fiber 9 gm., Fat 2 gm.,
Cholesterol 0, Calcium 41 mg., Sodium 444 mg.

Calories 271
From protein: 23%; From carbohydrate: 72%; From fat: 5%

Prolific Pizza Dough

This pizza crust is crisp, yet tender. Making this soy boosted pizza dough is a snap when using the food processor, however if you prefer the conventional method, it works just as well. Try this crust with your favorite toppings or when making calzones (see page 192).

◆ 16-INCH PIZZA (8 SERVINGS) ◆

1 1/4 cups whole wheat flour
1 1/4 cups unbleached flour
1/3 cup soy flour
1 tsp. salt

2 1/2 tsp. yeast
1 cup warm water
1 Tbsp. liquid Fruitsource or honey
vegetable oil cooking spray

FOOD PROCESSOR METHOD

Place the first 5 ingredients in the food processor, and pulse to mix. Place the water and Fruitsource in a small measuring cup. Warm in the microwave or for 3 minutes on the stovetop. It should be warm to the touch, no more than 125° (a little warmer than your finger). Add water to the food processor. Process until the mixture forms a ball. Turn onto a floured surface, and knead about 5 minutes, adding just enough white flour to make the dough smooth and not sticky. At this point you may place the dough in a lightly oiled plastic bag and store it in the refrigerator for up to 2 days.

• 195 •

CONVENTIONAL METHOD

Set aside 1 cup of unbleached flour. Combine the remaining flours in a large bowl with salt and yeast. Combine water and Fruitsource, and heat to 125°. Add the liquid to the dry ingredients, and mix well, adding just enough of the reserved flour so the dough pulls away from the sides of the bowl. Turn dough out onto a floured board, and knead until smooth and elastic. Lightly spray a large bowl with cooking spray. Place the dough in the prepared bowl. Cover the bowl with a clean towel, and set it in a warm place to rest for an hour or so. Place the dough on a lightly floured surface, and knead lightly for about 2 minutes.

BOTH METHODS

Roll dough into a circle about an inch larger than the perimeter of the pan. Pat dough into the pan, and fold the overlap, pinching to form a lip around the edge of the pan. Proceed with your recipe.

NUTRITION ANALYSIS
(PER SERVING)

Protein 7 gm., Carbohydrate 37 gm., Fiber 4 gm., Fat 1 gm.,
Cholesterol 0, Calcium 18 mg., Sodium 271 mg.

Calories 180
From protein: 14%; From carbohydrate: 80%; From fat: 6%

Quick 'n Healthy Ravioli

*Frozen, prepared ravioli and an easy-to-prepare sauce save time
while adding the goodness of soy to your dinner.*

◆ 6 TO 8 SERVINGS ◆

1 1/2 tsp. olive oil

1/8 tsp. crushed red pepper

1/2 cup chopped onion

4 cloves garlic, minced

1/4 cup chopped red bell pepper

2 28-oz. cans Italian-style crushed
    tomatoes

6-oz. can tomato paste

6 oz. white wine (fill tomato
    paste can)

4 fresh basil leaves, snipped

1 bay leaf

2 13-oz. pkg. frozen Soy Boy ravioli,
    do not thaw

In a 4-quart saucepan, heat oil and crushed pepper over medium-high heat 1 minute. Add the next 3 ingredients, and sauté 3 minutes. Add tomatoes, tomato paste, wine, and herbs. Lower heat and simmer until ready to serve. Prepare ravioli according to package directions. Drain and top with sauce.

◆ *196* ◆

NUTRITION ANALYSIS
(PER SERVING)

Protein 12 gm., Carbohydrate 43 gm., Fiber 3 gm., Fat 4 gm.,
Cholesterol 0, Calcium 128 mg., Sodium 617 mg.

Calories 252
From protein: 19%; From carbohydrate: 66%; From fat 15%

Pumpkin Ravioli Filling

The pumpkin filling encased in colorful dough makes an attractive presentation.

◆ 8 SERVINGS ◆

1/2 cup + 2 Tbsp. lite silken tofu
(extra firm), drained
1 cup canned pumpkin

3 Tbsp. prune purée
1 Tbsp. liquid Fruitsource or honey
1/4 tsp. nutmeg

Prepare one recipe Tomato Basil Pasta (see page 202). Place tofu in the food processor; add pumpkin, and blend. Add remaining ingredients, and process until smooth. Roll out 2 large sheets of dough. Place rounded teaspoonfuls of filling at regular intervals on the first sheet of dough. Cover with the second sheet of dough. Use your thumbs to gently press down the spaces between the mounds of filling. Dip the rim of a 3-inch diameter glass into a small bowl of flour. Use the glass to cut circles around each ravioli. Press the edges of each circle with a fork to close. Roll dough scraps into remaining dough. Ravioli may be made up to a day ahead before cooking. Drop into gently boiling salted water, to which 1 tablespoon oil has been added. Boil 12 to 15 minutes, carefully stirring occasionally. Serve topped with tomato sauce.

◆*197*◆

NUTRITION ANALYSIS
(PER SERVING WITH SAUCE)

Protein 11 gm., Carbohydrate 53 gm., Fiber 6 gm., Fat 4 gm.,
Cholesterol 0, Calcium 34 mg., Sodium 427 mg.

Calories 273
From protein: 15%; From carbohydrate: 73%; From fat: 11%

Soysational Pasta Dough

*This versatile pasta dough is a natural
for fettuccine or for Spinach Ravioli Filling.*

◆ 1 POUND ◆

1 cup lite silken tofu (extra firm),
   drained
1 cup semolina
1/2 tsp. salt

1/2 cup soy flour
2 Tbsp. unbleached flour
1 Tbsp. olive oil

Place tofu in food processor, and blend until smooth. Add semolina and salt, and process. Repeat with soy flour and unbleached flour. Add oil, and process. The dough may seem a little sticky. Turn dough onto a board sprinkled with unbleached flour, and knead for about 3 minutes or until dough appears elastic. Add unbleached flour sparingly, if necessary. Sprinkle with unbleached flour, and place in a plastic bag or wrap with plastic wrap. Allow dough to rest for an hour or more. Divide dough into 4 equal portions. Work with one portion at a time; keep remaining portions in the bag.

Hand-cut pasta: On a floured board, roll the dough into an oblong shape, about 7" x 16". Dough should be thin, but not translucent. (For filled pasta, roll dough to 1/16th-inch thick.) Divide sheets crosswise, and set aside to dry on wax paper in a warm place for about 30 minutes, or until dry and pliable but not brittle.

Sprinkle dough lightly with flour, and roll dough loosely, jelly-roll style. Use a sharp knife to cut according to the type of pasta desired. Remember that pasta will swell about double when cooked, so make cuts about half the diameter desired. Allow the cut pasta to dry for at least an hour by tossing it into a loose pile or laying flat on wax paper. This will prevent the pasta from sticking after it has been cut, and keep it firm after cooking.

Pasta machine (manual): Divide dough into 4 equal portions. Place one portion on a lightly floured board and return remaining portions to plastic bag. Roll dough into oval sheet. Sprinkle with flour and feed into the widest roller setting. Fold dough into thirds, and feed it through again; repeat several times at this setting. Continue to feed dough (without folding) through machine, setting the rollers one notch closer each time, until the sheet is 16" x 20" inches. Divide sheets crosswise, and set aside to dry on wax paper in a warm place for about 30 minutes, or until dry and pliable but not brittle. Sprinkle dough lightly with flour, and cut to desired shape by feeding through wide, thin, or narrow blades. Allow the cut pasta to dry for at least an hour by tossing it into a loose pile or laying flat on wax paper. This will prevent the pasta from sticking after it has been cut, and keep it firm after cooking.

Cooking homemade pasta: Cook pasta in about 6 quarts of water with 1 tablespoon oil and 1 teaspoon salt. Drop pasta into boiling water and bring to a second boil. Cook 3 to 5 minutes, stirring frequently. Drain and top with sauce.

NUTRITION ANALYSIS
(PER SERVING)

Protein 9 gm., Carbohydrate 25 gm., Fiber 2 gm., Fat 4 gm.,
Cholesterol 0, Calcium 21 mg., Sodium 215 mg.

Calories 176
From protein: 21%; From carbohydrate: 56%; From fat: 23%

Whole Wheat Pasta

This easy to make pasta is delicious topped with your favorite sauce.

◆ 1 POUND ◆

1 cup lite silken tofu (extra firm)
1 cup semolina
1/2 tsp. salt

1/2 cup whole wheat flour
1 Tbsp. olive oil

Place tofu in food processor and blend until smooth. Add semolina and salt, and process. Add whole wheat flour, and process again. Add oil while processing. Turn dough onto board sprinkled with semolina flour. Knead for about 3 minutes or until dough appears elastic. Sprinkle with semolina flour and place in zip lock bag or wrap with plastic wrap. Allow dough to rest for an hour or more.

Hand-cut pasta: Divide dough into 4 equal portions. Place one portion on a lightly floured board, and return remaining portions to plastic bag. Flatten the dough into an oval shape and roll the dough into an oblong sheet, about 7" x 16". Dough should be thin, but not translucent. (For filled pasta, roll dough to 1/16th-inch thick.) Divide sheets crosswise and set aside to dry on wax paper in a warm place for about 30 minutes, or until it is dry and pliable, but not brittle.

Sprinkle dough lightly with flour and roll up loosely, jelly-roll style. Use a sharp knife to cut according to the type of pasta desired. Remember that pasta will swell about double when cooked, so make cuts about half the diameter desired. Allow the cut pasta to dry by tossing into a loose pile or laying flat on wax paper in the open air for at least an hour. This will prevent the pasta from sticking after it has been cut, and keep it firm after cooking.

Pasta machine (manual): Divide dough into 4 equal portions. Place one portion on a lightly floured board, and return remaining portions to plastic bag. Flatten dough into an oval shape, sprinkle with flour, and feed it through the widest roller setting. Fold dough into thirds and feed it through again. Fold and roll dough several times at this setting. Continue to feed dough (without folding), setting rollers one notch closer together each time, until you have a sheet between 16 and 20 inches long. Cut dough crosswise and set sheets aside to dry, 30 minutes, on wax paper in a warm place. Lightly flour dough and cut to desired shape by feeding through wide, thin, or narrow blades. Allow the cut pasta to dry by tossing into a loose pile or laying flat on wax paper in the

◆ *200* ◆

open air for at least an hour. This will prevent the pasta from sticking after it has been cut, and keep it firm after cooking.

Cooking homemade pasta: Cook pasta in about 6 quarts. of boiling water with 1 tablespoon oil and 1 teaspoon salt. Drop pasta into boiling water and bring to a second boil. Cook 3 to 5 minutes, stirring frequently. Drain and top with sauce.

NUTRITION ANALYSIS
(PER SERVING)

Protein 8 gm., Carbohydrate 28 gm., Fiber 2 gm., Fat 3 gm.,
Cholesterol 0, Calcium 9 mg., Sodium 214 mg.

Calories 170
From protein: 18%; From carbohydrate: 66%; From fat: 17%

Tomato Basil Pasta

This colorful pasta is delightful cut into any shape.

◆ 4 SERVINGS ◆

1/2 cup lite silken tofu, extra firm, drained

6 Tbsp. tomato paste

1 cup semolina flour

1/2 cup whole wheat flour

1 1/2 tsp. dried basil

1/2 tsp. granulated garlic

1/2 tsp. salt

1 Tbsp. olive oil

25 oz.-jar fat-free tomato sauce

Place tofu in food processor and process with tomato paste. Add the next 5 ingredients and process. Add the oil and blend until dough sticks together. Turn dough onto board sprinkled with semolina. Knead until smooth, about 3 minutes. Place the dough in a zip lock plastic bag and set aside to rest for an hour.

Hand-cut pasta: Divide dough into 4 equal portions. Place one portion on a lightly floured board, and return remaining portions to plastic bag. Flatten the dough into an oval shape and roll the dough into an oblong sheet, about 7" x 16". Dough should be thin, but not translucent. Divide sheets crosswise and set aside to dry on wax paper in a warm place for about 30 minutes, or until it is dry and pliable, but not brittle. For filled pasta, roll dough on floured board to about 1/16-inch thick. (see Pumpkin Ravioli Filling).

Sprinkle dough lightly with flour and roll up loosely, jelly-roll style. Use a sharp knife to cut according to the type of pasta desired. Remember that pasta will swell about double when cooked, so make cuts about half the diameter desired. Allow the cut pasta to dry by tossing into a loose pile or laying flat on wax paper in the open air for at least an hour. This will prevent the pasta from sticking after it has been cut, and keep it firm after cooking.

Pasta machine (manual): Divide dough into 4 equal portions. Place one portion on a lightly floured board, and return remaining portions to plastic bag. Flatten dough into an oval shape, sprinkle with flour, and feed it through the widest roller setting. Fold dough into thirds and feed it through again. Fold and roll dough through several times at this setting. Continue to feed dough (without folding), setting rollers one notch closer together each time, until you have a sheet between 16 and 20 inches long. Cut dough crosswise and set sheets aside to dry about 30 minutes on wax paper in a warm place. Lightly flour dough and cut to desired shape by feeding through wide, thin, or narrow blades. Allow the cut pasta to dry by tossing into a loose pile or laying flat on wax paper in the open air for at least an hour or overnight. This will prevent the pasta from sticking after it has been cut, and keep it firm after cooking.

Cooking homemade pasta: Cook pasta in about 6 quarts of boiling water with 1 tablespoon oil and 1 teaspoon salt. Drop pasta into boiling water and bring to a second boil. Cook 3 to 5 minutes, stirring frequently. Drain and top with sauce.

NUTRITION ANALYSIS
(PER SERVING)

Protein 13 gm., Carbohydrate 64 gm., Fiber 7 gm., Fat 4 gm.,
Cholesterol 0, Calcium 34 mg., Sodium 593 mg.

Calories 335
From protein: 15%; From carbohydrate: 73%; From fat: 12%

Spinach Ravioli Filling

This variation on a spinach-cheese filling is delicious and nutritious.

◆ 6   S E R V I N G S ◆

10-oz. pkg. frozen spinach, thawed
1 1/4 cups lite silken tofu (firm),
  drained and patted dry
1/4 cup nutritional yeast
1/2 tsp. granulated garlic

1 rounded Tbsp. mellow white miso
3 scallions, minced
8 large fresh basil leaves, snipped
1/4 tsp. nutmeg

Prepare one recipe Soysational Pasta Dough (see page 198), rolling 2 large sheets of dough slightly thicker than for cut pasta. Place spinach in a fine mesh colander, and press out as much liquid as possible using paper toweling. Mash tofu with a potato masher in a large bowl. Stir in yeast, garlic, and miso. Add spinach, and mix well. Add remaining ingredients, and mix thoroughly.

Place rounded teaspoonfuls of filling at regular intervals on the first sheet of dough. Cover with the second sheet of dough. Use your thumbs to gently press down the spaces between the mounds of filling. Dip the rim of a 3-inch diameter glass into a small bowl of flour. Use the glass to cut circles around each ravioli. Press the edges of each circle with a fork to close. Roll dough scraps into remaining dough. Ravioli may be made up to a day ahead before cooking.

Drop ravioli into gently boiling salted water, to which 1 tablespoon oil has been added. Boil 12 to 15 minutes, stirring occasionally. Serve topped with tomato sauce.

NUTRITION ANALYSIS
(PER 2-OUNCE SERVING OF FILLING ONLY)

Protein 7 gm., Carbohydrate 5 gm., Fiber 1 gm., Fat 1 gm.,
Cholesterol 0, Calcium 45 mg., Sodium 85 mg.

Calories 50
From protein: 49%; From carbohydrate: 38%; From fat: 13%

Tasty Tempeh Calzones

Wrap a crisp textured pizza dough around a tasty tempeh filling and you have a deliciously hearty meal.

◆ 6 CALZONES ◆

1 recipe Prolific Pizza Dough
  (see page 196)
1 1/2 tsp. olive oil
1/4 tsp. crushed red pepper
1 cup chopped onion
6 cloves garlic, minced
1 cup thinly sliced carrots
1/2 recipe Seasoned Tempeh,
  crumbled (see page 148)

1 Tbsp. tamari
14.5-oz. can Cajun-style tomatoes
1/2 cup white wine
1/2 tsp. granulated garlic
1 tsp. dried marjoram
1 tsp. dried basil
1/2 tsp. dried thyme
vegetable oil cooking spray
cornmeal

While pizza dough is rising, make filling:

Heat olive oil and crushed pepper for 2 minutes in a medium saucepan over medium-high heat. Add onions, garlic, and carrots; sauté 5 minutes. Add tempeh, and cook 10 minutes, stirring frequently. Stir in tamari, tomatoes, and wine. Lower heat, and simmer 5 minutes. Add garlic, marjoram, basil, and thyme, and simmer until ready to fill calzones.

Preheat oven to 400°. Spray a baking pan with cooking spray, then dust it lightly with cornmeal. Divide dough into 6 equal portions. Work with one portion at a time; keep remaining dough covered with a clean towel. Roll each portion into a ball between palms of hands. Pat dough gently, and roll into a circle. Place filling on one side of the circle, then fold dough over the filling. Press the crescent closed with a fork. Place on prepared baking pan and bake 15 to 20 minutes, until lightly browned.

◆ *205* ◆

NUTRITION ANALYSIS
(PER CALZONE)

Protein 19 gm., Carbohydrate 55 gm., Fiber 7 gm., Fat 5 gm.,
Cholesterol 0, Calcium 70 mg., Sodium 632 mg.

Calories 344
From protein: 22%; From carbohydrate: 64%; From fat: 14%

Tempeh-Topped Pizza

*This delightful pizza features a savory topping
garnished with bell pepper strips and fresh basil.*

◆ 16-INCH PIZZA ◆

1 recipe Prolific Pizza Dough
(see page 195)
1 Tbsp. olive oil
1/2 cup chopped onion
3 cloves garlic, minced
1 bay leaf
1/2 recipe Seasoned Tempeh,
crumbled (see page 148)

1 Tbsp. tamari
vegetable oil cooking spray
25-oz. jar fat-free tomato sauce
1/2 large bell pepper, cut into strips
1/4 cup snipped fresh basil leaves
1 Tbsp. dried basil

In a 10" frying pan, heat oil over medium heat. Add the onions, garlic, and bay leaf;
sauté 3 minutes. Add the tempeh, and sauté mixture 8 minutes, stirring frequently. Add
the tamari; lower heat to simmer 5 minutes. Remove bay leaf before assembling pizza.

Preheat oven to 425°. Spray a 16" pizza pan with cooking spray. Roll out prepared
pizza dough to about 1/2 inch larger than pizza pan. Pat it into place on the pizza pan.
Fold the overlap, pinching to form a lip around the edge of the pan. Spread with tomato
sauce. Top the sauce with the tempeh mixture, and garnish with the pepper strips,
arranging them in a pinwheel fashion. Top with fresh basil and dried basil. Set aside for
20 minutes. Bake for 20 minutes or until topping and the crust are lightly browned.

NUTRITION ANALYSIS
(PER 2-SLICE SERVING)

Protein 14 gm., Carbohydrate 44 gm., Fiber 5 gm., Fat 5 gm.,
Cholesterol 0, Calcium 26 mg., Sodium 600 mg.

Calories 264
From protein: 21%; From carbohydrate: 64%; From fat: 15%

Vegetarian Italian Sausage With Ziti

Delectable chunks of savory Italian sausage made with versatile
soy make this traditional favorite into a healthful meal.

◆ 8 SERVINGS ◆

vegetable oil cooking spray

1 Tbsp. olive oil

1/4 tsp. crushed red pepper

1 small onion, chopped, about 1 cup

1/2 cup chopped green bell pepper

6 cloves garlic, minced

11.2-oz. pkg. Lean Links Italian, cut in 1/2-inch pieces (see Soyfoods Pantry)

2 28-oz. cans crushed tomatoes, Italian-style

28-oz. can diced tomatoes in juice

6-oz. can tomato paste

6 oz. water (fill tomato paste can)

1/4 cup burgundy wine

1 bay leaf

4 large basil leaves, snipped

1/2 tsp. dried basil

1/4 tsp. dried thyme

1 lb. ziti or your favorite pasta, cooked according to package directions

◆*207*◆

Spray a 5-quart saucepan with cooking spray, and add oil and crushed red pepper. Sauté over medium high heat, 2 minutes. Add the next 3 ingredients and sauté for 2 minutes. Add sliced sausage and sauté 10 minutes, stirring frequently. Add the next 7 ingredients, stirring well after each addition. Lower heat to simmer and cook sauce, covered, 25 minutes, stirring frequently. Add basil, thyme, and pasta, and simmer 10 minutes or until ready to serve.

NUTRITION ANALYSIS
(PER SERVING)

Protein 12 gm., Carbohydrate 41 gm., Fiber 5 gm., Fat 5 gm.,
Cholesterol 0, Calcium 104 mg., Sodium 660 mg.

Calories 251
From protein: 18%; From carbohydrate: 64%; From fat: 18%

Delectable Desserts

You can create luscious, low-fat desserts without eggs, cream, butter, or added fat. Serving delectable desserts made with wholesome soyfoods is a delicious way to incorporate their nutritional advantages into your diet. Here you will find rich-tasting, gourmet desserts that look decadent, but are low in fat and completely cholesterol- and dairy-free. Scrumptious cakes, pies, cookies, and frozen confections are guaranteed to tempt dessert lovers of all ages. These seductive sweets are easy to make using these innovative techniques and versatile ingredients.

Creamy pies and puddings are created with soymilk lite and the ever-versatile lite silken tofu. Elegant mousses and rich tasting ice creams are made both egg- and dairy-free by tapping the tremendous potential of the simple soybean. Make Marie's Incredible Chocolate Brownies or the innovative Pumpkin Fudge Brownies, and the rich taste and fabulous texture of these heavenly chocolate treats will knock your socks off. My Apricot Almond Delite is a marvelous snacking cake topped with a delicate, brandy scented "cream" that makes a perfect luncheon dessert.

This chapter will show you how to create decadent desserts with grace and style, to reduce fat considerably, eliminate cholesterol, and maximize nutrition without sacrificing flavor or texture. These memorable desserts will dazzle family and friends. Impress them you will, and the added nutritional benefit will inspire you to serve these desserts often. You don't have to abandon extravagant desserts when eating more healthfully; it's easy when you know how. ◆

Apple Almond Spice Cake

This cake makes an impression at any gathering!

◆ 16 SERVINGS ◆

vegetable oil cooking spray

1 medium Pippin or Granny Smith apple, peeled, and cut into 1/4-inch chunks

2 Tbsp. lemon juice

2 1/2 cups whole wheat pastry flour

1/3 cup soy flour

1 1/2 cups Sucanat or brown sugar

1 tsp. baking powder

1 tsp. baking soda

1/4 tsp. salt

1 tsp. cinnamon

1/2 tsp. ground ginger

1/8 tsp. ground nutmeg

1/8 tsp. ground cloves

1 1/4 cups lite silken tofu (firm), drained

1/2 cup prune purée

1/4 cup liquid Fruitsource or honey

1/2 cup soymilk lite

1 Tbsp. egg replacer powder

1/4 cup water

1/2 tsp. almond extract

1/2 tsp. vanilla extract

1/3 cup chopped almonds

1/4 cup soy grits

Preheat oven to 350°. Spray a tube pan with cooking spray. Place apple chunks in a medium bowl, and toss with lemon juice; set aside. Mix together the next 10 ingredients in a large bowl; set aside. Place tofu in food processor, and blend. Add prune purée, Fruitsource, and soymilk; pulse to mix, then blend. Whisk egg replacer powder with water in a small bowl until foamy. Add to tofu mixture along with extracts, and blend until smooth. Mix together almonds with soy grits in a small bowl; set aside. Quickly fold the tofu mixture into the dry ingredients. Fold in apple chunks and almond mixture, and pour into prepared pan. Bake 45 minutes or until tester comes out clean. Cool 20 minutes in pan, then remove to rack. Serve dusted with powdered sugar.

NUTRITION ANALYSIS
(PER SERVING)

Protein 6 gm., Carbohydrate 39 gm., Fiber 3 gm., Fat 3 gm., Cholesterol 0, Calcium 57 mg., Sodium 197 mg.

Calories: 196
From protein: 12%; From carbohydrate: 76%; From fat: 12%

Apple Crunch Cake

*Pippin apple slices and a crunchy pecan topping make
a beautiful presentation in this delicious coffee cake.*

◆ 1 2   S E R V I N G S ◆

vegetable oil cooking spray
1 cup soymilk lite
2 Tbsp. lemon juice
2 cups whole wheat pastry flour
1/3 cup yellow cornmeal
1/4 cup soy flour
1 tsp. baking powder
1 tsp. baking soda
2/3 cup Sucanat or brown sugar
1/4 tsp. salt
1/2 cup unsweetened applesauce
1 Tbsp. liquid Fruitsource or honey

1 Tbsp. egg replacer powder
1/4 cup water
1 tsp. vanilla extract
1 medium Pippin apple, peeled and
   thinly sliced
TOPPING:
1/3 cup pecans
1/3 cup Sucanat or brown sugar
2 Tbsp. soy grits
1/2 tsp. cinnamon
1/4 tsp. ground nutmeg
2 Tbsp. frozen apple juice concentrate (do not thaw)

◆ *211* ◆

Preheat oven to 350.° Spray an 8" or 9" square baking pan with cooking spray.
Place soymilk in a small bowl, and add lemon juice. Set aside. Mix together the next 7
ingredients in a medium bowl. Set aside. Place applesauce in a large bowl with
Fruitsource; mix well. Whisk egg replacer powder with water in a small bowl until
foamy. Add soymilk and vanilla; mix thoroughly. Fold dry ingredients into liquid ingredients just until mixed. Pour batter into prepared pan. Arrange apples in an overlapping
pattern. Mix topping ingredients together in a small bowl. Sprinkle over apples. Bake 25
to 30 minutes or until toothpick inserted in center comes out clean.

NUTRITION ANALYSIS
(PER SERVING)

Protein 5 gm., Carbohydrate 38 gm., Fiber 3 gm., Fat 4 gm.,
Cholesterol 0, Calcium 58 mg., Sodium 221 mg.

Calories 195
From protein: 10%; From carbohydrate: 75%; From fat: 16%

Apricot Almond Delite

Served with rich-tasting tofu cream, this luscious cake delivers
delicious chunks of brandied apricots and slivered almonds in every bite.

◆ 8 SERVINGS ◆

vegetable oil cooking spray

1/2 cup snipped apricots

1/4 cup apricot brandy

1 1/4 cups whole wheat pastry flour

1 cup Sucanat or brown sugar

1/2 tsp. baking soda

1/2 tsp. baking powder

1/2 tsp. cinnamon

1/8 tsp. salt

1/2 cup plus 2 Tbsp. lite silken tofu (firm)

1/4 cup prune purée

1/2 cup soymilk lite

1/2 tsp. almond extract

1/4 cup almond pieces

Preheat oven to 350.° Spray an 8" square pan with cooking spray. Place apricots in a small saucepan with the brandy. Cook over low heat until brandy is absorbed, about 3 minutes, stirring frequently. Set aside. In a large bowl, stir together flour with the next 5 dry ingredients. Set aside. Place tofu in the food processor, and blend. Add prune purée, and blend. Add soymilk and almond extract, and blend until smooth. Add the tofu mixture to the dry ingredients. Fold in apricots and almonds. Pour batter into prepared pan. Bake 25 minutes or until toothpick inserted into center comes out clean. Serve with Tofu Cream (next page).

◆ *212* ◆

NUTRITION ANALYSIS
(PER SERVING, INCLUDING TOFU TOPPING)

Protein 4 gm., Carbohydrate 36 gm., Fiber 2 gm., Fat 2 gm.,
Cholesterol 0, Calcium 47 mg., Sodium 153 mg.

Calories 185
From protein: 10%; From carbohydrate: 80%; From fat: 10%

Tofu Cream

Serve this topping with Apricot Almond Delite
or use to stuff dates or Calimyrna figs.

◆ A B O U T   1   1 / 2   C U P S ◆

1/2 cup plus 2 Tbsp. lite silken tofu
(firm), drained

3 Tbsp. maple syrup

1/4 cup orange juice

1 tsp. grated lemon zest

1 tsp. vanilla extract

1/4 cup fruit-sweetened apricot jam

1 tsp. apricot brandy

Place drained tofu in food processor; blend. Add remaining ingredients and blend until smooth.

NUTRITION ANALYSIS
(PER 3 TBSP. OF TOPPING)

Protein 1 gm., Carbohydrate 10 gm., Fiber 0,
Fat 0, Cholesterol 0, Calcium 7 mg., Sodium 20 mg.

Calories 48
From protein: 12%; From carbohydrate: 83%; From fat: 5%

◆ *213* ◆

Apricot Snack Bars

These delicious snack bars make great lunch box stuffers.

◆ 25 SNACK BARS ◆

vegetable oil cooking spray

1 cup soymilk lite

2 Tbsp. lemon juice

3/4 cup snipped dried apricots

1/2 cup golden raisins

1/3 cup apricot brandy

2 1/2 cups whole wheat pastry flour

1/3 cup soy flour

1 tsp. baking soda

1 tsp. baking powder

1/4 tsp. salt

1 tsp. cinnamon

1/2 cup unsweetened applesauce

2/3 cup Florida Crystals or sugar

1 Tbsp. egg replacer powder

1/4 cup water

1 tsp. vanilla extract

1/4 cup walnut pieces

1/4 cup soy grits

cinnamon

nutmeg

◆ *214* ◆

Preheat oven to 350°. Spray a 9" x 13" baking pan with cooking spray. Place soymilk in a small glass measuring cup; add lemon juice. Set aside. Place apricots and raisins in a small saucepan with brandy. Cover and simmer, stirring frequently, 5 minutes or until liquid is absorbed. Set aside.

In a medium bowl, stir together the next 6 ingredients. Set aside. Place the applesauce in a large bowl, and cream with the Florida Crystals. Whisk the egg replacer powder and water in a small bowl until foamy. Add to the applesauce mixture along with the vanilla; blend well. Fold the applesauce mixture into the dry ingredients alternately with the soymilk. Mix just until blended. Add the brandied fruit. Mix the walnut pieces and soy grits together. Add to batter. Do not overmix. Spread batter in prepared pan. Sprinkle generously with cinnamon and nutmeg. Bake 30 minutes or until toothpick inserted in center comes out clean.

NUTRITION ANALYSIS
(PER SNACK BAR)

Protein 4 gm., Carbohydrate 20 gm., Fiber 2 gm., Fat 1 gm.,
Cholesterol 0, Calcium 26 mg., Sodium 94 mg.

Calories 106
From protein: 13%; From carbohydrate: 75%; From fat: 11%

Black Forest Cake

Dried cherries and walnut pieces fill this rich chocolate cake
topped with a fudge glaze—outstanding!

◆ 1 2 S E R V I N G S ◆

vegetable oil cooking spray

2 cups whole wheat pastry flour

1 cup cocoa powder

1 tsp. baking soda

1 tsp. baking powder

1/2 tsp. salt

1 3/4 cups Florida Crystals or sugar

8-oz. pkg. dried cherries (about 1 3/4 cups)

1/3 cup walnut pieces

1 1/4 cups lite silken tofu (extra firm), drained

3/4 cup prune purée

1 cup strong coffee

2 tsp. vanilla extract

Preheat oven to 350.° Spray a Bundt pan with cooking spray. In a large bowl, mix together flour with the following 5 ingredients. Add cherries and walnut pieces, and set aside. Blend tofu in food processor until smooth. Add prune purée, and blend. Add coffee and vanilla, and blend. Fold tofu mixture into the dry ingredients. Turn into prepared pan, and bake for 40 minutes or until a toothpick inserted comes out clean. Cool 15 minutes in the pan, then invert onto a rack.

◆ *215* ◆

G L A Z E

3 Tbsp. tapioca flour (or arrowroot)

1/4 cup cocoa powder

2 Tbsp. Florida Crystals or sugar

3/4 cup liquid Fruitsource or rice syrup

In a small bowl, stir together the first 3 ingredients. Heat Fruitsource in microwave 1 minute. Whisk into cocoa mixture until smooth. Drizzle onto cooled cake.

NUTRITION ANALYSIS
(PER SERVING)

Protein 8 gm., Carbohydrate 72 gm., Fiber 7 gm., Fat 4 gm.,
Cholesterol 0, Calcium 58 mg., Sodium 268 mg.

Calories 324
From protein: 9%; From carbohydrate: 81%; From fat: 10%

Cake Newton

This cake features a fig filling made with luscious Calimyrna figs.

◆ 20 "NEWTONS" ◆

vegetable oil cooking spray
2 cups whole wheat pastry flour
3/4 cup yellow corn meal
1/3 cup soy grits
1 tsp. baking powder
1 tsp. baking soda
1/2 tsp. salt
1/2 cup prune purée
1 cup Florida Crystals or sugar
1 Tbsp. egg replacer powder

1/4 cup water
1 tsp. vanilla extract
1 cup soymilk lite
FILLING:
8-oz. pkg. Calimyrna figs
1/4 cup frozen apple juice
  concentrate
1 cup golden raisins
1/2 cup date pieces
1/4 cup prune purée

Preheat oven to 350°. Spray a 9" square baking pan with cooking spray. Mix flour and the following 5 ingredients in a medium bowl. Set aside. Place prune purée in a large bowl, and cream with Florida Crystals. Whisk egg replacer powder with water in a small bowl until foamy. Whisk into the prune mixture along with the vanilla and soymilk. Fold the dry ingredients into the liquid ingredients just until mixed.

Stem figs and slice into thirds. Place sliced figs and remaining filling ingredients in a food processor; process until mixed (filling will be thick). Spoon half of the batter into the pan. Place filling over batter by pressing handfuls together, then gently placing over batter. Filling needn't form a solid covering. Top with remaining batter. Bake 45 to 50 minutes or until tester comes out clean.

◆ *216* ◆

NUTRITION ANALYSIS
(PER 3-OUNCE SLICE)

Protein 4 gm., Carbohydrate 43 gm., Fiber 4 gm., Fat 1 gm.,
Cholesterol 0, Calcium 28 mg., Sodium 153 mg.

Calories 187
From protein: 8%; From carbohydrate: 88%; From fat: 4%

Cherry Truffles

*You can make these chewy fudge truffles in advance
for a dinner party or just to have a very special treat on hand.*

◆ ONE DOZEN TRUFFLES ◆

1 cup dried cherries

1/2 cup date pieces

1/2 cup golden raisins

1/4 cup apricot brandy

1 1/4 cups lite silken tofu (extra firm), drained

1/3 cup prune purée

1/2 cup Liquid Fruitsource or honey or rice syrup

1/3 cup cocoa powder

3 Tbsp. agar flakes

1/2 cup white grape juice concentrate, thawed

1/2 cup whole dry roasted almonds (unsalted)

3/4 cups Sunspire organic dark chocolate chips

TOPPING:

1/4 cup cocoa powder

3 Tbsp. tapioca powder or arrowroot

2 Tbsp. Florida Crystals or sugar

1/2 cup liquid Fruitsource or honey

1 tsp. vanilla extract

◆ *217* ◆

Place the first three ingredients in a small saucepan with the brandy. Heat over medium-low heat until the brandy is absorbed. Set aside. Place tofu in food processor, and blend until smooth. Add prune purée, and blend. Place Fruitsource in a small glass measuring cup, and heat 1 minute in the microwave. Whisk in cocoa, and blend to make a smooth syrup. Add to food processor; blend. Whisk agar flakes into juice concentrate. Add to the tofu mixture; blend. Fold tofu mixture into brandied fruit, and mix thoroughly. Add almonds. Fold in chocolate chips. Spoon into 2-inch paper cups, and place in miniature muffin tins or square pans. In a small bowl, mix together cocoa powder, tapioca powder, and Florida Crystals. Place the Fruitsource in a small glass measuring cup; microwave 30 seconds. Whisk into dry ingredients; add vanilla. Spoon topping over truffles and place the truffles in the freezer, uncovered, for at least 2 hours.

NUTRITION ANALYSIS
(PER 2-TRUFFLE SERVING)

Protein 3 gm., Carbohydrate 28 gm., Fiber 2 gm., Fat 4 gm.,
Cholesterol 0, Calcium 24 mg., Sodium 216 mg.

Calories 155
From protein: 7%; From carbohydrate: 69%; From fat: 24%

Chocolate Almond Fruitcake

A thick fudge glaze accents this festive chocolate cake. Rich with crunchy almonds and brandied fruit, this luscious cake is a welcome finale.

◆ 24 SERVINGS ◆

vegetable oil cooking spray
2 Tbsp. lemon juice
1 1/4 cups soymilk lite
1 cup snipped apricots
1/2 cup golden raisins
1/2 cup apricot brandy
2 1/2 cups whole wheat pastry flour
1/2 cup soy grits
1/4 tsp. salt
1 tsp. cinnamon

1/2 cup unbleached flour
1 cup Wonderslim cocoa
1 1/4 cups lite silken tofu (extra firm), drained
2/3 cup prune purée
1 Tbsp. egg replacer powder
1/4 cup water
1 tsp. vanilla extract
1/2 tsp. almond extract
1/2 cup almond pieces

◆ 218 ◆

Preheat oven to 350°. Spray a 9" x 13" baking pan with cooking spray. In a small bowl, add lemon juice to soymilk, and set aside. Combine apricots, raisins, and brandy in a small saucepan. Simmer fruit 3 to 5 minutes, stirring often, until liquid is absorbed; set aside. Mix the next 6 ingredients in a medium bowl; set aside. Place tofu in a food processor and blend. Add prune purée and blend until smooth. In a small bowl, whisk egg replacer with water; add to tofu mixture along with vanilla, soymilk, and almond extract. Fold tofu mixture into dry ingredients. Fold in fruit and almond pieces, just until mixed. Pour into prepared pan. Bake 40 minutes or until toothpick inserted in center comes out clean. Cool completely in pan, and top with Cinnamon Almond Fudge Glaze (recipe and nutrition analysis follow).

Cinnamon Almond Fudge Glaze

Serve this topping with Chocolate Almond Fruitcake.

3 Tbsp. tapioca flour or arrowroot

1/3 cup Wonderslim cocoa

1/2 cup liquid Fruitsource or honey

1 tsp. cinnamon

1 tsp. vanilla extract

1/2 tsp. almond extract

In a small bowl, stir together tapioca flour and cocoa; set aside. Heat Fruitsource 40 seconds in microwave or simmer in saucepan 2 minutes. Whisk hot Fruitsource into cocoa mixture until smooth; whisk in remaining ingredients. Drizzle onto cooled cake.

NUTRITION ANALYSIS
(PER SERVING OF CAKE WITH GLAZE TOPPING)

Protein 6 gm., Carbohydrate 33 gm., Fiber 4 gm., Fat 3 gm.,
Cholesterol 0, Calcium 22 mg., Sodium 50 mg.

Calories 189
From protein: 14%; From carbohydrate: 72%; From fat: 14%

Chocolate Chip Cranberry Bliss

*Dust this luscious cake with powdered sugar
or drizzle with Fudgy Chocolate Glaze (page 228).*

◆ 16 SERVINGS ◆

vegetable oil cooking spray
1 cup soymilk lite
2 Tbsp. lemon juice
3 cups whole wheat pastry flour
1/4 cup yellow cornmeal
1 tsp. baking soda
1 tsp. baking powder
1/4 tsp. salt
1 tsp. cinnamon
1/2 cup Sunspire organic dark
   chocolate chips
1/2 cup dried cranberries

1 1/4 cups lite silken tofu (extra
   firm), drained
1/4 cup unsweetened applesauce
1/4 cup liquid Fruitsource or honey
1 Tbsp. egg replacer powder
1/4 cup water
1 1/2 cups Florida Crystals or sugar
1 tsp. vanilla extract
1/2 tsp. almond extract
1/3 cup almond pieces
1/4 cup soy grits

◆ *220* ◆

Preheat oven to 350°. Spray a tube pan with cooking spray. Place soymilk in a small glass measuring cup; add lemon juice. Set aside. Mix together the next 8 ingredients in a large bowl. Set aside. Place tofu in food processor; blend until smooth. Add applesauce and Fruitsource; pulse to mix, then blend. Whisk egg replacer powder with water in a small bowl until foamy. Add to tofu mixture; blend. Add Florida Crystals and extracts, and blend. Fold the liquid ingredients into the dry just until mixed. Mix almond pieces and soy grits in a small bowl. Fold into batter. Do not overbeat. Pour batter into prepared pan. Bake 45 to 50 minutes or until toothpick inserted in center comes out clean. Cool 20 minutes in pan, then remove to rack to finish cooling.

NUTRITION ANALYSIS
(PER SERVING)

Protein 7 gm., Carbohydrate 43 gm., Fiber 4 gm., Fat 5 gm.,
Cholesterol 0, Calcium 40 mg., Sodium 163 mg.

Calories 232
From protein:12%; From carbohydrate: 70%; From fat:19%

Chocolate Ice Cream

*Make this delectable frozen dessert in advance;
it's quite rich tasting and very easy to assemble.*

◆ 8 SERVINGS ◆

1 1/4 cups lite silken tofu (extra firm), drained

2 frozen bananas (peel and break into 2-inch pieces before freezing)

1/3 cup cocoa powder

1/2 cup liquid Fruitsource or honey

1 cup white grape juice concentrate, thawed

2 rounded Tbsp. agar flakes

Place tofu in food processor, and blend. Add frozen bananas, and blend until smooth. Place cocoa in a small bowl. Warm Fruitsource in a small glass measuring cup for 50 seconds in microwave. Whisk Fruitsource into cocoa to make a smooth syrup. Add syrup to tofu, and blend. Stir agar into juice concentrate. Add to food processor; blend until smooth. Pour mixture into a covered container, and place in the freezer at least 4 hours or overnight.

Remove from freezer. Let stand 15 minutes, then place frozen chunks in food processor. Blend, then return to freezer for at least 2 hours. Serve with Fudgy Chocolate Glaze (page 228).

◆ *221* ◆

NUTRITION ANALYSIS
(PER 1/2-CUP SERVING)

Protein 4 gm., Carbohydrate 36 gm., Fiber 2 gm., Fat 1 gm.,
Cholesterol 0, Calcium 12 mg., Sodium 40 mg.

Calories 159
From protein: 9%; From carbohydrate: 85%; From fat: 6%

Chocolate Chip Cookies

*These delicious cookies are moist and bursting
with flavor. My son Justin thinks they are terrific!*

◆ MORE THAN 7 DOZEN COOKIES ◆

vegetable oil cooking spray

2 1/2 cups whole wheat pastry flour

1/2 cup yellow cornmeal

1 1/2 cups Sucanat or brown sugar

1 tsp. baking soda

1 tsp. baking powder

1 tsp. cinnamon

1/4 tsp. salt

1 1/4 cups lite silken tofu (extra
firm), drained

1/3 cup liquid Fruitsource or honey

2 Tbsp. egg replacer powder

1/3 cup water

1/2 cup soymilk lite

1 Tbsp. vanilla extract

1 cup Sunspire organic dark
chocolate chips

3/4 cup golden raisins

◆ 222 ◆

Preheat oven to 350.° Spray baking sheets with cooking spray. Mix together flour and the following 6 dry ingredients in a large bowl. Set aside. Blend tofu in a food processor. Add Fruitsource. Pulse, then process to blend. Whisk egg replacer powder with water in a small bowl until foamy. Add to the tofu mixture along with soymilk and vanilla. Blend until smooth. Fold the tofu mixture into the dry ingredients. Mix thoroughly. Fold chocolate chips and raisins into cookie batter. Drop by rounded tablespoons onto prepared cookie sheets. Bake 10 minutes or until lightly browned. Cool 1 minute on tray and finish cooling on racks.

NUTRITION ANALYSIS
(PER 2-COOKIE SERVING)

Protein 2 gm., Carbohydrate 19 gm., Fiber 1 gm.,
Fat 2 gm., Cholesterol 0, Calcium 21 mg., Sodium 85 mg.

Calories 97
From protein: 8%; From carbohydrate: 75%; From fat: 17%

Cranberry Almond Cake

Top off your holiday meal with this moist and marvelous cranberry treat.

◆ 16 SERVINGS ◆

vegetable oil cooking spray
3 cups unbleached flour
3/4 cup yellow cornmeal
1 1/2 tsp. baking soda
2 tsp. baking powder
1/2 tsp. salt
1/3 cup Sucanat or brown sugar
1/3 cup almond pieces

1 1/4 cups lite silken tofu (extra firm), drained
1/2 cup unsweetened applesauce
1 cup soymilk lite
2 cups Florida Crystals or sugar
1 Tbsp. grated orange zest
1 tsp. vanilla extract
1/2 tsp. almond extract
1 cup chopped fresh cranberries

Preheat oven to 350°. Spray a tube pan with cooking spray; lightly flour the pan. In a large bowl, mix together the flour with the following 6 ingredients. Set aside. Place tofu in food processor, and blend. Add the remaining cake ingredients, except cranberries, to the food processor. Blend until smooth. Gently fold tofu mixture into the dry ingredients. Add cranberries. Pour batter into prepared tube pan. Bake 45 minutes or until lightly browned and a toothpick inserted in center comes out clean. Cool 20 minutes in pan and remove to rack to finish cooling.

TOPPING

4 cups cranberries, fresh or frozen
1 1/2 cups orange juice
1 1/2 cups Sucanat or brown sugar

1 tsp. orange blossom water
1 Tbsp. grated orange zest

In a medium saucepan, cook cranberries and orange juice for 15 minutes or until the cranberries begin to loose their shape and thicken. Add remaining ingredients, and simmer 5 minutes. Chill. Topping may be made a day or two in advance.

NUTRITION ANALYSIS
(PER SERVING)

Protein 5 gm., Carbohydrate 61 gm., Fiber 3 gm., Fat 2 gm.,
Cholesterol 0, Calcium 79 mg., Sodium 290 mg.

Calories 282
From protein: 7%; From carbohydrate: 86%; From fat: 7%

Cranberry Oatmeal Cookies

These are great oatmeal cookies, with all the flavor and texture you expect and none of the excess fat or calories. Dried cranberries add a special touch!

◆ 5 1/2 DOZEN COOKIES ◆

vegetable oil cooking spray
2 1/2 cups whole wheat pastry flour
2 cups rolled oats
1 1/2 cups Sucanat or brown sugar
1 tsp. baking soda
1 tsp. baking powder
1 tsp. cinnamon
1/2 tsp. salt
1 1/4 cups lite silken tofu, drained

1/3 cup liquid Fruitsource or honey
1 Tbsp. egg replacer powder
1/4 cup water
1 Tbsp. vanilla extract
1/4 cup soymilk lite
1 Tbsp. canola oil
1 cup dried cranberries
1/3 cup soy grits

◆ *224* ◆

Preheat oven to 350.° Spray cookie sheets with cooking spray. Mix together flour with the following 6 ingredients in a large bowl. Set aside. Place tofu in food processor, and blend. Add Fruitsource. Pulse, then blend. Whisk egg replacer with water in a small bowl until foamy. Add to tofu mixture along with vanilla, soymilk, and oil. Blend until smooth. Fold the liquid ingredients into the dry. Add cranberries and soy grits. Mix thoroughly. Drop by rounded tablespoons onto cookie sheets. Bake 10 minutes or until lightly browned. Cool 1 minute on pan, then finish cooling on racks.

NUTRITION ANALYSIS
(PER 2-COOKIE SERVING)

Protein 3 gm., Carbohydrate 21 gm., Fiber 2 gm., Fat 1 gm.,
Cholesterol 0, Calcium 24 mg., Sodium 107 mg.

Calories 104
From protein: 11%; From carbohydrate: 79%; From fat: 10%

East Indian Spice Cake

This unique and delicious dessert is served with a delightful cream topping.

◆ 12 SERVINGS ◆

vegetable oil cooking spray
3/4 cup soymilk lite
1 Tbsp. lemon juice
1 cup whole wheat pastry flour
1 cup yellow cornmeal
1 cup Sucanat or brown sugar
1 tsp. baking powder
1 1/2 tsp. cinnamon
3/4 tsp. ground cardamom
1/2 tsp. ground ginger

1/4 tsp. ground nutmeg
1/8 tsp. ground cloves
1/4 tsp. salt
1/2 cup lite silken tofu (firm),
    drained
1/3 cup prune purée
1/3 cup mild molasses
cinnamon
nutmeg

Preheat oven to 350°. Spray an 8" square or round pan with cooking spray. Combine soymilk and lemon juice in small glass measuring cup; set aside. In a large bowl, mix together the next 10 ingredients. Set aside. Place 1/2 cup tofu in food processor, and blend; reserve the remaining tofu. Add prune purée, and blend. Add soymilk and molasses; blend until smooth. Fold tofu mixture into dry ingredients. Pour into prepared pan. Sprinkle with cinnamon and nutmeg. Bake 25 to 30 minutes or until toothpick inserted in center comes out clean.

◆ 225 ◆

MOLASSES CREAM TOPPING

3/4 cup lite silken tofu
1/2 cup Veganrella cream cheese
    (or low-fat cream cheese)

2 Tbsp. mild molasses
1/4 cup Florida Crystals or sugar
1 tsp. vanilla extract

Place tofu in food processor, and blend. Add cream cheese, and blend. Add remaining ingredients, and blend until smooth. Refrigerate until ready to serve.

NUTRITION ANALYSIS
(PER SERVING)

Protein 4 gm., Carbohydrate 47 gm., Fiber 2 gm., Fat 3 gm.,
Cholesterol 0, Calcium 77 mg., Sodium 171 mg.

Calories 227
From protein: 8%; From carbohydrate: 81%; From fat: 11%

Frozen Fudge Cheesecake

Completely dairy-free, this luscious frozen ice cream pie is outstanding!

◆ 1 6 S E R V I N G S ◆

NO-BAKE PIE CRUST:

6 1/4-oz. pkg. Health Valley fat-free apple spice cookies

1/2 cup wheat germ

1/4 cup date pieces

1/4 cup frozen apple juice concentrate, thawed

FILLING:

2 1/2 cups lite silken tofu (extra firm), drained

8-oz. pkg. Veganrella or low-fat cream cheese

1/3 cup prune purée

1 cup liquid Fruitsource or honey

1/2 cup cocoa powder

1 Tbsp. vanilla extract

◆ *226* ◆

Place cookies in a food processor, and pulse to make crumbs. Add wheat germ, and process to mix. Add date pieces, and process to make a loose crumb. Pour juice concentrate through feed tube; mix thoroughly. Press mixture into a deep dish pie plate to form crust. Refrigerate.

Place tofu in a food processor, and blend until smooth. Add cream cheese, and process. Add prune purée, and process again. Heat Fruitsource in a small saucepan (over low heat for about 3 minutes) or in the microwave (on high for 90 seconds). Remove from heat, and whisk in cocoa powder to make a smooth syrup. Add syrup to tofu mixture along with vanilla. Process thoroughly. Pour into prepared pie crust. If there's any filling left over, pour into freezer pop containers for great fudgesicles! Freeze for at least 4 hours or overnight to give the tofu time to absorb all of the rich flavor.

NUTRITION ANALYSIS
(PER SERVING)

Protein 5 gm., Carbohydrate 32 gm., Fiber 3 gm., Fat 4 gm.,
Cholesterol 0, Calcium 7 mg., Sodium 100 mg.

Calories 175
From protein: 10%; From carbohydrate: 70%; From fat: 20%

Fudgy Chocolate Walnut Ring

*Completely caffeine free, this luscious glazed chocolate cake
is lovely garnished with fresh strawberries.*

◆ 16 SERVINGS ◆

vegetable oil cooking spray
1 cup soymilk lite
2 Tbsp. lemon juice
2 1/2 cups whole wheat pastry flour
1 3/4 cups Wonderslim Cocoa (see page 28)
1 tsp. baking soda
1 tsp. baking powder
1 tsp. cinnamon
1/4 tsp. salt

1 1/4 cups. pkg. lite silken tofu, firm
1/2 cup unsweetened applesauce
1/4 cup liquid Fruitsource
1 1/2 cups Florida Crystals or sugar
2 tsp. vanilla extract
1 Tbsp. egg replacer
1/4 cup water
1/2 cup walnut pieces*
1/4 cup soy grits (see page 20)

Preheat oven to 350°. Spray a tube pan with cooking spray. Place soymilk in a small bowl or measuring cup; add lemon juice. Set aside. Mix the next 6 ingredients in a large bowl. Set aside. Place tofu in food processor and blend until smooth. Add the next 4 ingredients and pulse to mix, then blend. Whisk egg replacer powder and water in a small bowl until foamy. Add to tofu mixture along with soymilk, and blend thoroughly. Fold liquid ingredients into dry ingredients, just until mixed. Mix together nuts and soy grits; add to batter. Do not overbeat. Pour batter into prepared pan and bake 50 minutes or until tester comes out clean. Cool in pan 20 minutes, then cool completely on rack. Glaze with Fudgy Chocolate Glaze (recipe follows).

*Also delicious with almond pieces. Just add 1/2 teaspoon of almond extract, in addition to the vanilla extract, to the glaze ingredients.

◆ 227 ◆

NUTRITION ANALYSIS
(PER SERVING, INCLUDING GLAZE)

Protein 9 gm., Carbohydrate 44 gm., Fiber 3 gm., Fat 4 gm.,
Cholesterol 0, Calcium 46 mg., Sodium 267 mg.

Calories 238
From protein: 14%; From carbohydrate: 71%; From fat: 15%

Fudgy Chocolate Glaze

This is a quick and easy glaze with a rich chocolate flavor.

3 Tbsp. tapioca flour or arrowroot

1/2 cup liquid Fruitsource

1/3 cup Wonderslim cocoa

1 tsp. vanilla extract

Mix together tapioca flour and cocoa in a small bowl. Set aside. Heat Fruitsource in microwave 40 seconds or until hot (or in saucepan for a minute or so over low heat). Pour hot Fruitsource into cocoa mixture, whisking as you go. Whisk until a smooth syrup is formed and add extract. Cool slightly and drizzle over cooled cake. Refrigerate glazed cake until ready to serve.

Ginger-Spiced Fruit and Nut Bars

Aromatic and flavorful, these cookie bars are chock full of goodness.

◆ 25 COOKIE BARS ◆

vegetable oil cooking spray
1 cup snipped dried apricots
1/3 cup water
1 1/2 cups whole wheat pastry flour
1/4 cup soy flour
1/4 cup yellow cornmeal
1 tsp. baking soda
1 tsp. baking powder
1/4 tsp. salt
1 tsp. cinnamon
1/2 tsp. ground ginger
1/4 tsp. ground allspice
1/4 tsp. ground nutmeg

1/8 tsp. ground cloves
1/3 cup unsweetened applesauce
2 Tbsp. liquid Fruitsource or honey
1 cup Florida Crystals or sugar
1 Tbsp. egg replacer powder
1/4 cup water
1/4 cup soymilk lite
2 tsp. vanilla extract
1 Tbsp grated fresh gingerroot
1 Tbsp. grated lemon zest
3/4 cup dried blueberries
1/3 cup cashew pieces
1/4 cup soy grits

• 229 •

Preheat oven to 350.° Spray a 9" x 13" pan with cooking spray. Place apricots in a small saucepan with water, and bring to a boil. Reduce heat and simmer for 5 minutes, or until all liquid is absorbed. Set aside. Mix together the next 11 ingredients in a medium bowl; set aside. Place applesauce in a large bowl, and mix thoroughly with Fruitsource. Cream applesauce mixture with Florida Crystals. Whisk egg replacer with water in a small bowl until foamy. Whisk into applesauce mixture, then add soymilk, vanilla, gingerroot, and lemon zest. Fold dry ingredients into liquid. Add apricots, blueberries, cashews, and soy grits. Pour batter into prepared pan. Bake 25 minutes or until lightly browned and tester comes out clean.

NUTRITION ANALYSIS
(PER COOKIE BAR)

Protein 2 gm., Carbohydrate 20 gm., Fiber 1 gm., Fat 1 gm.,
Cholesterol 0, Calcium 21 mg., Sodium 89 mg.

Calories 101
From protein: 9%; From carbohydrate: 78%; From fat: 13%

Glazed Apple Custard Pie

Rich-tasting custard topped with fresh cinnamon-glazed apples makes a lovely presentation in this delightful pie.

◆ 8 SERVINGS ◆

CRUST

6.25-oz. box Health Valley fat-free apple spice cookies

1/2 cup wheat germ

1/4 cup date pieces

1/4 cup frozen apple juice concentrate

Place cookies in food processor, and process to crumb. Add wheat germ, and pulse to mix. Add date pieces, and blend. Add juice concentrate, and process until mixed thoroughly. Press into a deep dish pie plate. Freeze until ready to fill.

FILLING

2 1/2 cups lite silken tofu, drained and patted dry

1/4 tsp. cinnamon

1 Tbsp. vanilla extract

1 cup soymilk lite, separated

3/4 cup frozen apple juice concentrate

2 1/2 Tbsp. agar flakes

1/2 cup maple syrup

vegetable oil cooking spray

3 cups Granny Smith or Pippin apples, peeled and sliced

1 Tbsp. lemon juice

Blend tofu in food processor until smooth. Add cinnamon and vanilla. Set aside. Heat 3/4 cup of soymilk with juice concentrate in a medium saucepan. Whisk agar flakes into remaining 1/4 cup soymilk. Add to saucepan, whisking constantly over medium-low heat. When showing signs of thickening, add to tofu mixture, and blend. Add maple syrup, and mix thoroughly. Pour into pie shell. Spray a 10" frying pan with cooking spray. Cook and carefully stir apple slices over medium heat for 3 minutes. Add lemon juice. When apples are crisp-tender (about 5 to 8 minutes) remove pan from heat, and set aside.

GLAZE

1/2 cup frozen apple juice concentrate, thawed

1/4 tsp. cinnamon

1 1/2 tsp. cornstarch

Combine all glaze ingredients in a medium saucepan over low heat. Whisk constantly for 5 to 8 minutes, or until glaze thickens. Arrange apple slices in a circular pattern over custard, and pour glaze over all. Refrigerate for at least 4 hours or overnight.

NUTRITION ANALYSIS
(PER SERVING)

Protein 9 gm., Carbohydrate 70 gm., Fiber 5 gm., Fat 2 gm.,
Cholesterol 0, Calcium 37 mg., Sodium 135 mg.

Calories 322
From protein: 11%; From carbohydrate: 83%; From fat: 6%

• *231* •

Glazed Chocolate Carrot Cake

Accented by a fudgy chocolate glaze, this cake is fantastic!

◆ 1 2   S E R V I N G S ◆

vegetable oil cooking spray
1 cup soymilk lite
2 Tbsp. lemon juice
2 1/2 cups whole wheat pastry flour
1 tsp. baking soda
1 tsp. baking powder
1/2 tsp. salt
1/2 cup unbleached flour

1/2 cup cocoa powder
2 cups Sucanat or brown sugar
1 1/4 cups lite silken tofu (firm), drained
1/2 cup prune purée
2 tsp. vanilla extract
2 cups grated carrots

Preheat oven to 350.° Spray a tube pan with cooking spray. Place soymilk in a small glass measuring cup, and add lemon juice. Stir together whole wheat flour and the next 3 ingredients in a large bowl. Sift the unbleached flour and cocoa into the flour mixture. Add Sucanat. Stir together, then set aside. Place tofu in food processor; blend. Add prune purée, and process. Add vanilla and half of the soymilk; blend. Fold the tofu mixture into the dry ingredients alternately with the remaining soymilk. Pour batter into the prepared pan. Bake for 50 minutes or until toothpick inserted in center comes out clean. Cool 20 minutes in pan; then remove to rack to finish cooling.

GLAZE

3 Tbsp. tapioca flour or arrowroot
1/3 cup liquid Fruitsource or honey

1/4 cup cocoa powder

Place flour in a medium bowl. Set aside. Heat Fruitsource in microwave 20 seconds or in saucepan until hot. Whisk into flour until smooth. Gradually whisk in cocoa until smooth. Let sit 5 minutes. Spoon over cooled cake.

NUTRITION ANALYSIS
(PER SERVING)

Protein 7 gm., Carbohydrate 65 gm., Fiber 6 gm., Fat 2 gm.,
Cholesterol 0, Calcium 73 mg., Sodium 329 mg.

Calories 291
From protein: 10%; From carbohydrate:85%; From fat: 5%

Marie's Incredible Chocolate Brownies

*My daughter Kyra's favorite, these outrageous brownies
will disappear as fast as you make them.*

◆ 30 BROWNIES ◆

vegetable oil cooking spray
2 Tbsp. lemon juice
1 1/2 cups soymilk lite
2 cups unbleached flour
2 tsp. baking soda
2 tsp. baking powder
2 cups Wonderslim cocoa powder

1/2 tsp. salt
3 cups Sucanat or brown sugar
1 1/4 cups lite silken tofu (firm or
   extra firm), drained
1 3/4 cup prune purée
1 Tbsp. vanilla extract
1/2 cup walnut pieces

Preheat oven to 350°. Spray a 9" x 13" baking pan with cooking spray. In a glass measuring cup, add lemon juice to soymilk; set aside. In a large bowl, stir together the next 6 ingredients. Set aside. Purée the tofu in a food processor or blender until smooth. Add prune purée, and blend. Add one cup of the soymilk along with the vanilla extract; blend. Add the tofu mixture to the dry ingredients alternately with the reserved 1/2 cup of soymilk; mix thoroughly. Fold in walnut pieces. Pour batter into prepared pan. Bake 40 to 45 minutes.

◆ *233* ◆

NUTRITION ANALYSIS
(PER SERVING)

Protein 2 gm., Carbohydrate 30 gm., Fiber 1 gm., Fat 2 gm.,
Cholesterol 0, Calcium 42 mg., Sodium 204 mg.

Calories 141
From protein: 6%; From carbohydrate: 82%; From fat: 12%

Lemon Blueberry Delite

*Sweet dried blueberries are suspended in a lovely lemon cake
with a luscious blueberry topping—superb!*

◆ 12 SERVINGS ◆

vegetable oil cooking spray
1 cup soymilk lite
2 Tbsp. lemon juice
3 cups unbleached flour
1 1/2 tsp. baking soda
1 tsp. baking powder
1/2 tsp. salt
1 1/4 cups lite silken tofu (firm),
  drained

1/2 cup unsweetened applesauce
3 Tbsp. lemon juice
1 Tbsp. grated lemon zest
1/4 tsp. lemon extract
1 tsp. vanilla extract
1 1/2 cups Florida Crystals or sugar
2/3 cup dried blueberries

• 234 •

Preheat oven to 350°. Spray a tube pan with cooking spray. Place soymilk in a small glass measuring cup; add lemon juice, and set aside. Sift flour with the next 3 ingredients in a large bowl. Set aside. Place tofu in food processor, and blend. Add the next 5 ingredients, and process. Add Florida Crystals, and blend until smooth. Fold tofu mixture into the dry ingredients alternately with the soymilk, just until mixed. Fold in blueberries, being careful not to overmix. Bake 45 to 50 minutes or until a toothpick inserted comes out clean. Cool 20 minutes in the pan, then remove onto a rack to complete cooling. Serve with Lemon Blueberry Delite Topping (recipe follows).

NUTRITION ANALYSIS
(PER SERVING, INCLUDING TOPPING)

Protein 6 gm., Carbohydrate 62 gm., Fiber 2 gm., Fat 1 gm.,
Cholesterol 0, Calcium 40 mg., Sodium 314 mg.

Calories 278
From protein: 8%; From carbohydrate: 89%; From fat: 3%

Lemon Blueberry Delite Topping

♦ 3 CUPS ♦

6-oz. pkg. fresh blueberries
 (1 1/2 cups)
1 cup white grape juice concentrate,
 thawed
1/2 cup Florida Crystals or sugar

1/4 tsp. lemon extract
1 tsp. grated lemon zest
2 Tbsp. cornstarch
3 Tbsp. cold water

Rinse blueberries. Place berries and juice concentrate in a medium saucepan over medium heat. Bring to a boil, then add the next 3 ingredients. Cook for 10 minutes or until berries soften and the mixture is dark. Combine the cornstarch and water in a small bowl. Add to the blueberries. Reduce heat, and simmer for 10 to 12 minutes or until sauce is thickened. Refrigerate until ready to use. Spoon over a slice of Lemon Blueberry Delite cake or any dessert that would be complemented by blueberries.

NUTRITION ANALYSIS
(PER 2-OZ. SERVING)

Protein 0, Carbohydrate 16 gm., Fiber 1 gm., Fat 0,
Cholesterol 0, Calcium 4 mg., Sodium 3 mg.

Calories 61
From protein: 2%; From carbohydrate: 96%; From fat: 2%

♦ *235* ♦

Middle Eastern "Honey" Cake

This delicious cake fills the house with the heady aroma of roses.

◆ 2 4 S E R V I N G S ◆

vegetable oil cooking spray
3 cups unbleached flour
1 1/2 tsp. baking powder
1 tsp. baking soda
1 tsp. cinnamon
1/2 tsp. salt
1 1/2 cups Sucanat or brown sugar

1 1/4 cups lite silken tofu (extra firm), drained
1 cup prune purée
3/4 cup liquid Fruitsource or honey
1 Tbsp. grated orange zest
2 tsp. rose water
1/3 cup soymilk lite
1/2 cup walnut pieces

Preheat oven to 350.° Spray a 9" x 13" pan with cooking spray. Combine flour with the next 5 ingredients in a large bowl. Place tofu in food processor; blend until smooth. Add prune purée, and blend. Add Fruitsource, orange zest, and rose water; blend. Add tofu mixture to dry ingredients alternately with the soymilk. Fold in walnuts. Pour into prepared pan. Bake 45 minutes or until toothpick inserted in the center comes out clean.

◆ *236* ◆

NUTRITION ANALYSIS
(PER SERVING)

Protein 3 gm., Carbohydrate 34 gm., Fiber 1 gm., Fat 2 gm.,
Cholesterol 0, Calcium 37 mg., Sodium 163 mg.

Calories 162
From protein: 7%; From carbohydrate: 82%; From fat: 10%

Mocha Mousse Magic

This smooth, rich-tasting dessert mousse is elegant.

◆ 1 2   S E R V I N G S ◆

2 1/2 cups lite silken tofu (firm), drained

8-oz. pkg. Veganrella cream cheese or low-fat cream cheese

2 frozen bananas

3/4 cup liquid Fruitsource or honey

1/3 cup cocoa powder

1 Tbsp. vanilla extract

1/2 cup cold soymilk lite

2 Tbsp. agar flakes

1/2 cup Florida Crystals or sugar

1/2 cup strong coffee (cold)

1/3 cup Sunspire Crystal dark chocolate chips (optional)

Place drained tofu in food processor; blend. Add cream cheese, and blend. Break frozen bananas into 3-inch chunks, and add to blended tofu. Pulse to break up chunks, then blend. Heat Fruitsource in microwave for 45 seconds or in a saucepan for 2 minutes over low heat. Place cocoa in a small bowl. Whisk in hot Fruitsource and vanilla. Add syrup to tofu mixture, and blend. Place soymilk in a small microwave-safe bowl or saucepan. Stir in agar, and heat mixture just to the boiling point. Add to tofu mixture along with Florida Crystals and coffee. Add chocolate chips, and pulse just to mix. Pour mousse into a covered container, and freeze overnight.

When ready to serve, use a knife to cut chunks out of frozen mixture. Remove only what you will be serving, and return remainder to freezer. Place chunks in food processor, and pulse, then process to blend to a mousse-like consistency. Serve immediately. Garnish with fresh mint leaves if desired.

◆ *237* ◆

NUTRITION ANALYSIS
(PER SERVING)

Protein 5 gm., Carbohydrate 27 gm., Fiber 1 gm., Fat 5 gm.,
Cholesterol 0, Calcium 5 mg., Sodium 108 mg.

Calories 166
From protein: 10%; From carbohydrate: 63%; From fat: 27%

Orange Blossom Pecan Cake

The scent of orange blossoms fills the house while this cake bakes. Dust with powdered sugar and garnish with edible flowers for a very special presentation.

◆ 12 SERVINGS ◆

vegetable oil cooking spray

2 cups whole wheat pastry flour

1/3 cup soy flour

1/2 cup yellow cornmeal

1 tsp. baking soda

1 tsp. baking powder

1 tsp. cinnamon

1/4 tsp. salt

1 1/2 cups Sucanat or brown sugar

1 1/4 cups lite silken tofu (firm), drained

1/2 cup unsweetened applesauce

1/3 cup liquid Fruitsource or honey

1/2 cup orange juice (preferably fresh squeezed)

2 tsp. orange zest

1 tsp. orange blossom water

1 tsp. vanilla extract

1 Tbsp. egg replacer powder

1/4 cup water

1/4 cup soymilk lite

1/3 cup pecan pieces

1/4 cup soy grits

Preheat oven to 350°. Spray a tube pan with cooking spray. Mix flour with the next 7 ingredients in a large bowl. Set aside. Place tofu in food processor, and blend. Add applesauce and Fruitsource. Pulse to mix, then blend. Add the next 4 ingredients, and process. Whisk egg replacer with water in a small bowl. Add to tofu mixture. Fold the liquid ingredients into dry alternately with soymilk. Mix pecan pieces with soy grits, and fold quickly into batter. Pour into prepared pan. Bake 45 minutes or until tester comes out clean. Cool in pan 20 minutes; remove to rack to finish cooling. Dust with powdered sugar before serving.

NUTRITION ANALYSIS
(PER SERVING)

Protein 7 gm., Carbohydrate 47 gm., Fiber 4 gm., Fat 4 gm., Cholesterol 0, Calcium 66 mg., Sodium 251 mg.

Calories 245
From protein: 11%; From carbohydrate: 74%; From fat: 15%

Peach Ice Dream

*You'll love the brandied peaches and
creamy texture of this dairy-free confection.*

◆ 8 SERVINGS ◆

16-oz. pkg. frozen peaches
1/4 cup peach brandy
1 1/4 cups lite silken tofu (firm),
    drained

1 cup apple juice concentrate, thawed
2 rounded Tbsp. agar flakes
1/2 tsp. almond extract
1/2 cup maple syrup

Heat peaches in a medium saucepan over medium heat. When thawed, add brandy, and continue to cook over low heat until liquid is absorbed. Blend tofu in food processor. Add peaches to tofu, and blend. Whisk agar flakes into juice concentrate. Add to tofu mixture. Add almond extract and maple syrup, and blend. Pour into a covered container, and freeze at least 4 hours or overnight.

Remove from freezer, and let sit 15 minutes. Place frozen chunks in food processor, and blend until smooth. Return to freezer for 4 hours or overnight. Serve garnished with mint leaves.

◆ *239* ◆

NUTRITION ANALYSIS
(PER 5 1/4-OUNCE SERVING)

Protein 3 gm., Carbohydrate 28 gm., Fiber 1 gm., Fat 1 gm.,
Cholesterol 0, Calcium 19 mg., Sodium 46 mg.

Calories 142
From protein: 9%; From carbohydrate: 79%; From fat: 4%

Pumpkin Cranberry Ring

Cranberries add a piquant sweetness to this moist pumpkin cake.

◆ 1 2   S E R V I N G S ◆

vegetable oil cooking spray
2 cups whole wheat pastry flour
1/2 cup soy flour
1 1/2 cups Sucanat or brown sugar
1 tsp. baking powder
1 tsp. baking soda
1 tsp. cinnamon
1 tsp. ground ginger
1/2 tsp. ground nutmeg
1/4 tsp. ground cloves
1/2 tsp. salt

1 1/4 cups lite silken tofu (extra firm), drained
1/2 cup prune purée
1 cup canned pumpkin
1/4 cup liquid Fruitsource or honey
1 tsp. vanilla extract
1 Tbsp. egg replacer powder
1/4 cup water
3/4 cup soymilk lite
1 cup dried cranberries

◆ *240* ◆

Preheat oven to 350°. Spray a tube pan with cooking spray. Mix together the first 10 ingredients in a medium bowl. Place tofu in food processor, and blend. Add prune purée and pumpkin; blend. Add Fruitsource and vanilla; pulse to mix, then blend. Whisk egg replacer and water in a small bowl until foamy. Add to tofu mixture along with soymilk, and blend until smooth. Fold liquid ingredients into dry, just until mixed. Fold in cranberries. Bake 50 minutes or until toothpick inserted comes out clean. Cool 20 minutes in pan; remove to rack to finish cooling. Dust with powdered sugar.

NUTRITION ANALYSIS
(PER SERVING)

Protein 6 gm., Carbohydrate 56 gm., Fiber 4 gm., Fat 2 gm.,
Cholesterol 0, Calcium 73 mg., Sodium 309 mg.

Calories 255
From protein: 10%; From carbohydrate: 85%; From fat: 6%

Pumpkin Fudge Brownies

*Pumpkin brownies with chocolate fudge swirls deliver
exceptional flavor, texture, and nutrition.*

◆ 30 BROWNIES ◆

vegetable oil cooking spray
1 cup soymilk lite
2 Tbsp. lemon juice
2 1/2 cups unbleached flour
1/2 cup oat bran
1 tsp. baking soda
1 tsp. baking powder
1/2 tsp. salt
1 tsp. cinnamon
1/4 tsp. ground nutmeg
1 tsp. ground ginger

1/8 tsp. ground cloves
2 cups Sucanat or brown sugar
1 1/4 cups lite silken tofu (extra
  firm), drained
2/3 cup prune purée
2/3 cup canned pumpkin
2 tsp. vanilla extract, separated
1/4 cup boiling water
1/4 cup cocoa powder
1 Tbsp. liquid Fruitsource or honey

Preheat oven to 350.° Spray a 9" x 13" baking pan with cooking spray. Place soymilk in a glass measuring cup. Add lemon juice, and set aside. In a large bowl, stir together the next 10 ingredients, and set aside. Place tofu in food processor and blend. Add prune purée and pumpkin; process. Add soymilk and 1 teaspoon of vanilla. Blend until smooth. Fold the tofu mixture into the dry ingredients. Remove 1 1/2 cups of the batter to a medium bowl. Whisk together boiling water and cocoa. Blend the remaining teaspoon of vanilla along with Fruitsource into the cocoa mixture. Fold cocoa mixture into the 1 1/2 cups of reserved batter.

Spread two-thirds of the pumpkin batter on the bottom of the prepared pan. Spoon dollops of the fudge batter on top, leaving spaces between dollops. Spoon dollops of the remaining pumpkin batter in an alternating fudge-pumpkin pattern. Run a butter knife through the batters to form a swirling marble pattern. Bake 30 minutes. Cool and cut into squares.

NUTRITION ANALYSIS
(PER SERVING)

Protein 2 gm., Carbohydrate 24 gm., Fiber 1 gm., Fat 1 gm.,
Cholesterol 0, Calcium 28 mg., Sodium 130 mg.

Calories 106
From protein: 9%; From carbohydrate: 87%; From fat: 4%

Spiced Fruitcake

*This special party cake is topped with a creamy vanilla icing and
filled with brandied apricots, date pieces, and chopped walnuts.*

◆ 1 6 S E R V I N G S ◆

vegetable oil cooking spray
1 cup apricots, snipped
1/2 cup apricot brandy
1 cup soymilk lite
2 Tbsp. lemon juice
3 cups whole wheat pastry flour
1/2 cup wheat germ
1 tsp. baking soda
1 tsp. baking powder
1/4 tsp. salt

2 tsp. cinnamon
1/4 tsp. ground nutmeg
1 /14 cups lite silken tofu (firm),
    drained
2 cups brown sugar
2 tsp. vanilla extract
1/2 cup unsweetened applesauce
1/2 cup prune purée
1/2 cup date pieces
1/3 cup chopped pecans

◆ 242 ◆

Preheat oven to 350.° Spray a 9" x 13" pan with cooking spray. Place the apricots
in a small saucepan, stir in brandy, and bring to a low boil over medium heat. Reduce
heat, and simmer until brandy is absorbed (about 5 minutes). Pour soymilk into a glass
measuring cup, and add lemon juice. Set aside. Stir together the next 7 ingredients in a
large bowl. Set aside. Blend the tofu in a food processor until smooth. Add soymilk,
brown sugar, vanilla, applesauce, and prune purée. Blend. Fold the tofu mixture into the
dry ingredients. Fold the brandied apricots into the batter, along with dates and pecans.
Pour into the prepared pan. Bake for 35 minutes or until a toothpick inserted in the
center comes out clean. Cool in pan and top with Creamy Vanilla Icing (recipe follows).

NUTRITION ANALYSIS
(PER SERVING—WITH ICING)

Protein 7 gm., Carbohydrate 60 gm., Fiber 5 gm., Fat 3 gm.,
Cholesterol 0, Calcium 47 mg., Sodium 156 mg.

Calories 295
From protein: 10%; From carbohydrate: 81%; From fat: 9%

Creamy Vanilla Icing

*This rich tasting frosting has a cream cheese frosting
consistency, and is very attractive garnished with fruit.*

◆ 2 3 / 4 C U P S ◆

1/2 cup frozen apple juice
concentrate

3 Tbsp. agar flakes

1 1/4 cups lite silken tofu (firm or
extra firm), drained

1 tsp. grated lemon zest

1 Tbsp. lemon juice

1 tsp. vanilla extract

1/3 cup liquid Fruitsource or honey

Place juice concentrate in a small saucepan; add agar flakes, and bring to a low boil over medium heat, stirring until dissolved. Lower heat and simmer, stirring frequently, until thickened, about 5 minutes. Place tofu in food processor, and blend until smooth. Add lemon zest, lemon juice, vanilla, and Fruitsource. Process until smooth, scraping down once or twice. Add thickened juice concentrate, and blend until smooth. Frost cake, and decorate with sliced strawberries, saving a berry with greens intact for the center.

◆ *243* ◆

NUTRITION ANALYSIS
(PER SERVING—ICING ONLY)

Protein 1 gm., Carbohydrate 8 gm., Fiber 0, Fat 0,
Cholesterol 0, Calcium 3 mg., Sodium 20 mg.

Calories 295
From protein: 14%; From carbohydrate: 80%; From fat: 6%

◆ *244* ◆

Resource Guide

Flours, grains, and natural foods products—
    Arrowhead Mills
    Box 2059
    Hereford, TX 79045
    (806) 364-0730

EnerG® egg replacer, tapioca flour, and allergy free products—
    EnerG Foods, Inc.
    500 First Ave. South
    P.O. Box 84487
    Seattle, WA 98124-5787
    (800) 331-5222

Fruitsource natural sweetener and fat replacer—
    Fruitsource
    1803 Mission St., Ste. 404
    Santa Cruz, CA 95060
    (408) 464-9891

TVP in styles that include beef and chicken, ground, chunks, and strips; also a
    variety of natural food products, all available by catalog—
    Harvest Direct
    505 West Depot Ave.
    Knoxville, TN 37917
    (800) 835-2867

Soya Granules (soy grits)—
    Fearn Natural Foods
    3015 West Vera Ave
    Milwaukee, WI 53209
    (414) 352-3333

Dairy free products, including Rice Dream, original and vanilla rice milk—
   Imagine Foods
   350 Cambridge Ave., Ste. 350
   Palo Alto, CA 94306
   (800) 333-6339

Flour, tools, equipment, and books—
   The Baker's Catalog
   King Arthur Flour
   P.O. Box 876
   Norwich, VT 05055-0876
   (800) 827-6836

Variety of soy-based products, including tempeh, deli slices, and Gimme Lean—
   Lightlife Foods, Inc.
   P.O. Box 870
   Greenfield, MA 01302
   (800) 274-6001

Bragg Liquid Aminos—
   Live Food Products
   P.O. Box 7
   Santa Barbara, CA 93102
   (805) 968-1028

TVP granules, chunks, and flakes, and organic granules and 1/2-inch chunks—
   The Mail Order Catalogue
   Box 180
   Summertown, TN 38483
   (800) 695-2241

Mori Nu Silken Tofu Lite—
   Morinaga Nutritional Foods, Inc.
   2050 West 190th St., Ste. 110
   Torrance, CA 90504
   (310) 787-0200

Tofu-based dressings and Nayonaise—
  Nasoya Foods, Inc.
  Loeminster, MA 01453
  (800) 229-TOFU

Florida Crystals, less-refined cane sugar products—
  The Natural Source
  2200 Front St.
  Melbourne, FL 32901
  (800) 784-2721

Soy Boy Ravioli and Not Dogs—
  Northern Soy, Inc.
  545 West Ave.
  Rochester, NY 14611-2424
  (716) 235-8970

Sucanat unrefined cane sugar—
  Sucanat North America Corp.
  26 Clinton Drive, #117
  Hollis, NH 03049
  (603) 595-2922

The Soy Deli, reduced-fat soyfoods made with organic soybeans—
  Quong Hop & Co.
  161 Beacon St.
  S. San Francisco, CA 94080
  (415) 761-2002

Veganrella cream cheese alternative—
  Sharon's Finest
  P.O. Box 5020
  Santa Rosa, CA 95402
  (707) 576-7050

Variety of salad dressings made with soy—
  Simply Delicious, Inc.
  8411 Hwy. NC 86 North
  Cedar Grove, NC 27231
  (919) 732-5294

Prune purée products—
   Sokol and Co.
   5315 Dansher Rd.
   Countryside, IL 60525
   (708) 482-8250

Confections, including organic dark chocolate chips—
   Sunspire
   2114 Adams Ave.
   San Leandro, CA 94577
   (510) 569-9731

Variety of soy products, including Ready Ground Tofu and Savory Tofu—
   Tree of Life
   1750 Tree Blvd.
   P.O. Box 410
   St. Augustine, FL 32085-0410
   (904) 825-2009

Variety of natural deli and tofu products—
   Wildwood Natural Foods
   135 Bolinas Rd.
   Fairfax, CA 94930
   (800) 499-TOFU (8638)

Variety of natural and organic foods, including Soymilk Lite—
   Westbrae Natural Foods
   1065 Walnut
   Carson, CA 90746
   (800) SOYMILK

Yves Canadian veggie bacon, veggie burgers, etc.—
   Yves Veggie Cuisine
   1138 East Georgia Street
   Vancouver, BC V6A 2A8 Canada
   (604) 251-1345

Recommended Reading

Barnard, Neal. *The Power of Your Plate*. Summertown, TN: The Book Publishing Company, 1990.

Barnard, Neal. *Food for Life*. New York: Harmony Books, 1993.

Barnard, Neal. *Eat Right Live Longer*. New York: Harmony Books, 1995.

Messina, Mark and Messina, Virginia. *The Simple Soybean and Your Health*. New York: Avery Publishing Group, 1994.

Messina, Virginia and Messina, Mark. *The Vegetarian Way*. New York: Crown Books, 1996.

McDougall, John. *The McDougall Program*. New York: Plume Books, 1991.

McDougall, John and McDougall, Mary. *The New McDougall Cookbook*. New York: Dutton, 1993.

McDougall, John. *The McDougall Program for a Healthy Heart*. New York: Dutton, 1996.

Ornish, Dean. *Dr. Dean Ornish's Program for Reversing Heart Disease*. New York: Random House, 1990.

Ornish, Dean. *Eat More, Weigh Less*. New York: HarperCollins, 1993.

Ornish, Dean. *Everyday Cooking with Dr. Dean Ornish*. New York: HarperCollins, 1996.

Robbins, John. *Diet For A New America*. Walpole, NH: Stillpoint Publishing, 1987.

Robbins, John. *May All Be Fed*. New York: William Morrow and Co., 1992.

Shurtleff, William and Aoyagi, Akiko. *The Book of Tofu*. New York: Ballantine Books, 1979.

Shurtleff, William and Aoyagi, Akiko. *The Book of Miso*. New York: Ballantine Books, 1981.

Bibliography

Akizuki, Tatsuichiro. (translated by Herman Aihara): *Macrobiotic Monthly* 1968; 8(5):6-12.

Akizuki, Tatsuichiro. *Physical Constitution and Food: The Way to Health*. Tokyo: Kurei Shuppan-bu, 1980.

Akizuki, Tatsuichiro: How we survived Nagasaki. *East West Journal* 1980; Dec.: 10, 12-13.

Anderson, J.J.; Ambrose, W.W.; Garner, S.C.: Orally dosed genestein from soy and prevention of canellous bone loss in two ovariectomized rat models. *Journal of Nutrition* 1995; 125(3S):799S.

Anderson, James W.; Johnstone Bryan M.; Cook-Newell, Margaret E.: Meta-analysis of soy protein intake on serum lipids. *New England Journal of Medicine* 1995; 333(5): 276-82. March supplement.

Anthony, M.S.; Clarkson, T.B.; Weddle, D.L.; Wolfe, M.S.: Effects of soy protein phytoestrogens on cardiovascular risk factors in rhesus monkeys. *Journal of Nutrition* 1995;125(3S): 803S-04S. March supplement.

Barnard, Neal. *Food for Life*. New York: Harmony Books, 1993.

Barnard, Neal. *Eat Right Live Longer*. New York: Harmony Books, 1995.

Barnard, Neal: Hormone replacement increases cancer risk. *Good Medicine* 1995; 4(3):14-15.

Barnes, Stephan: Effect of genestein on in vitro and in vivo models on cancer. *Journal of Nutrition* 1995; 125(3S):771S-76S. March supplement.

Barnes, Stephan; Peterson, Greg, T: Biochemical targets of the isoflavone genistein in tumor cell lines. *Proceedings of the Society for Experimental Biology and Medicine* 1995; 208(1):103-08.

Campbell, Colin: The latest from the China diet and health study. *Good Medicine* 1995; 3(3):10-14.

Constantinou, A.; Huberman, E.: Genistein as an inducer of tumor cell differentiation: possible mechinisms for action. *Proceedings of the Society for Experimental Biology and Medicine* 1995; 208(1):109-15.

Fotsis, T.; Pepper, M; Aldercreutz, H; Hase, T.; Montesano, R.; Schweigerer, L.: Genistein, a dietary ingested isoflavanoid, inhibits cell proliferation and in vitro angiogenesis and angiogenic diseases. *Journal of Nutrition* 1995; 125(3S): 800S. March supplement.

Giovannucci, E.; et al.: Intake of carotenoids and retinol in relation to risk of prostate cancer. *Journal of the National Cancer Institute* 1995; 87:1767-76.

Hartwell, Jonathon L.: Plants used against cancer: a survey. *Lloydia* 1967-1971; 30(4):379-46; 31(2):71-170; 32(1):79-107; 32(2):153-205; 32(3):247-96; 33(1):97-194; 33(3):288-392.

Herman, Aldercreutz, T; Goldin, B.R.; Gorbach, S.L.; et al.: Soybean phytoestrogens intake and cancer risk. *Journal of Nutrition* 1995; 125(3S):757S-770S. March supplement.

Kennedy, Ann R.: The evidence for soybean products as cancer preventive agents. *Journal of Nutrition* 1995; 125(3S):733S-43S. March supplement.

McDougall, John; Litzau, K; Haver, E; Saunders, V; Spiller, G.: Rapid reduction of serum cholesterol and blood pressure by a twelve day, very low fat, strictly vegetarian diet. *Journal of the American College of Nutrition* 1995; 14:491-96.

Messina, Mark; Messina, Virginia; Setchell, Kenneth R. *The Simple Soybean and Your Health.* Garden City Park, NY: Avery Publishing Group, Inc., 1994.

Messina M.; Erdman Jr., J., eds: First international symposium on the role of soy in preventing and treating chronic disease. *Journal of Nutrition* .1994; 125(3S):677S-808S. March supplement.

Messina, M.: Putting protein in perspective. *The Soy Connection* (United Soybean Board). 1994; 2(1):1-2.

Messina, M.: Fiber, soyfoods, and health. *The Soy Connection* (United Soybean Board). 1995; 3(2):1-2.

Messina, M.; Messina, V.: Soybeans linked to health benefits. *Vegetarian Voice* 1995; 20(4):10-11.

Mindell, Earl. *Earl Mindell's Food as Medicine*. New York: Simon & Schuster (A Fireside Book), 1994.

Mindell, Earl. *Earl Mindell's Soy Miracle*. New York: Simon & Schuster (A Fireside Book), 1995.

Molteni, Agostino; Brizio-Molteni, L.; Persky. V. In vitro hormonal effects of soybean isoflavones. *Journal of Nutrition* 1995; 125(3S):751S-770S. March supplement.

Northrup, Christiane. *Heal Your Symptoms Naturally*. Potomoc, MD: Phillips Publishing Inc., 1995.

Northrup, Christiane: Should you switch to a natural estrogen? *Health Wisdom For Women* 1995; 2(10):1-3.

Ornish, Dean. *Dr. Dean Ornish's Program For Reversing Heart Disease*. New York: Random House, 1990.

Ornish, Dean. *Eat More, Weigh Less*. New York: Harper Collins, 1993.

Peterson, Greg: Evaluation of the biochemical targets of genistein in tumor cells. *Journal of Nutrition* 1995; 125(3S):790S-97S. March supplement.

Petrakis, N.; Wiencke, J.; Coward, L.; Kirk, M.; Barnes, S.: A clinical trial of the chemoprotective effect of a soy beverage on women at high risk for breast cancer. *Journal of Nutrition* 1995; 125(3S):800S. March supplement.

Setchell, K.D.R.; Borriello, S.P.; Hulme, P; et al.: Nonsteroidal estrogens of dietary origin; possible roles in hormone dependent disease. *American Journal of Clinical Nutrition* 1984; 40(3):569-78.

Slavin, Joanne, L.: Health benefits of soy fiber. *The Soy Connection* (United Soybean Board) 1995; 3(2)1-4.

Steele, Vernon E., ; Pereira, M.A.; Sigman, C.C.; Kelloff, G.J.: Cancer chemoprevention agent development strategies for genistein. *Journal of Nutrition* 1995; 125(3S):713S-16S. March supplement.

Tufts University Diet and Nutrition Newsletter. Scientists spotlight phytoestrogens for better health. 1995; 12(2):3-6.

Urban, D. Grizzie, W.E.; Coward, L.; Kirk, M.; Barnes, S.: A clinical trial of the chemopreventive effect of soy beverage on men at high risk for prostate cancer. *Journal of Nutrition* 1995; 125(3S):800S.

Wei, Huachen; Ronald, Cai, Quiyin; Barnes, S; Wang, Y.: Antioxidant and antipromotional effects of the soybean isoflavone genistein. *Proceedings of the Society for Experimental Biology and Medicine* 1995; S208(1):124-30.

Zava, David T.: The phytoestrogen paradox. *The Soy Connection* (United Soybean board) 1994; 3(1):1, 4.

Index

◆258◆

COLOR THEORY
Made Easy

COLOR THEORY
Made Easy

A NEW APPROACH TO COLOR THEORY
AND HOW TO APPLY IT
TO MIXING PAINTS

Jim Ames

WATSON-GUPTILL PUBLICATIONS

New York

To my family

First published in 1996 in the United States by Watson-Guptill
Publications, a division of BPI Communications, Inc., 1515
Broadway, New York, NY 10036-8986.

Library of Congress Cataloging-in-Publication Data for this title can
be obtained by writing to the Library of Congress, Washington, DC.

Manufactured in China

ISBN 0-8230-0754-5

2 3 4 5 / 00 99

Senior Editor: Marian Appellof
Associate Editor: Dale Ramsey
Designer: Jay Anning
Production Manager: Hector Campbell

ACKNOWLEDGMENTS

When I think of how the science of color was unfolded to me during my research of the past seven years, I am humbled and inspired. The encounter challenged and enlightened me, and I was in awe of the mathematical and physical laws of color, which are universal and exact. My studies were an exciting experience that reinforced my belief in God. I thank God for leading me into this work of observing and interpreting the laws of color for artists. I hope I have interpreted them correctly.

Seven years is a long time to put a family through all that research and deliberation that ensued. My wife Diane listened to countless hours of debate and put up with my thousands of hours of study. She always supported me. My daughter Terry Chiles and her husband Ed have always been behind me as well. My two grandchildren Jon and Tiffany are probably the first children to tell their elementary school teachers that cyan, magenta, and yellow are nature's true primary colors.

I would not have discovered the approach to color I have laid out in the following pages if it had not been for my son Jim. He intrigued me with aspects of traditional theory and constantly questioned the results of my prism researches. He also refined some of my crude analyses of color theory. I am very grateful to him.

Many others encouraged me: Gary Rett shared my investigations into prisms with me; Ron Gaffe came to my aid with legal matters; Terry Musclow helped me understand how fluorescent color is perceived; Ginny Lagather edited my prism research papers. Rolf Anselm introduced me to Dr. Mary Cox of the University of Michigan at Flint, and Dr. Cox, a professor of physics, gave me the book *Seeing the Light: Optics in Nature, Photography, Color,* *Vision, and Holography,* by David Falk, Dieter Brill, and David Stork. To all these people who helped me so much, I offer my sincere thanks.

My watercolor class guided me also in my pursuit of an accurate color theory. They kept me from getting too scientific in my explanations, so that I realized what is and isn't important in writing a book on color for artists. Their input has been greatly appreciated.

I thank all the artists who have given me their encouragement. Space doesn't permit me to name them all, but I must name four special artists: Jane Chan was the one who got me started when she painted a rose in my class. Ron Smalley, M.D., supplied me with copies of medical research papers on vision. Larry Deitering and Bill Anderson gave me their reactions to my text, and Larry contributed his ideas on a transparent color wheel. Bill assisted me in testing paints from various manufacturers and helped me find a satisfying way to define cool and warm colors on the color wheel.

The paint companies Daniel Smith, Grumbacher, Da Vinci, and Holbein graciously sent me their watercolor paints for my tests. Special mention is due to Joe Miller and his great art supply company, Cheap Joe's, for keeping me fully provided with materials I needed.

I salute the people at Watson-Guptill, my publishers: Candace Raney believed in me; Marian Appellof organized the book; and Dale Ramsey did an excellent job of editing. Jay Anning, the designer, and Hector Campbell, the production manager, made the book look wonderful.

I suspect I've forgotten to mention some important people. To all I have acknowledged here and those I've forgotten to name, my hearty thanks.

Jim Ames, A.W.S.
Flint, Michigan
January 1996

CONTENTS

INTRODUCTION

This book is the result of my study of color over a seven-year period, during which I have worked as a commercial artist, as a fine artist, and as a teacher of a watercolor class at the Flint Institute of Arts in Michigan. It all began during one of my classes when a student was trying to paint a pink rose with a cadmium red. The result was that she was painting dull pink petals. When I teach, I always try to separate the commercial artist from the fine artist, but the commercial artist in me intervened in this instance and critiqued the painting by saying: "You won't be able to get that clean-looking pink for the petals because you don't have a magenta paint."

She asked: "What is magenta?"—to which I replied that it is a fuchsia, a pinkish red that is used in the printing industry. The following week she came to class with a tube of Winsor & Newton permanent magenta. This watercolor paint, unfortunately, was not the magenta that I knew. I promised the class I would do some research on color and get back to them.

As I followed through then and in the succeeding years, it amazed me how much confusion there is about color and how often contradictory statements are written and published. I learned that I had to make a fresh start.

Around this time my son Jim was at the University of California at Berkeley getting his PhD in biochemistry. I had begun my color research doing some reading about the physics of color, and my son and I had a friendly argument as to whether white light is triadic in nature or is a continuum. I thought the triadic theory made sense, and he favored the continuum theory. He suggested we settle the dispute with our own prism studies.

The prism led to a new way of considering color theory and to untold hours of prism experiments. I concluded that Isaac Newton, the great progenitor of our thinking on the subject, was mistaken when he assigned color to light—specifically the primary colors red, green, and blue. I now believe that color—all the color in nature—is best understood as phenomena in the brain in which cyan, magenta, and yellow are the primaries. Light is colorless energy to which our eyes react, sending signals to the brain that *subtract* proportions of cyan, magenta, and yellow from its perception of what we see.

My watercolor class has proved that the physics of color is something that artists generally do not understand or care about. So why bring this up in a book about color for artists? Because this cyan–magenta–yellow theory is the foundation for a fresh approach to mixing color. You don't have to understand it totally—and I have kept my explanations as simple as possible—but once you believe that all color is proportions of cyan, magenta, and yellow in your brain and that all matter, including paints, carries what I call a cyan–magenta–yellow coding, then the color wheel becomes an accurate tool, you learn the meaning of pure hues and shaded colors, and color mixing becomes easy to learn.

COLOR THEORY: FINDING A FRESH APPROACH

One

Color theory—our understanding of the nature of light and color—came into being as modern physical science developed around the seventeenth century. In this chapter we will examine the traditional concepts of color theory that originated with the great physicist Isaac Newton (1642–1727), and then we'll take a fresh look. We'll try to establish some universal concepts that improve upon the traditional approach. As you will see, the confusion that color theory causes artists begins with the identification of the primary colors and the concepts that attempt to explain how the other colors of the spectrum come into being and are perceived.

Having answered the fundamental questions about color theory, we will then begin to apply this fresh understanding to our work as artists. This will prepare us for lessons in color mixing and painting in the succeeding two chapters.

TRADITIONAL COLOR THEORY

The foundation for our present-day thinking about color was laid by Isaac Newton, who conducted some landmark experiments with prisms. Newton carefully observed the effects produced when a beam of sunlight passed through a glass prism. The prism divided the white light into the colors seen in the rainbow—that is, into the color spectrum. Before Newton's time, people thought that prisms embodied some sort of "latent" power to color the white light passing through it. Newton was able to show this assumption to be false by passing the light through a second prism, which reassembled the colored light into white light.

From these experiments, Newton concluded that light is the *source* of color. He also identified seven basic colors in the light spectrum: red, orange, yellow, green, cyan, indigo, and purple.

THE ADDITIVE SPECTRUM

The physicist Thomas Young (1773–1829) carried Newton's experiments further and discovered that, when mixed together, just three of the colors produce white light: red, green, and blue. Since Young's discovery, red, green, and blue have been considered the *primary colors* in what is called the *additive* spectrum. Also referred to as the solar spectrum and the rainbow spectrum, the additive spectrum is that of visible light, which consists of electromagnetic radiation of wavelengths ranging in length from 400 to 740 nanometers (nm). The shortest wavelength light rays, around 400 to 500, look purple to blue. The medium wavelengths, around 500 to 600nm, appear green to yellow. The long wavelengths, approximately 600nm to 740nm, we see as orange to red.

Why is this spectrum called *additive*? Because when added to each other, the three primaries of this spectrum give us transparent light (what we call white light).

Moreover, any two primaries, when added to each other, produce one of light's *secondary* colors. For example, the addition of green light to blue produces cyan; the addition of red light to blue produces magenta; and the addition of green light to red produces yellow. Thus the secondary colors of light are cyan (a greenish blue), magenta (a red-violet), and yellow.

Note that the additive concept in traditional color theory has to give way to another concept when we deal not with light but with pigments.

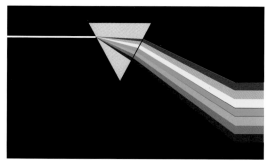

Isaac Newton's famous experiments with a prism brought him to conclude that there are seven basic colors of light.

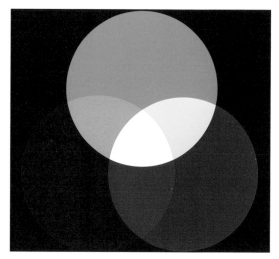

In the additive spectrum, the primaries are red, green, and blue.

THE SUBTRACTIVE SPECTRUM

Cyan, magenta, and yellow—the three secondary colors of the additive spectrum—become the primary colors of the *subtractive* spectrum (see illustration top right). According to this aspect of traditional theory, when light illuminates an object, colors are *subtracted* from the light rays because the object *absorbs* them. The colors that reach the eyes are those that are reflected, not absorbed, by the object.

When the primaries of the subtractive spectrum—cyan, magenta, and yellow—are blended, we get black. When we blend two of these primaries together we get red, green, or blue. Thus red, green, and blue (the same hues as the primary colors of the additive spectrum) are the secondary colors of the subtractive spectrum.

This is a theory that makes sense when we examine color pigments.

And yet there is a third spectrum that fine artists traditionally use—let's call it the artists' spectrum.

THE ARTISTS' SPECTRUM

Traditional color theory, on which most artists' color wheels are founded today, designates blue, red, and yellow as the primary hues. Moreover, there are many variations of blue, red, and yellow being propounded today as the primaries (see illustration bottom right). Exactly *why* these have long been the artists' primaries is hard to say at this point. Artists may have simply believed so since antiquity and never deeply considered an alternative.

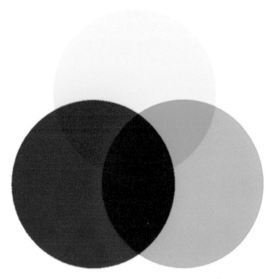

The subtractive spectrum is a useful concept when it comes to explaining the behavior of pigments in painting and color printing; it also applies to color filters used in photography. Because light is absorbed by an object, including a puddle of pigment-rich paint or a camera's filter, color is subtracted from the light.

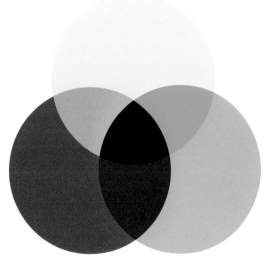

Numerous variations of blue, red, and yellow turn up on color wheels for artists. Here, the blue is actually cyan.

OTHER ASPECTS OF COLOR THEORY

Since Newton's day, discoveries and theories concerning other dimensions of color besides their relationships within the spectrum have emerged. Various systems for the application of the theories developed.

In 1866 the German scientist Hermann von Helmholtz (1821–1894) demonstrated that every color has three different qualities, or dimensions: hue, value, and intensity.

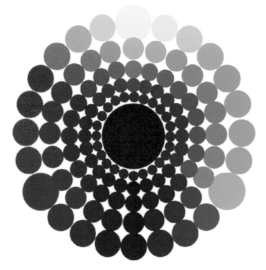

This color wheel shows twenty-four hues in the outermost color discs, plus their shades grading to black (center).

Hue

Hue is the quality that designates a color. Hue tells us that turquoise is the color it is—it is not yellow-green, or something else, and so on. Hue also denotes a color's position on the spectrum or on a color wheel. In this sense, there are technically millions of hues. In order to keep the understanding of color simple, we'll limit the number of hues in our upcoming discussions of the color wheel to twenty-four (or to twelve, for some wheels).

Value

Value is the lightness or darkness of a color. For an artist, value is a very important dimension because the use of color in composition is so closely tied to the artist's arrangement of darks and lights. Thus one must understand value when mixing colors.

The true color of an object, without reference to conditions that darken or lighten it, is called its *local color*. For instance, a barn is painted red, and on a sunny day it looks red. But on a rainy day, the same barn is a darker, muted color—not the same red. What is the local color of the barn? The answer is the color that you see when white light (like sunshine on a cloudless day at noon) illuminates the barn with no refracting of the rays. In other words, the local color is red, without reference to conditions that can darken or lighten it.

| YELLOW | YELLOW-GREEN | CYAN | TURQUOISE | GREEN | ORANGE | MAGENTA | BLUE | COOL RED | WARM RED | MAUVE-VIOLET | PURPLE |

A computer was used to convert these tomatoes of different colors into black-and-white ones. Notice that each color has its own tone value, with yellow the lightest and the purple the darkest—as the graded bar at the bottom shows.

Sometimes the case is made that the color you're seeing at a given moment is the only color the barn is. The real point in that argument is that an interpretive power lies at the disposal of artists; they have the ability to interpret color as they see fit—unless their intention has been to assign themselves the task of painting a rigidly accurate representation of the subject.

The darkening of a color produces a *shade*. Prussian blue, for instance, is a shade of blue; it is low in value. If you were to do a painting of the barn on a rainy day, you'd avoid its local color and, probably, use a shade of red— alizarin crimson, perhaps.

The lightening of a color produces a *tint*. Peach, for instance, is a tint of orange; it is high in value. If you were to paint a sunny highlight on the barn's door, you'd use a red tint—perhaps pink.

Intensity

Intensity refers to the brightness, or *saturation*, of a color. A brilliant yellow, a very vibrant red, and a strong, rich blue—these are said to be intense, or saturated. Duller versions of these hues are, of course, lacking in intensity. A color that is at 100 percent saturation is one that is as bright as possible.

Note that brightness does not refer to value. Colors can be bright yet quite different in value, as our illustration of the tomatoes shows. An intense yellow is light and therefore high in value, but an intense purple is dark and therefore low in value. Moreover, colors can be different in intensity yet the same in value (see illustration below).

Helmholtz didn't work out a practical system for applying his concepts in art, and we will deal more with applications of these concepts later, when we consider the mixing of colors. After Helmholtz, around the turn of the century, Albert H. Munsell (1858–1915), an American instructor in art, took things further. Munsell realized that everyone who wants to use color correctly must recognize and understand Helmholtz's observations. Using Helmholtz as a starting point, Munsell developed a complete system for the analysis and organization of color. His color theory, which he described with the aid of a calibrated "Color Tree" and a color-notation system, is used throughout the world, especially in industry. On his Color Tree, Munsell placed the most intense colors on the farthest reaches of the limbs. The darkest values were at the base of the tree; the lightest at the top.

Interestingly enough, though there are three primaries, Munsell identified ten basic colors— not a multiple of three. And two hues that artists rely upon, yellow-orange and pure violet, do not appear in Munsell's system. In the following pages, we'll look at color with a fresh perspective and, at the same time, try to avoid such problems.

Moving left to right, in these three balls only the intensity, not the value, has changed.

LOOKING AT COLOR THEORY ANEW

Traditional color theory says that the color is in the light. As we have seen, Isaac Newton propounded the idea that we see the color of—let us say—an orange because that fruit (assuming it is illuminated by sunlight at noon) reflects the light energy in the spectrum which we see as orange, while all other parts of the spectrum are absorbed. In other words, the orange absorbs 100 percent of the blue light and 50 percent of the green light. It reflects 100 percent of the red light and 50 percent of the green light. The percentages of red and green light together make orange.

My own studies of color, however, have convinced me that the red–green–blue additive theory derived from Newton's ideas and traditionally employed by artists is an inaccurate one that leads to countless difficulties in understanding color. Not the least of these difficulties is that we must wrestle with two sets of primaries: the red–green–blue of the additive

and the cyan–magenta–yellow of the subtractive spectrums.

Let's consider a fresh approach, then, that should make color theory easier for us to use as artists.

THE "CODE CARRIER" CONCEPT

A key component of an alternate color theory is that light is a colorless, triadic *code carrier*. Harold Kueppins, a highly respected German color theorist, has described this concept best.

Beginning with the idea that the universe is colorless—that is, nature consists of colorless matter and colorless energy—Kueppins has claimed that colors exist *only* as an observer's sensory perception. This means that the rays of light energy that stimulate the human retina are not colors but, rather, information transmitters (they could perhaps be compared to a

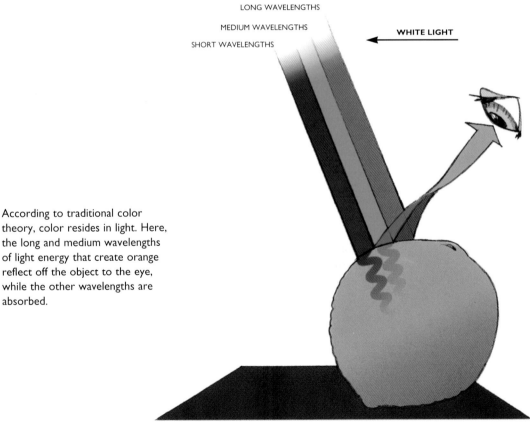

LONG WAVELENGTHS

MEDIUM WAVELENGTHS

SHORT WAVELENGTHS

WHITE LIGHT

According to traditional color theory, color resides in light. Here, the long and medium wavelengths of light energy that create orange reflect off the object to the eye, while the other wavelengths are absorbed.

magnetic tape). Light is the information carrier. Only after the "input" is received by the eye and converted according to the eye's pre-programming can there be interpreted information: our sensation of color.

Kueppins designates the basic colors as white, cyan, magenta, yellow, red, green, purple, and black. These colors, he believes, are the eight possibilities resulting from three primary colors: red, green, and purple. They represent the most extreme color sensations that our visual system can produce.

My own research with a prism disagrees with Kueppins's on the issue of his three primaries, red, green, and purple. Neither do I believe that matter is colorless. Also, I have concluded that Kueppins's eight basic colors (six hues plus black and white) should really be expanded to fourteen. I would add the following colors: turquoise, lime green, orange, cool red, mauve-violet, purple, and purple-blue.

A Universal Theory

As we're about to see, the human eye is "programmed" for a spectrum in which cyan, magenta, and yellow are the primary colors. In nature, cyan, magenta, and yellow produce all other colors, and in the use of pigments—those used in the art of printing and in painting—the same is true. It's really very simple: *An accurate color theory must reflect this universality of cyan, magenta, and yellow as primaries and serve to explain all color situations in nature and in art.*

Color resides in the brain with cyan, magenta, and yellow. Matter, far from being colorless, carries a cyan, magenta, and yellow code for the color it possesses. Light rays reflected off matter are the stimuli that trigger perceptions of the cyan, magenta, and yellow in our brains and allow us to recognize color. We'll examine these concepts more completely in the next few pages.

Black and white and the twelve colors shown between them are the basic ones produced by various combinations of the primaries cyan, magenta, and yellow.

BLACK

CYAN

TURQUOISE

GREEN

LIME GREEN

YELLOW

ORANGE

WARM RED

COOL RED

MAGENTA

MAUVE-VIOLET

PURPLE

PURPLE-BLUE

WHITE

COLOR CODES AND COLOR PERCEPTION

As I've implied, to attain a more accurate color theory, I believe we must depart from the traditional interpretation of the source of color. Color is not in the light, but in the cortex of the brain as a coding of percentages of cyan, magenta, and yellow. An electrical impulse is always turned on between the brain and the neural cells that are connected to photosensitive cells, or *receptors*, in the retina of the eye. The color receptors are cone-shaped cells and are commonly referred to as *cones*. (Besides the cones there are receptors called *rods* which are color-blind but extremely light-sensitive.) We see color when light, with its various proportions of electromagnetic energy, *interrupts* the electrical impulse by way of the cones. This can be explained in terms of *codes*.

We've seen that light contains three different wavelengths of energy that are intertwined in a continuous flow: 100 percent long, 100 percent medium, and 100 percent short rays. We can label light at this stage as **Code 1**.

Every object is coded with various percentages of cyan, magenta, and yellow. When light strikes an object, some wavelengths are absorbed by the object, and others are reflected. The object from which the light is reflected we'll call **Code 2**. Light's three wavelengths become separated by their interaction with the coded matter. That is, it is no longer continuous but is now in three separate and distinct states of long, medium, and short wavelengths. When light reaches the eye, it has been *encoded* as a result of its being reflected off the object. The reflected light, which is now different from the light that illuminated the object, we can label **Code 3**. Thus, Code 1 has interacted with Code 2, resulting in Code 3.

Traditional color theory calls the cones that respond to reflected long wavelengths the red cones; the cones that respond to medium wavelengths the green cones; and the cones that respond to the short rays the blue cones. But my theory is that the cones do not match up with the color source. I think they are best understood as collectors of the light's units of energy, as follows:

- The cone that responds to *long* wavelengths is the *cyan* cone.

LONG
MEDIUM
SHORT

CODE 1

Light contains different wavelengths of colorless energy.

CODE 2

A cyan, magenta, and yellow–coded object. Orange is coded 0 percent cyan + 50 percent magenta + 100 percent yellow.

CODE 3

Light encoded by its interaction with the object is reflected.

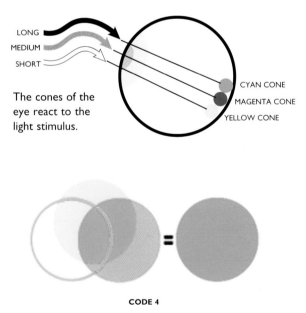

LONG
MEDIUM
SHORT

The cones of the eye react to the light stimulus.

CYAN CONE
MAGENTA CONE
YELLOW CONE

CODE 4

The brain is a decoder of the cyan, magenta, and yellow information (see page 19).

- The cone that responds to *medium* wavelengths is the *magenta* cone.

- The cone that responds to *short* wavelengths is the *yellow* cone.

To take our example of the orange: It is coded 0 percent cyan + 50 percent magenta + 100 percent yellow (see illustration, page 18).

Every orange when illuminated must absorb like amounts of the light energy and reflect the rest. For example, the orange's 50 percent magenta code means that the object will absorb 50 percent of the light's medium-length wave energy and reflect 50 percent of that same wave energy to the eyes.

The eye has millions of photoreceptor cells in the retina. The cyan, magenta, and yellow cones receive the encoded light once it is reflected from the orange. This light's 50 percent medium-wave energy, entering the eye, would turn off 50 percent of the electrical impulse traveling between the affected cones and the brain. This blocks 50 percent magenta and leaves 50 percent magenta still active as perceived color in the brain. There is no cyan coded in the orange, so a 100 percent long-wave reflection causes a turn-off of the brain's cyan.

The orange absorbs 100 percent of the short-wave energy in the illumination, so the eye receives none and the brain's perceived yellow remains at 100 percent. The brain's color center (**Code 4**) responds by saying, in effect: "You blocked off my cyan, and you cut my magenta in half, but I still experience 100 percent yellow, so the color I register is orange (0 percent cyan + 50 percent magenta + 100 percent yellow = orange)."

Color in the Brain

I recently read in a computer magazine an explanation of the way the subtractive spectrum works. According to the author of the article, magenta ink printed on white paper looks magenta because it absorbs all the colors except magenta. The light passes through the ink and reflects off the white paper to your eyes and they perceive magenta. Let's retrace our steps for a better explanation.

What happens is this: Magenta ink absorbs the 100 percent medium-wave light energy (green to yellow) and reflects the short and long (blue-purple and red). These short and long waves act not upon the magenta cones but upon the cyan and yellow cones in your eyes, blocking their signal to the brain. The brain now has cyan and yellow shut off while the magenta is still on. You see the color as magenta because the brain still has magenta active.

The brain is the key to understanding color. Code 3, the reflected light, is now encoded as a result of the magenta pigment's code. The eye's millions of cones collect Code 3, working in groups of three—that is, one cone in each group works in unison with the long, one with the medium, and one with the short wavelengths in Code 3.

A theory developed by some scientists says there is constant electrical energy between the cones and the brain. Actually, the electrical impulse is between the brain and the neural cells that receive information from the cones, and it is always turned on until light's energy affects the cones and blocks it.

The brain receives the coded information and interprets it; it is like a program for decoding. Thus the information the brain receives is the blocking or the flowing of an electrical signal.

The human brain is programmed to perceive black as long as electrical signals for all three of the primaries remain uninterrupted. That is, 100 percent cyan + 100 percent magenta + 100 percent yellow = black. It is because light's energy blocks—or subtracts—the electrical impulse to the brain that we see color.

White and Black

White light can be anywhere from very bright to very dim, at which point we begin to call it black. To understand this let's assign 100 units of energy to each of the three wavelength groups, short (S), medium (M), and long (L). Thus 300 units of light would be a bright white light (100S + 100M + 100L = 300 units of light.)

Let's assume that at 300 units, the white light would blind you; it's at a level we cannot tolerate. At around 240 units (80S + 80M + 80L = 240 units) is what we should consider the ideal light that gives us the true color of an object. As we approach 0 units, the whiteness turns to a neutral value, or a gray. At 0 we arrive at a pure black.

PERCEIVING RED, GREEN, AND BLUE

Traditional color theory holds that the primary colors in light are red, green, and blue. Here is the way I believe we perceive those colors—not as true primaries but as combinations of cyan, magenta, and yellow.

A reflection of 100 percent long-wave light energy looks **red** because it blocks the 100 percent cyan in the brain, leaving 100 percent magenta and 100 percent yellow to create the sensation of red.

LONG RAY
MEDIUM RAY
SHORT RAY

0% CYAN
100% MAGENTA
100% YELLOW

A reflection of 100 percent medium-wave light energy looks **green** because it blocks the 100 percent magenta in the brain, leaving 100 percent cyan and 100 percent yellow to create the sensation of green.

LONG RAY
MEDIUM RAY
SHORT RAY

100% CYAN
0% MAGENTA
100% YELLOW

A reflection of 100 percent short-wave light energy looks **blue** (really a blue-purple) because it blocks the 100 percent yellow in the brain, leaving 100 percent cyan and 100 percent magenta to create the perception of blue (blue-purple).

LONG RAY
MEDIUM RAY
SHORT RAY

100% CYAN
100% MAGENTA
0% YELLOW

PERCEIVING THE PRIMARIES CYAN, MAGENTA, AND YELLOW

Taking a more accurate approach, here is how
we perceive cyan, magenta, and yellow, the true
primaries found in nature:

A reflection of 100 percent short-
and 100 percent medium-wave
light energy looks **cyan** because it
blocks the 100 percent magenta
and yellow in the brain, leaving
100 percent cyan to create the
sensation of that color.

LONG RAY
MEDIUM RAY
SHORT RAY

100% CYAN
0% MAGENTA
0% YELLOW

LONG RAY
MEDIUM RAY
SHORT RAY

A reflection of 100 percent short- and
100 percent long-wave light energy
looks **magenta** because it blocks the
100 percent cyan and yellow in the
brain, leaving 100 percent magenta to
create the sensation of that color.

0% CYAN
100% MAGENTA
0% YELLOW

A reflection of 100 percent
medium- and 100 percent long-
wave light energy looks **yellow**
because it blocks the 100 percent
cyan and magenta in the brain,
leaving 100 percent yellow to
create the sensation of that color.

LONG RAY
MEDIUM RAY
SHORT RAY

0% CYAN
0% MAGENTA
100% YELLOW

PIGMENT COLORS

A color theory based on the primaries cyan, magenta, and yellow is nothing new. In fact, since modern-day color printing was developed, printers have used inks of cyan, magenta, and yellow, plus black, as their standard for printing all the other colors.

In color printing, these four primary colors are printed as minuscule dots in transparent ink. The dots are clustered next to and on top of one another, and the effect to the naked eye is of thoroughly blended colors. Indeed, this is the technique used in the printing of this book. Ironically, some art books will make the blanket assertion in discussions of pigments that the three primaries are red, yellow, and blue—yet these books are printed with the same cyan, magenta, and yellow (plus black) inks we've been talking about. Some art book authors call the true cyan, magenta, and yellow primaries "balanced primary colors" and then, once they've mentioned them, turn their emphasis to other primary schemes like red, yellow, and blue. This only confuses matters.

But though the printing-ink primaries are cyan, magenta, and yellow, the inks themselves are not perfectly true to nature. First of all, creating pigments that absolutely match our theory's true primaries is almost impossi-

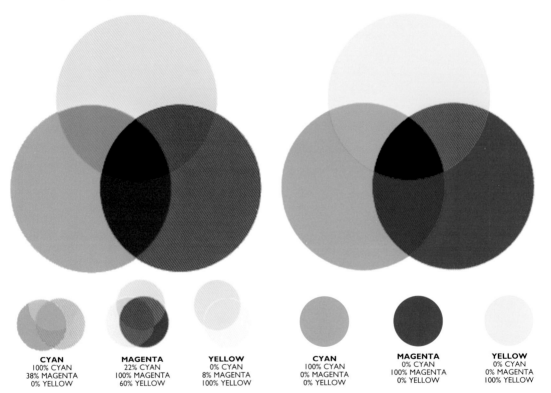

CYAN, MAGENTA, AND YELLOW PRINTING INKS

PURE CYAN, MAGENTA, AND YELLOW

CYAN	MAGENTA	YELLOW	CYAN	MAGENTA	YELLOW
100% CYAN	22% CYAN	0% CYAN	100% CYAN	0% CYAN	0% CYAN
38% MAGENTA	100% MAGENTA	8% MAGENTA	0% MAGENTA	100% MAGENTA	0% MAGENTA
0% YELLOW	60% YELLOW	100% YELLOW	0% YELLOW	0% YELLOW	100% YELLOW

In printing, the primary colors are cyan, magenta, and yellow. Yet printers' inks are slightly adjusted, or "de-purified." The large circles on the left represent the slightly adjusted printers' primaries, achieved through the slight mixtures shown at bottom. The large circles on the right as well as the small circles represent the more accurate inks for the three primaries.

ble. Yet pigments exist that come so close that a search for perfection would be pointless.

Secondly, the inks are slightly adjusted and thus are impure. There are several reasons for the adjustments, which have to do with the consistency, lightfast quality, flow, and other ink-technology issues. However, another reason is that printed pictures are supposed to mimic what we normally see, and they would have more of a fluorescent glow or neon effect if done with true cyan, magenta, and yellow inks—a lot like the inks being used in some felt-tip "neon" highlighting markers on the market today. The world we see everyday is, after all, mainly of colors that are a mix.

The illustration on page 22 shows the amount of "contamination" in each of the printers' primaries (left) and compares them to truer cyan, magenta, and yellow primaries (right).

What does this impurity mean? For one example, because the inks are adjusted, printers cannot print the brightest possible oranges: The 22 percent cyan in the magenta ink's makeup dulls the color slightly.

We can now begin to turn from theory to the artistic application of our understanding of color. Let's start with a consideration of the pigment-based colors that artists use as compared to the true cyan, magenta, and yellow primaries that are found in light.

ARTISTS' COLORS: SOME PRELIMINARIES

A number of artists select colors without including those which come close to the true primaries we have been discussing. For instance:

- Many artists do choose a cyan for their palettes, available in artist's colors such as Holbein peacock blue. But many others use Winsor blue, Prussian blue, or even an ultramarine—colors that include as much as 50 percent magenta and even some yellow in them.

- Many choose a cool red and not a true magenta, and the cool reds, like rose madder,

have various amounts of cyan and yellow in them. Nature's true magenta, of course, has no trace of these other primaries whatsoever. A magenta is available in artists' colors such as Holbein Opera or Winsor & Newton permanent rose. Using red instead of magenta has made it impossible for many artists' color wheels to make sense.

- The primary yellow that is found in nature is, as it happens, the same as the yellow referred to in traditional color theory. This color is available in artists' colors such as Grumbacher lemon yellow. Some artists lean toward a gamboge or cadmium yellow, which have a small percentage of magenta in them.

We'll be examining artists' colors in depth in Chapters 2 and 3. Right now we'll continue to explore some color basics and look at what belongs on an accurate artists' color wheel.

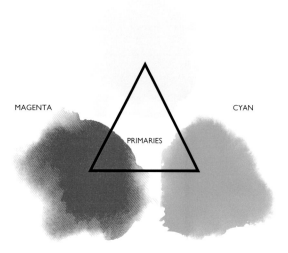

The key to applying color theory is that every color comes from various percentages of the three primaries cyan, magenta, and yellow—the starting point for the mixing of colors.

THE COLOR WHEEL

The artists' color wheel is a device that bridges theory and practice.

All color wheels start with the primaries cyan, magenta, and yellow. To create the other colors on the basis of these three you derive three more, then six more, and so on, up to twenty-four. (After twenty-four one is simply splitting hairs trying to define new colors).

Here are some fundamental concepts that will apply to the mixing of colors:

- The *primary colors* are so called because they cannot be made from any other color.

- *Secondary colors* are those formed by mixing equal parts of any two primaries, both at 100 percent saturation. There are three secondary colors: warm red, green, and purple.

- *Tertiary colors* are those formed by mixing one primary that is at 100 percent saturation and any other primary that is at 50 percent saturation. There are six tertiary colors: cool red, orange, lime green, turquoise, purple-blue, and mauve-violet.

- *Quaternary colors* are formed by mixing one

primary that is at 100 percent saturation with any other primary that is at either 25 percent or 75 percent saturation. There are twelve quaternary colors: cherry red, red, red-orange, orange-yellow, yellow-green, warm green, cool green, blue-green, blue, ultramarine blue, purple-mauve, and red-violet.

The closer together colors are in their location on the color wheel, the more related and harmonious they are, because each color contains some of the other color lying next (or *contiguous*) to it. By the same token, colors which are separated from each other are more distantly related.

The colors that are *directly* opposite each other across the wheel are known as *complements*. They produce black or gray when mixed together—in fact, quite interesting grays are made when you thin these mixtures with water (or add white).

As we've seen, in his theory Hermann von Helmholtz identified hue, value, and intensity as the dimensions of color. Color wheels help artists to explore these dimensions and to make decisions about mixing colors.

It's important to learn what primary, secondary, tertiary, and quaternary colors are. Constructing a color wheel, especially an elaborate one like this, is a useful learning exercise. Study the various proportions of the primaries in the colors on the wheel until you can recognize the makeup of a hue. For instance, warm red is a secondary pure hue that is 100% yellow and 100% magenta.

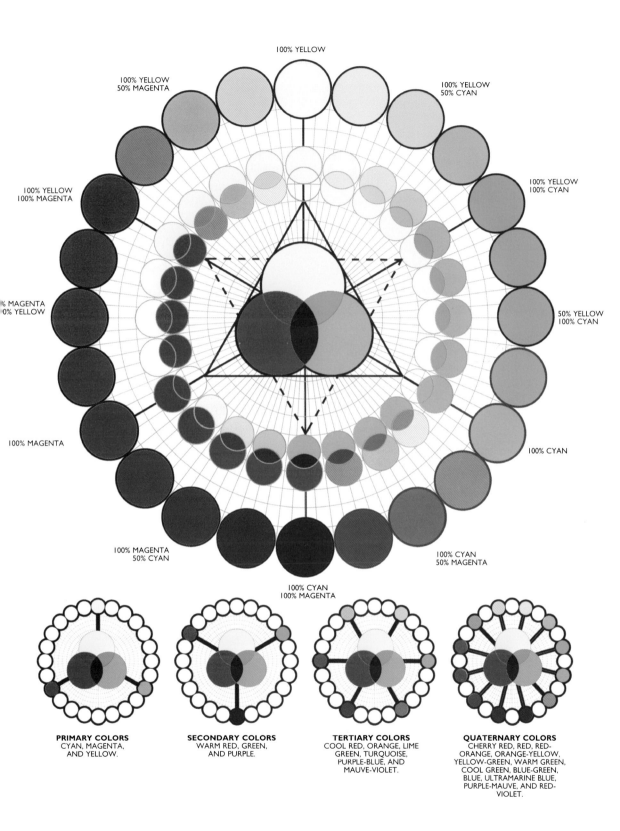

100% YELLOW

100% YELLOW
50% MAGENTA

100% YELLOW
50% CYAN

100% YELLOW
100% MAGENTA

100% YELLOW
100% CYAN

% MAGENTA
0% YELLOW

50% YELLOW
100% CYAN

100% MAGENTA

100% CYAN

100% MAGENTA
50% CYAN

100% CYAN
50% MAGENTA

100% CYAN
100% MAGENTA

PRIMARY COLORS
CYAN, MAGENTA,
AND YELLOW.

SECONDARY COLORS
WARM RED, GREEN,
AND PURPLE.

TERTIARY COLORS
COOL RED, ORANGE, LIME
GREEN, TURQUOISE,
PURPLE-BLUE, AND
MAUVE-VIOLET.

QUATERNARY COLORS
CHERRY RED, RED, RED-
ORANGE, ORANGE-YELLOW,
YELLOW-GREEN, WARM GREEN,
COOL GREEN, BLUE-GREEN,
BLUE, ULTRAMARINE BLUE,
PURPLE-MAUVE, AND RED-
VIOLET.

PURE HUES

The pure hues of the color wheel are the primaries cyan, magenta, and yellow and the colors that are created from two of the primaries. A pure hue does not have a third primary in its mixture. The pure hues are bright and said to be "clean-looking" colors.

A pure hue will always consist of at least one primary at 100 percent saturation. It can have a second primary in its mixture with a saturation from 0 to 100 percent. For instance, orange is approximately 50 percent magenta + 100 percent yellow (see illustration at bottom of page). Warm red is 100 percent yellow + 100 percent magenta.

Of course, you don't have to be a math whiz to learn color. Approximations are good enough. Orange is composed of a lot of yellow and some magenta. You need to know when you look at yellow-green that it has a lot of yellow and a little cyan. Purple-blue has 100 percent cyan and some magenta in its make-up.

The pure hues that are mixtures of two primaries can be grouped according to the three primaries: Group 1 comprises mixtures of magenta and yellow; Group 2 comprises mixtures of yellow and cyan; and Group 3 comprises mixtures of magenta and cyan, as this color wheel shows.

Besides the primaries, there are three groups of pure hues. Group 1 comprises mixtures of magenta + yellow; Group 2 comprises mixtures of yellow + cyan; and Group 3 comprises mixtures of magenta + cyan.

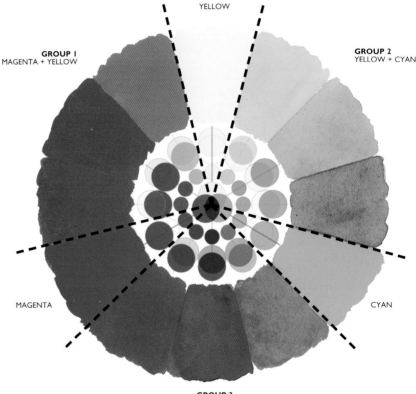

YELLOW

GROUP I
MAGENTA + YELLOW

GROUP 2
YELLOW + CYAN

MAGENTA

CYAN

GROUP 3
MAGENTA + CYAN

A pure hue is a primary or a color mixed from one primary at 100 percent saturation and another of 0 to 100 percent saturation. This orange is 50 percent magenta + 100 percent yellow.

SHADES

Shades are achieved by mixing three primaries together. A "shaded color" is a pure hue darkened by adding the primary or primaries that it does not already contain. At least one primary must be at 100 percent saturation, while the other two can vary in degree of saturation. For instance, the secondary color red is composed of 100 percent magenta plus 100 percent yellow. Add any percentage of the missing primary cyan and you get a shade of the color red.

Shades include, typically, all the browns, such as burnt sienna; olive green; and dark blues such as Prussian blue. Black should be ranked as a shade because it is actually composed of color; it consists of the three primaries cyan, magenta, and yellow, all at 100 percent saturation.

To mix a shade you can add a "missing" primary, as suggested above. Otherwise, another good formula for mixing a shade is as follows: Add a primary color that is not a component of the pure hue to that pure hue's cooler neighbor, or *contiguous* color, on the color wheel. This will be explained more fully in Chapter 3 (see page 77).

BLACK

Shades are produced by mixing three primaries— and the three primaries add up to black when they are all mixed at 100 percent saturation (center).

WARM RED

100% MAGENTA   100% YELLOW

WARM RED   100% CYAN

SHADED RED

If you understand what a pure hue is, then learning what a shade is will be easy. The mix that creates warm red, a pure hue, does not contain cyan, so adding cyan to it (right) gives you a shaded red.

TINTS

A tint is simply any pure hue, shaded hue, or black that has been lightened. You create a tint by adding water to watercolors to lighten them and by adding white to opaque mediums like oil.

Tints of the pure hues are considered *pastel* colors: pink, pale yellow, peach, light blue, aqua, lilac, and many more clean-looking, light colors. Peach, for instance, is a mixture consisting of a small percentage of magenta and a small percentage of yellow thinned with water or lightened with white. Pink is a small percentage of magenta and water or white.

Since a tint is simply a lightening of a color, a tint can be made of a shade as well as of a pure color. Tints of black, of course, give us grays.

Tints of pure hues yield the pastel colors, and tints of black produce grays.

GRAY

The peach shown here is a tint created from tints: a magenta of roughly 30 percent saturation and a yellow of about 40 percent saturation—a pink and a pale yellow.

MAGENTA TINT   ORANGE TINT   YELLOW TINT   ORANGE TINT   EARTH COLOR   CYAN TINT

A tint of a shade will always consist of all three primaries in various proportions that are well below a 100 percent saturation. Here, orange tint was created (left), then it was shaded with the "missing" tinted primary—cyan. An earth color is the result.

BASIC APPLICATIONS

Color mixing can be easy once you have grasped the foregoing basics of pure hues, shades, and tints. With the aid of the color wheel you should always be able to keep in mind the relations of your colors to the primaries cyan, magenta, and yellow. Let's briefly examine the concepts of hue, value, and intensity as you would apply them to your work. Then we'll consider one last quality of color, temperature.

Hues

To keep our wheel simple, I've limited the number of pure hues here to twenty-four. The color wheel below shows the twenty-four pure hues graded all the way to black, for a total of 121 hues (remember, we are counting black).

The aid this gives the artist in mixing color will by now have become obvious. A glance at the wheel informs you, for instance, that orange is a *pure* hue, and that burnt sienna is a *shade* of orange.

Value

Value is the lightness or darkness of a color. As we have learned, a color at its greatest intensity may be light or dark when placed on a scale of values. An artistic arrangement of darks and lights could therefore be accomplished entirely with intense, pure colors. But, of course, normally an artist would compose a picture with light- and dark-valued colors of varying intensities from bright to dull—pure hues and shades and tints as well as grays and tints of shades.

Darks and lights become more powerful elements in composition because they help us to define shapes more readily—as in the illustration of the cube opposite.

Intensity

Intensity, the degree of saturation of a color, ranks behind value in importance in a painting because the eye reads value differences more easily than those of intensity. For instance, a yellow and a magenta both of 100 percent saturation both look very bright, but because the yellow is lighter in value the eye may not detect the fact that both colors are equal in

intensity. A dull magenta next to an intense purple is lighter in value, but its lower intensity may not be easy to discern. Value differences interfere with the eye's judgment of intensity differences (see illustrations on page 30).

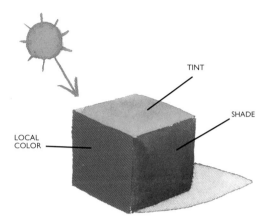

Artists define the form of an object by using lights and darks. On this cube a tint of its local color, red-orange, defines its highlighted side. Its shadowed side is rendered with a shade of the local color. This shade was produced by adding the primary color that is not a component of the red-orange—cyan—to a contiguous color of the red-orange—warm red.

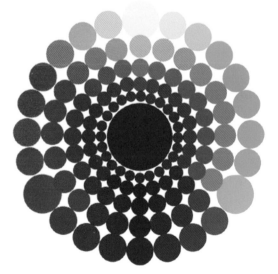

This color wheel shows twenty-four pure hues in the outermost circles, plus their shades graded all the way to black.

This composition is an arrangement of colors all used at full intensity. Note that the yellow draws the eye more powerfully than any other color because it is the lightest in value.

This composition attempts to arrange the colors according to intensity. The range is from bright to deeply shaded. The banana still dominates—but is it because of its bright yellow or lighter value? It's hard to tell.

Now the same composition is based on an arrangement of values. There are intense and shaded colors, but the balance achieved is due to the even distribution of lights and darks.

COLOR TEMPERATURE

Color temperature is a term that refers to the warmth or coolness of a color. The traditional artist's color wheel divides warm and cool colors by splitting the color wheel in half, as shown on page 31. The left half is considered warm in temperature; the right half is considered cool.

In seeking a more accurate theory we would differ from this. The warm-temperature hues are located in the top one-third of the color wheel, where every hue contains a 100 percent saturation of yellow. The bottom two-thirds are where the cool hues are located; these have a

100 percent saturation of either magenta or cyan.

The hues in the bottom two-thirds have either no yellow or a yellow saturation below 100 percent.

Every hue from the secondary warm red and the primary yellow to the secondary green is thus considered a warm hue.

We now have a color theory that is accurate and permits us to work with a set of primary colors that are basic to nature. In Chapter 2, we'll look at the colors we paint with and see how the pigments and the colors of nature correspond.

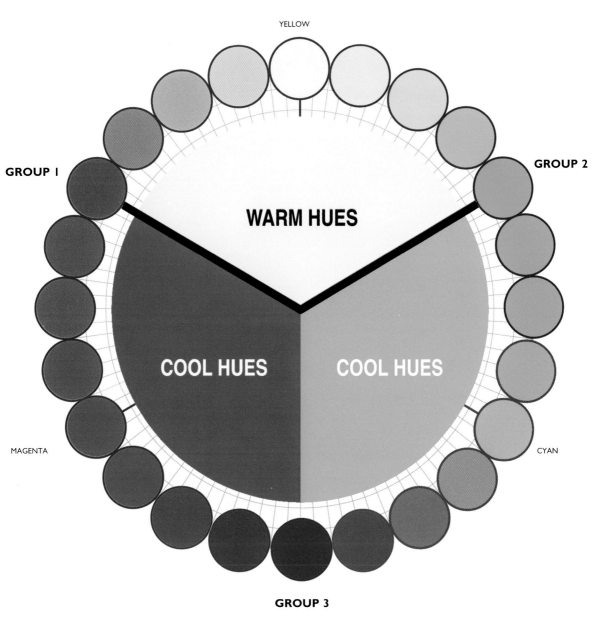

YELLOW

GROUP 2

GROUP 1

WARM HUES

COOL HUES

COOL HUES

MAGENTA

CYAN

GROUP 3

Traditionally, an artist's color wheel divides equally into warm and cool colors.

As the bottom two-thirds of this color wheel makes clear, every hue lacking a 100 percent yellow is cool in nature.

CHOOSING YOUR PAINTS

Looking for the best artists' colors among the many paints available can be confusing. This chapter will help you to understand paints in terms of a color wheel consisting of twenty-four colors. There are, of course, colors besides these; however, I will cover the supply of colors I have found on the market that are accurate in terms of the primaries cyan, magenta, and yellow.

The color wheel that we will use as our standard is based upon the true primaries in nature, not upon the pigments employed in the printing of this book or in the paints we'll be trying to match to the wheel. On the wheel are the following twenty-four colors:

- The primary colors: cyan, magenta, and yellow.

- The secondary colors: warm red, green, and purple.

- Five of the six tertiary colors: cool red, orange, lime green, turquoise, and mauve-violet.

- Five of the twelve quaternary colors: red, orange-yellow, cool green, blue, and ultramarine blue.

- Shades of cool red, orange, orange-yellow, yellow, lime green, green, blue, and mauve-violet.

COLORS AND PAINTS

In the following pages I discuss the twenty-four colors on the wheel (page 35), beginning with the three primaries and classifying the rest in three groups, each comprising a specific range of pure hues and some shades derived from them:

- Group 1: the reds and oranges (magenta + yellow)

- Group 2: the greens and turquoise (yellow + cyan)

- Group 3: the blues, purple, and mauve (magenta + cyan)

To write this book I experimented with colors of seven brands of paint to determine the amounts of saturation of cyan, magenta, and yellow the colors have. However, this doesn't mean that I have seen every last paint and studied them all. And let me make clear, too, that I am not a chemist for a paint manufacturer, and I don't consider myself a health expert when it comes to toxicity in paints. I'm an artist who seeks to show you how to recognize color using the true primaries cyan, magenta, and yellow as your guiding principle. To help you do this, I have created charts list-

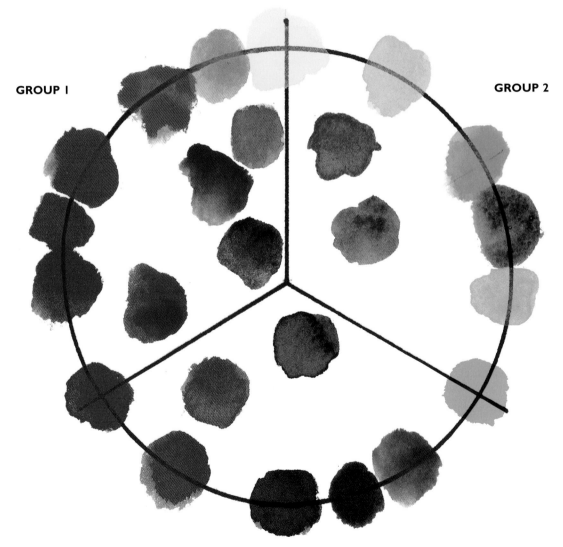

GROUP I

GROUP 2

GROUP 3

ing seven different brands of paint for twenty-three of the colors on our color wheel (pages 58–65). In the following pages I will discuss many of these paints. With these charts you can go beyond this text and select paints whose colors are close to those of the color wheel and therefore close to the true primaries and mixtures of them.

I include only twenty-three because I found no acceptable turquoise paints. Two manufacturers add to the confusion by calling their cyan hues turquoise. There are a number of other omissions in the charts, too, because acceptably accurate paints could not be found—or were not on the market at all. And finally, I did not study black—it is not needed on your palette.

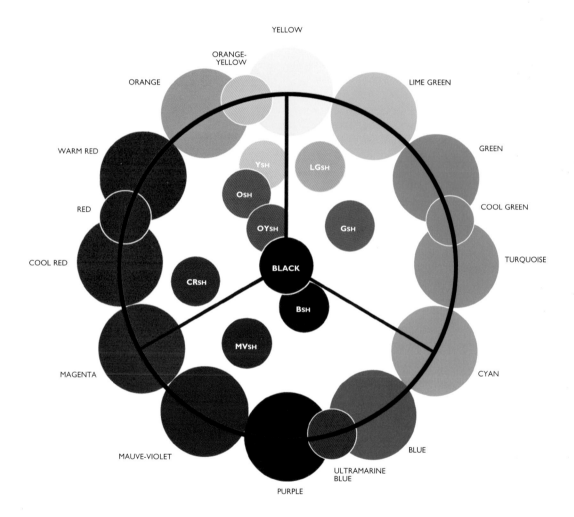

The twenty-four colors on the wheel at left, including the primaries cyan, magenta, and yellow, other pure hues, and a number of shades derived from them, are basic to watercolor painting. As we shall see, your palette need not contain paints for all of them.

The color wheel above shows the twenty-four colors in position. Black is added at the center. Shades are labeled with abbreviations of their names (sh = shade). The wheel at left shows the colors painted in patches of watercolor; the computer-generated wheel above shows the corresponding colors as combinations of cyan, magenta, and yellow—it represents the true colors of nature (albeit by way of today's color-printing process).

PAINT-QUALITY CONSIDERATIONS

Watercolor paints currently available on the market range in quality from excellent to not so good. For certain colors, often there is no difference in quality between brands. In other cases, a certain brand spreads better than another or is cleaner-looking, even though it was made with the same pigment as several other brands. Some student-grade paints are made with pigments that are identical to those used in their professional-grade counterparts, but to keep their price down they are formulated with a cheaper binder or perhaps fillers, which can affect the way they handle.

For example, Winsor & Newton makes both the professional-grade Winsor blue and the cheaper, student-grade W&N Cotman intense blue with the very same pigment. You cannot see any difference in quality when both are used fresh out of the tube. However, Winsor blue that has dried on the palette returns to its original intensity immediately when water is added to it, whereas the Cotman intense blue does not; it is workable, but it is not as vibrant as it was when fresh.

One characteristic of paint that the manufacturer's label will make reference to is *lightfastness*. This and several related terms are worth describing for future reference:

- Fugitive: A paint that after some period of exposure to light will fade significantly, change hue, or both, is often called *fugitive*. In some cases, fugitive colors totally disappear.

- Lightfast: Refers to a paint that is not affected by exposure to light.

- Permanent: Refers to a paint that is not affected by exposure to light and will maintain its hue and intensity, theoretically, forever. The term *durable* also refers to this attribute.

Permanence is a dubious assertion to make about anything, but the term is often used. Paints are assigned permanency ratings on a scale of 1 to 4, with 4 being excellent.

The American Society for Testing and Materials (ASTM), which has developed and promoted industry standards, devised lightfastness tests that most manufacturers subscribe to. It is the results of such test procedures that the lightfastness rating on the label of the paint is referring to. Even so, manufacturers can give puzzling information about lightfastness. For instance, Grumbacher's two alizarin crimson paints are both labeled "fugitive," whereas Winsor & Newton's alizarin crimson, which is made with the same pigment, is labeled "moderately durable."

Another quality issue to consider is that some paints can pose health risks if they aren't handled carefully. Most manufacturers list any health risks on the tubes' labels. I believe that if you read the full text of the health warnings you can quickly become paranoid. I have too little expertise to know ultimately whether a paint is safe for you to use. You should, as an artist who knows how you intend to use your paints, at the very least make yourself aware of the health factors.

For example, you may decide to exclude cerulean blue from your palette because it is regarded as a health hazard. The American Society for Testing and Materials has determined that cerulean blue is harmful to the user if it is absorbed by the skin or by inhalation. Artists are also cautioned against overheating this paint. If a paint poses a truly chronic health hazard, the law requires that it carry a health warning label. If you see an Art and Craft Materials Institute (ACMI) certification seal on the product label, then you can conclude that ASTM tests for safety have been applied to the paint.

COLOR ACCURACY AND SELECTION

To test the accuracy of colors, you can perform the following steps, as I did for my study of the paints discussed below: First, you would paint circular swatches of colors with clean, pure water on pure white paper. With these swatches illuminated by daylight or with a 50 Kelvin light—a standard that is used in the photographic and other industries as a perfect white light—you would then view each color through a prism. The color you'll see through the prism will either separate or will not according to its closeness to the true primaries.

In the illustration at right, for example, the circle on the left represents a true magenta: Holbein Opera. Next to it is a circle that represents a permanent rose, a common choice of artists. Both are depicted here as they would look through a prism. Note that on a north–south axis, cyan and yellow seem to emerge from the circle on the right but not from the one on the left. This is how the prism shows whether or not the color accurately matches the true primary magenta. When seen through a prism, the Holbein Opera shows no evidence that the other primaries are contained in it, while the permanent rose does. Thus the Opera is a more accurate magenta. Unfortunately, it is not sufficiently lightfast for artwork.

Having done the prism tests to determine which colors are most accurate in terms of the primaries cyan, magenta, and yellow, I would be wrong to say that there is only one correct palette. Artistic choices are personal choices. I do think the most important thing to remember is that all colors come from various proportions of cyan, magenta, and yellow. It is possible to paint with just these three colors, but

few artists do, and some paint with thirty or more. I have developed my approach to show you, the individual artist, a way to choose your own palette.

Yet there are still always some artists who will want to be told what paints to use on their palettes. Therefore, toward the end of this chapter I present my personal palette, a selection of sixteen paints that are lightfast and require no health warnings on their labels.

About Pigments

Pigments are organic and inorganic substances either found in nature or made synthetically, which, as microscopic ingredients of paints, give paints their color. The Society of Dyers and Colourists, a British organization, has developed a system of naming pigments that will help us in our understanding of their differences and in our palette choices.

On paint labels you will find a *Colour Index* name that includes a number—for example, PY42, which is an accepted designation for the pigment yellow ochre. This pigment may lend its name to a paint, as in the case of Holbein yellow ochre. But you'll often find that a paint made with the exact same pigment may be called something else, as in the case of Daniel Smith Mars yellow—it, too, is made with PY42. Thus one really gets one's bearings concerning pigments when considering them by their Colour Index names, rather than by the sometimes confusing names manufacturers assign to them. Though I will keep you posted in the succeeding pages on what many of these "proprietary" names are, we'll be dealing with the generic pigment names and Colour Index designations.

Here are Holbein Opera (left) and Winsor & Newton permanent rose (right) as they look viewed through a prism. The permanent rose misses being a true magenta by the amounts of cyan and yellow in it; these are made visible by the prism as colors emerging from the permanent rose. By comparison, Opera, with no other primary emerging from it, is a true magenta.

THE PRIMARY COLORS

Let's begin with the primaries, which are the most critical, for they should be as accurate as possible. The true cyan, magenta, and yellow built into our brain really glow. The inks and paints that are closest to nature's primaries are the so-called fluorescent ones. (Unfortunately, the primaries in this book are not printed with fluorescent inks; in this regard we are limited by the usual printer's restrictions.)

The three primaries in the illustration below are shown in relation to the color wheel. I painted in position the three paints I have picked for my personal palette as coming closest to each primary: Grumbacher Thalo blue, for cyan; Winsor & Newton permanent rose, for magenta; and Grumbacher lemon yellow, for yellow. Unlike the fluorescent colors, these are lightfast paints. The mixture of these paints shows how they combine to produce various colors.

Pure hues are shown here on the color wheel and with my paints. The color wheel shows the primaries cyan, magenta, and yellow. Below the wheel I have mixed other pure colors from the primaries.

YELLOW
GRUMBACHER LEMON YELLOW

MAGENTA
W&N PERMANENT ROSE

CYAN
GRUMBACHER THALO BLUE

GRUMBACHER LEMON YELLOW

GRUMBACHER THALO BLUE

W&N PERMANENT ROSE

CYAN

The cyan paints are unique in that they fall into two categories. One group is dark at full strength, while the other group is medium at full strength. The illustration shows that all of them make a vibrant light cyan (note the tints of 20 percent saturation).

In the dark group (A), Holbein peacock blue is the best match for cyan. But my favorite cyan choice is Grumbacher Thalo blue, made with the superior pigment. The pigments for the group A cyans are the phthalocyanine (*phthalo* for short) blues such as PB15 and PB17. They have slight chemical differences, but among them only PB15 carries no health warning. These pigments give color to paints that carry many different names, according to manufactur-er—for instance, Winsor & Newton's phthalo blue PB15 paints are called Winsor blue and W&N Cotman intense blue; Da Vinci's is phtha-lo blue, Grumbacher's is Thalo blue, and so on. The pigment PB15 yields a very intense blue that at full strength is dark, like Prussian blue (PB27), but unlike Prussian blue it is vivid and clean-looking when lightened.

As the illustration shows, a wash of Winsor blue is duller than Thalo blue, turquoise, or peacock blue. The greens derived from them are, not unexpectedly, duller too. Even so, Winsor blue is a great paint to have on your palette to make dark colors. If you use it, be sure you also have a cyan paint like any of the other paints recommended here.

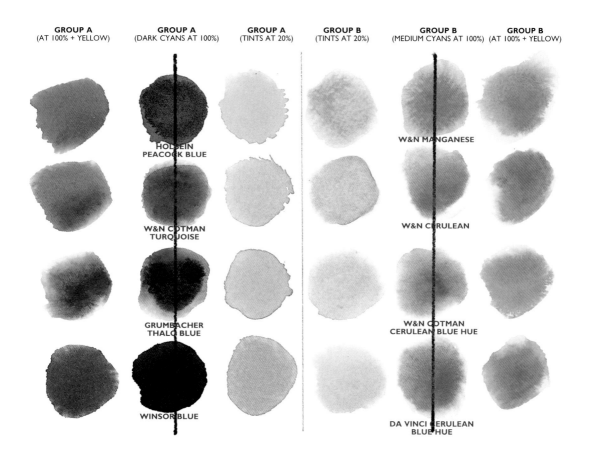

GROUP A (AT 100% + YELLOW)	GROUP A (DARK CYANS AT 100%)	GROUP A (TINTS AT 20%)	GROUP B (TINTS AT 20%)	GROUP B (MEDIUM CYANS AT 100%)	GROUP B (AT 100% + YELLOW)
	HOLBEIN PEACOCK BLUE			W&N MANGANESE	
	W&N COTMAN TURQUOISE			W&N CERULEAN	
	GRUMBACHER THALO BLUE			W&N COTMAN CERULEAN BLUE HUE	
	WINSOR BLUE			DA VINCI CERULEAN BLUE HUE	

These paints serve as full-strength and tinted cyan. As I also show (far left and far right) they are ideal in making pure dark greens and yellow-greens when mixed with yellow.

The illustration shows that W&N Cotman turquoise is nearly as close to cyan as Holbein peacock blue. Grumbacher Academy paints also offer a color called turquoise that is just like W&N Cotman turquoise. (Don't get confused by the name. These two paint colors really are cyan!) Both are good selections for an accurate cyan, and they handle equally well. I recommend you use either one of these two paints or one of the clean-looking, full-strength phthalo blues, which you will find on page 58. I picked Grumbacher Thalo blue, made with the safest phthalo blue, PB15, for my personal palette's cyan.

In the medium group (B), the cerulean blues have a base of PB15. The Da Vinci and Cotman colors look very similar to the Winsor & Newton cerulean blue and are called cerulean blue hue. (The word *hue* denotes that a paint is made not with the pigment suggested by the name but with one that imitates it.) The Da Vinci, which is lightened by adding titanium white, or the Cotman, which uses less of the pigment, are not as accurate for cyan as Winsor & Newton manganese blue, which uses full-strength PB35. They cannot make dark green or purples because their pigmentations are too low in their saturation of cyan.

The illustration shows that this group of paints is lighter at full strength than the darker group's, yet their tinted color is the same.

I used to think that cerulean blue (PB35) was a good choice for cyan, and many artists choose it. But as you can see it cannot make a deep rich green (purples are not satisfactory either). Cerulean's closeness to true cyan isn't as great as that of the other cyans available, such as PB15. It also carries a health warning.

As for manganese blue (PB33), it is an accurate cyan, but the paint is rather gummy and does not flow or cover very well. Some artists like to exploit the textures that result from this poor spreading ability.

MAGENTA

As noted, Holbein Opera is the most accurate we have for the primary magenta, and though it is insufficiently lightfast and excluded from my palette, I used it for the illustration below. I mixed great oranges and reds with Opera and varying proportions of yellow paint.

The best alternative to Opera—which is made of the magenta and violet pigments

| MAGENTA | COOL RED | RED | WARM RED | ORANGE | ORANGE-YELLOW | YELLOW |

Using watercolor, I mixed magenta (here, Holbein Opera) with yellow to obtain the red to yellow colors in this band. The varying proportions are marked by the trios of circles—note the absence of cyan (third circle) in any of these pure hues.

YELLOW MIXED ORANGE QUINACRIDONE VIOLET PV19

YELLOW MIXED ORANGE OPERA

CYAN MIXED MAUVE-VIOLET QUINACRIDONE VIOLET PV19

CYAN MIXED MAUVE-VIOLET OPERA

Compare two magentas as Holbein Opera and quinacridone violet PV19 are mixed to create orange (top two mixtures). Below, observe even more dramatically how the presence of yellow in the pigment PV19 results in a dull mauve-violet when it is mixed with cyan.

PR122 and PV10, respectively—is made with a pigment called quinacridone violet PV19. This pigment is not ideal, though, for the prism reveals that there is considerable yellow and cyan in its makeup. Still, PV19 is the best we have that is lightfast. It is the pigment used in the permanent rose paints made by Winsor & Newton and Da Vinci, in Grumbacher Thalo red, in Daniel Smith quinacridone rose, and other magenta paints. Despite the word "violet" in its name, it is quite reddish.

The illustration on page 41 demonstrates how the presence of cyan in PV19 results in a dull orange when it is mixed with yellow. Compare the results obtained with Opera in the same illustration.

All the tests I did with PV19 paints yielded the same results. They are all transparent, too. Winsor & Newton's permanent rose is the magenta most available to me, so I have chosen it for my personal palette.

Some artists use rose madder for magenta, but I have never seen a rose madder that I personally liked. Made of a natural red pigment NR9, rose madder is not true enough, evidencing even more cyan and yellow in prism tests than quinacridone violet. It also spreads poorly and has a gummy quality.

YELLOW

My prism studies show that the paints available for the primary yellow are the most accurate of the three primaries. Cadmium yellow lemon paints are very good, but they have a health warning label, so I eliminate them from my palette.

A good yellow pigment for thin, transparent watercolor washes is made with aureolin PY40. (Most brands will use the word "aureolin" as the name for their paint.) Used at full strength it has a small amount of cyan and magenta. If I were adding a second yellow to my palette (I'm not), I would pick this paint for a transparent yellow. However, the best yellow, which I do put on my palette, is arylide yellow light, made with the pigment PY3. All the PY3 arylide paints I tested were quite accurate—I saw no cyan in them as I viewed them through the prism, but they all had a trace of magenta. Because the magenta was so slight, these PY3 arylide paints could be considered a primary yellow. In watercolor, all are semi-transparent.

A common proprietary name for yellow made with this pigment is Hansa yellow. For my personal palette, I picked Grumbacher lemon yellow.

Prism tests revealed extremely small cyan and/or magenta levels in these lemony yellow watercolors.

W&N
CADMIUM LEMON

W&N
AUREOLIN

GRUMBACHER
LEMON YELLOW

REDS, ORANGES, AND THEIR SHADES

It's important that you begin to look at color as various proportions of cyan, magenta, and yellow. As you do, you will develop the ability to mix color through simple common sense.

As already pointed out, the color wheel divides into three groups. For Group 1, the reds and oranges and the shades of those colors, the paint manufacturers confront the artist with a wider choice of available products than for Groups 2 and 3.

Group 1 is unique in that its shaded colors—browns, ochres, and crimsons—appear radically different from the pure colors they are derived from. I have placed each color on the color wheel, right, relative to the primary, secondary, tertiary, and quaternary colors.

THE PURE HUES

Pure hues of this group are composed of either 100 percent magenta plus 0 to 100 percent yellow, or 100 percent yellow plus 0 to 100 percent magenta.

For instance, orange is a tertiary color: a 50 percent magenta plus 100 percent yellow and no cyan. Another way to think of this is two parts yellow and one part magenta. But all you really need to understand is that orange has a lot of the primary yellow, plus some of the primary magenta, and no cyan. You need not strive to make an exact interpretation of a color.

You can make orange from the magenta pri-

mary and the yellow primary, but the intensity of this orange isn't as great as using a prepared orange from a manufacturer because of the small amount of cyan in the permanent rose, our magenta. It is this cyan that dulls the orange.

Study the illustration at the bottom of the page to see how the Group 1 pure hues mix to make a range of oranges.

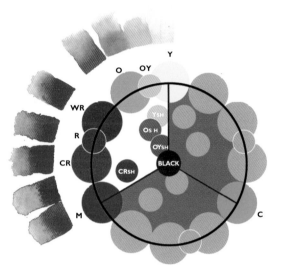

The pure hues of Group I are composed of various percentages of saturation of the two primary colors magenta and yellow.

Y	YELLOW
OY	ORANGE-YELLOW
O	ORANGE
WR	WARM RED
R	RED
CR	COOL RED
M	MAGENTA
C	CYAN
YSH	YELLOW SHADE
OYSH	ORANGE-YELLOW SHADE
OSH	ORANGE SHADE
CRSH	COOL RED SHADE

Magenta and the pure hues of Group I are mixed here with the primary yellow, making orange.

YELLOW — MAGENTA

YELLOW — COOL RED

YELLOW — RED

YELLOW — WARM RED

YELLOW — ORANGE

Cool Red is a tertiary color: Its saturation proportions for the primaries are a 100 percent magenta and a 50 percent yellow.

Manufacturers make numerous cool red paints using the pigment naphthol red PR112, which is rated moderate for lightfastness. These paints test out as quite accurate for true cool red.

Winsor red matches these cool reds with a naphthol pigment designated PR2 FRR. Daniel Smith offers three paints that qualify as accurate: their permanent red, made with naphthol red PR170; their perylene red, made with perylene maroon PR178; and their pyrrol scarlet, made with the pigment PR255. All these paints are identical in color and any one would make a good selection for your palette's cool red. Winsor red is my personal choice.

Red is a quaternary color: Its saturation proportions for the primaries are a 100 percent magenta and a 75 percent yellow.

I dropped red, best known in the form of cadmium red light, medium, and deep, from my personal palette because warm red and cool red gave me enough reds to work with. The cadmium reds are made with the cadmium-based pigment PR108, which is accompanied by a health warning label.

Warm Red is a secondary color: Its saturation proportions for the primaries are a 100 percent magenta and a 100 percent yellow.

Cadmium red lights, made by many manufacturers, are beautiful warm reds, but they carry the health warning and are not in my personal palette. Vermilion paints fall into the warm red category, but they are expensive and contain mercury, which is a toxic substance. There is a pigment called naphthol AS (PR188), which makes a warm red paint that Winsor & Newton puts out as scarlet lake and Daniel Smith as organic vermilion. Grumbacher vermilion deep hue is made with combinations of pigments.

Winsor & Newton bright red, which I have used for years as my personal choice, has naphthol red PR4 and arylide yellow PY1 in it.

Orange is a tertiary color: Its saturation proportions for the primaries are a 50 percent magenta plus a 100 percent yellow.

Cadmium oranges dominate this category with a beautiful orange. Unfortunately I can't use them because they, too, carry a health warning label.

W&N Cotman cadmium orange hue uses the substitute pigments arylide yellow PY1 and pyrazolone PO1. Daniel Smith permanent orange is made with a pigment called benzimidazolone orange H5G (PO62). Both the Cotman and Daniel Smith paints have a very true orange that is lightfast and presents no health hazards. Daniel Smith permanent orange is the one I use on my personal palette.

Orange-Yellow is a quaternary color: Its saturation proportions for the primaries are a 25 percent magenta plus a 100 percent yellow.

Once again the cadmiums dominate this category; they are great paints, but I don't use them because of the health warning.

Gamboge is a very good orange-yellow, but check the lightfastness; it varies from brand to brand because this color can come from so many different pigments. Daniel Smith Hansa yellow deep is made with arylide yellow RN (PY65); it is an accurate orange-yellow and the one I have chosen for my personal palette.

SHADED COLORS

The Group 1 shades—the crimsons and browns—are the pure reds and oranges with the addition of the "missing" primary, cyan.

From our study of the pure hues we know that the colors from lime green to the primary cyan to mauve-violet on the color wheel contain some percentage of cyan. Notice in the illustration on the bottom of page 45 that any of the seven colors in this range, from lime green to mauve-violet, can give us brown when blended into an orange.

Note also that by adjusting the percentages of red and yellow I have made virtually the same brown each time. That is, each brown ends up having roughly the same cyan, magenta, and yellow percentages in it. Each paint from lime green to mauve-violet, in addition to the cyan, has either some magenta and/or yellow in its makeup. Lime green has a lot of yellow in its makeup, so I reduced the yellow in the red–yellow mixture

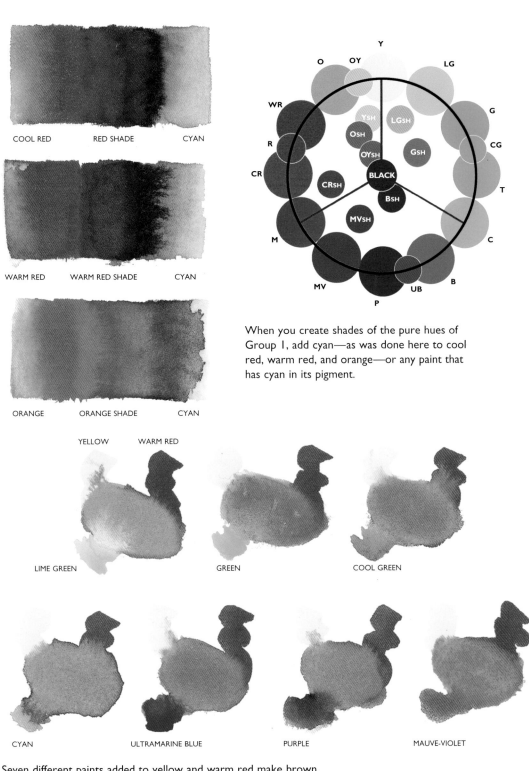

COOL RED   RED SHADE   CYAN

WARM RED   WARM RED SHADE   CYAN

ORANGE   ORANGE SHADE   CYAN

Y
O   OY   LG
WR   G
R   YSH   LGSH   CG
CR   OSH   GSH   T
OYSH   BLACK   C
CRSH   BSH
MVSH   B
M   UB
MV   P

When you create shades of the pure hues of Group 1, add cyan—as was done here to cool red, warm red, and orange—or any paint that has cyan in its pigment.

YELLOW   WARM RED

LIME GREEN   GREEN   COOL GREEN

CYAN   ULTRAMARINE BLUE   PURPLE   MAUVE-VIOLET

Seven different paints added to yellow and warm red make brown, because they add cyan to each. Remember, all three primaries together make black, so you are effectively darkening the color once the cyan blends with the magenta and yellow already there.

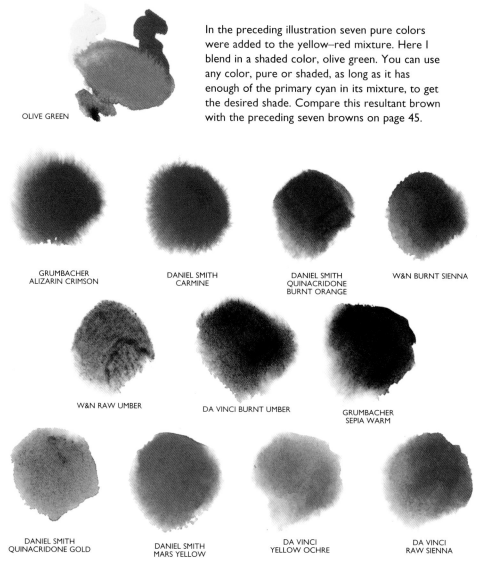

OLIVE GREEN

In the preceding illustration seven pure colors were added to the yellow–red mixture. Here I blend in a shaded color, olive green. You can use any color, pure or shaded, as long as it has enough of the primary cyan in its mixture, to get the desired shade. Compare this resultant brown with the preceding seven browns on page 45.

GRUMBACHER
ALIZARIN CRIMSON

DANIEL SMITH
CARMINE

DANIEL SMITH
QUINACRIDONE
BURNT ORANGE

W&N BURNT SIENNA

W&N RAW UMBER

DA VINCI BURNT UMBER

GRUMBACHER
SEPIA WARM

DANIEL SMITH
QUINACRIDONE GOLD

DANIEL SMITH
MARS YELLOW

DA VINCI
YELLOW OCHRE

DA VINCI
RAW SIENNA

A variety of red, orange, and yellow shades are widely obtainable as tube colors. They are made with the pigments of the pure hues of Group 1 plus black, and/or pigments ranging in color from lime green to blue to mauve-violet on the color wheel—a range that contains some percentage of cyan.

to which I added lime green. Mauve-violet has a lot of magenta in its makeup, therefore I cut back on the red in the red–yellow mixture to which I add mauve-violet. You may wish to repeat this exercise on your own as a color-mixing lesson. I will explain more about how to make beautiful browns in Chapter 3.

Let's take a brief look at the Group 1 shades individually.

There are many tube paints available for these shades, so I have only represented them by selections in the illustration above. A shaded paint does not have to be as accurate as a pure-hue paint, so I am not as particular in my recommendations of shades as I am with pure hues. You may want to learn the cyan, magenta, and yellow proportions for this group of shades and then go to pages 60–61, which will show you many paints that could be used.

Cool Red Shade is a 100 percent magenta, plus a yellow of about 70 percent and a cyan of about 40 percent.

The most popular cool red shade is made with the pigment alizarin crimson PR83. As already noted, some art books call this color primary red, but notice how much yellow it contains compared to magenta. Its darker quality signals that cyan is also present and a check with a prism bears this out. Winsor & Newton says that their alizarin crimson is lightfast, so I've made it my personal choice of a cool red shade. It is an important color to put on your palette, but since many manufacturers report that it can fade considerably, you may want to replace it with Daniel Smith carmine, made of a more lightfast pigment called benzimidazolone carmine HF3C (PR176).

Orange Shade is represented by burnt sienna and is a 100 percent yellow plus an 80 percent magenta and a 30 percent cyan. Made with the pigment brown iron oxide PBr7, burnt sienna dominates this shade category. You will sometimes see it referred to as Van Dyke brown.

I personally think this color should have a deep reddish yellow quality. Holbein, Winsor & Newton, and W&N Cotman fit this definition very well. I think the Daniel Smith, Grumbacher, and Grumbacher Academy versions are too dull and flat in color. Daniel Smith offers a very rich reddish brown color they call quinacridone burnt orange that is very close to burnt sienna; it is made with the pigment quinacridone PO48.

I've chosen Winsor & Newton burnt sienna for the orange shade in my personal palette. I like its richness and transparency.

Orange-Yellow Shade is a 100 percent yellow plus a roughly 55 percent magenta and a darkening 30 percent cyan.

This shade category is dominated by two dusky browns, raw umber and burnt umber, but also includes the sepias. Burnt umber, which is a derivative of raw umber, looks like a darker version of that shade. Winsor & Newton burnt umber has a redder cast than others' because of an added red iron oxide (PR101). Frankly, you don't need these shades in a tube color because you can make them so easily with other paints, but pick one of them if you want a prepared brown.

I consider Van Dyke brown a shade of orange-yellow. Most Van Dyke browns and sepias are made by mixing brown with black. These paints are nice to have, but check to make sure they are lightfast. Like all paints, they have personalities that appeal to different artists. This is why you should always be experimenting with new paints. I love to paint brown fields and couldn't get along without Winsor & Newton raw umber, whose yellowish brown doesn't look like the other available raw umbers. It has a broken-up texture when you paint a wash with it and it supplies a natural look like no other paint can do. Many artists would thus reject this paint, but its on my personal palette as the orange-yellow shade.

Yellow Shade is a 100 percent yellow plus a 35 percent magenta and about a 10 percent cyan. The most used color in this shade category is yellow ochre. There are three good yellow ochres:

- The most common is made with an iron oxide processed from a natural mineral. Look on the label for the pigment PY43 to get this natural yellow ochre, a semi-opaque paint.

- A good synthetic version of yellow ochre is Mars yellow, made of yellow oxide PY42, which tends to be more opaque.

- A third possibility here is raw sienna, made with the brown pigment PBr7, a natural iron oxide that has been calcined (roasted, essentially). Raw sienna is a little redder than the preceding yellow ochres.

I don't think there is a big difference between these three choices. This is probably why manufacturers substitute pigments freely in all three categories. A paint may be called yellow ochre but the pigment will be that of Mars yellow, and so on. My favorite is one of these in which the manufacturer has "switched" the pigments: Winsor & Newton raw sienna, made with the pigment yellow ochre PY43. It has a deep, rich yellow cast.

I would be remiss if I didn't tell you about Daniel Smith quinacridone gold, made with quinacridone orange PO49. This paint is a richer, deeper yellow ochre you just might want to have.

GREENS, TURQUOISE, AND SHADES OF GREEN

Group 2's pure hues are mixtures of yellow and cyan. Its shaded colors are the olive greens, derived from mixtures of the pure hues from lime green to turquoise on the color wheel and magenta in varying proportions. I have placed these colors on the color wheel below relative to the primary, secondary, tertiary, and quaternary colors.

THE PURE HUES

The pure hues in Group 2 are either 100 percent yellow plus 0 to 100 percent cyan, or 100 percent cyan plus 0 to 100 percent yellow. None of the paints introduced here has any magenta in it—it is the "missing" primary.

Study the cyan, magenta, and yellow makeup for these colors so you can recognize them at a glance.

The pure hues of Group 2 are available in paints that are based on the cool green phthalocyanine pigments PG7 and PG36, which contain the naturally green metal copper. These pigments are very strong; they will stain the fibers of the paper, canvas, or other surface to which they are applied. (You will find that some artists avoid these paints because the word "staining" sounds so negative; I think we should just think of them as strong pigments.)

Some artists are not fond of the acid-looking color of the phthalo greens. I believe they are some of the best pigments we have, and you'll see them in most of the pure-hue paints from lime green to turquoise. As for the acid-looking color, rarely do you use it without mixing it with other colors.

Phthalo green is sold under many different names, such as Winsor green, Grumbacher Thalo green, Holbein viridian hue, Daniel Smith phthalo green, and so on.

The pure hues of Group 2 are composed of various percentages of saturation of the two primary colors cyan and yellow.

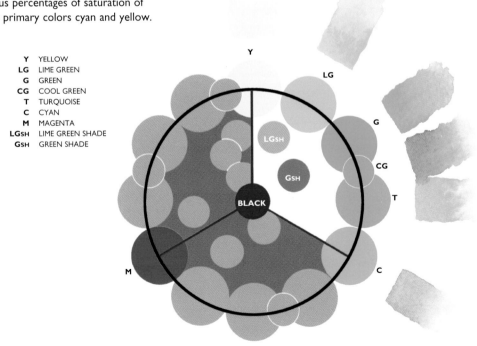

Y	YELLOW
LG	LIME GREEN
G	GREEN
CG	COOL GREEN
T	TURQUOISE
C	CYAN
M	MAGENTA
LGSH	LIME GREEN SHADE
GSH	GREEN SHADE

GRUMBACHER LEMON YELLOW   DANIEL SMITH PHTHALO GREEN   GRUMBACHER THALO BLUE

Here, I have made a range of greens and turquoises using cyan and yellow (top swatches) and using phthalo green PG7, cyan, and yellow. The varying proportions are indicated in the trios of circles; of course, no magenta (first circle) is used in the pure hues of this group.

Lime Green is a tertiary color: Its saturation proportions for the primaries are a 100 percent yellow and a 50 percent cyan.

Grumbacher is the only company offering this color; they call it Thalo yellow-green. It is made with phthalo green PG7 and a light arylide yellow (PY3). Of the colors we have considered so far, this is one I don't include in my personal palette; in my judgment, separate tubes of lime green and green are not needed

because they can be mixed so easily with a cool green (see the illustration above). Moreover, the premixed watercolor paints don't spread very well.

Green is a secondary color: Its saturation proportions for the primaries are a 100 percent cyan and a 100 percent yellow.

There are many greens made by all the manufacturers. They are all created from mixtures of phthalo green and arylide yellow. Again, greens are easily mixed, so I don't include any of the premixed paints in my personal palette. Of course, you should feel free to use them if you wish.

Cool Green is a quaternary color: Its saturation proportions for the primaries are a 100 percent cyan and a 75 percent yellow.

These, in my opinion, are the best greens. I flipped a coin and picked a Daniel Smith paint made with phthalo green (PG7) for my personal palette. In other words, you can take your pick among those cool greens made with phthalo green.

Another cool green is viridian, made with a pigment derived from chromium oxide (PG18). Sometimes called emerald green, it is, to me, a weaker, milder green than phthalo green, so I omit it from my selection.

Turquoise is a secondary color: Its saturation proportions for the primaries are a 100 percent cyan and a 50 percent yellow.

I include turquoise here, but do not list it in the chart on page 62. First, I could find only one paint for turquoise: Daniel Smith cobalt teal oxide. It is made with a pigment derived, obviously, from cobalt: PG50. Second, I don't even include this paint in my personal palette because I feel I can create as good a version by mixing phthalo green with my cyan, Grumbacher Thalo blue.

SHADED COLORS

The Group 2 shades—known best by their tube-color names sap green and Hooker's green (also olive green)—are the pure lime green and green hues with the addition of the "missing" primary, magenta. Shades of cool green and

In the three bands of color at right, lime green, green, and cool green have been mixed with magenta to produce shades. Opposite, in the large pool of color, Winsor & Newton burnt sienna and Daniel Smith permanent orange—also sources of the "missing" magenta—have been blended with Daniel Smith phthalo green and Grumbacher lemon yellow.

LIME GREEN   SHADE   MAGENTA

GREEN   SHADE   MAGENTA

COOL GREEN   SHADE   MAGENTA

turquoise are not particularly valued in the form of premixed tube colors; you would simply make shades of these yourself by adding the missing primary to them.

Actually, magenta or a color containing it can be the added color (see illustration below). For instance, burnt sienna and orange (from Group 1) have a lot of magenta in their pigment. The illustration shows that adding these two paints to a mixture of cool green and primary yellow gives us many of the shades for Group 2. To make shades we could use black also—any color that has enough magenta in it.

For the shaded paints in Group 2 there are many tube paints available.

Lime Green Shade is a 100 percent yellow and a 40 percent cyan, plus a darkening magenta of approximately 40 percent. This shade is available as sap green from most of the manufacturers (Grumbacher Academy calls it olive green hue).

Sap green is made with mixtures of pigments such as phthalo green PG7 and yellow iron oxide PY42. It is not needed on your palette, for it can be easily mixed, but use it if you want.

Green Shade is represented by Hooker's green, which is said to be named after the artist who first used it; it dominates this category among the tube colors. There was originally a pigment

DANIEL SMITH PHTHALO GREEN

GRUMBACHER LEMON YELLOW

W&N BURNT SIENNA

DANIEL SMITH PERMANENT ORANGE

that was special to Hooker's green, but it was not lightfast. Instead of relying on that pigment, present-day Hooker's greens are made with phthalo greens and arylide yellows and/or other pigments. These paints are very good to use, especially when mixed with burnt sienna for an even darker, richer quality.

Hooker's green light is a more yellowish shade, and Hooker's green dark is more bluish. I use Winsor & Newton Hooker's green dark for my personal palette. It is made with a combination of phthalo green PG7, a yellow pigment called tartrazine lake (Y23), and an "acid green" naphthol.

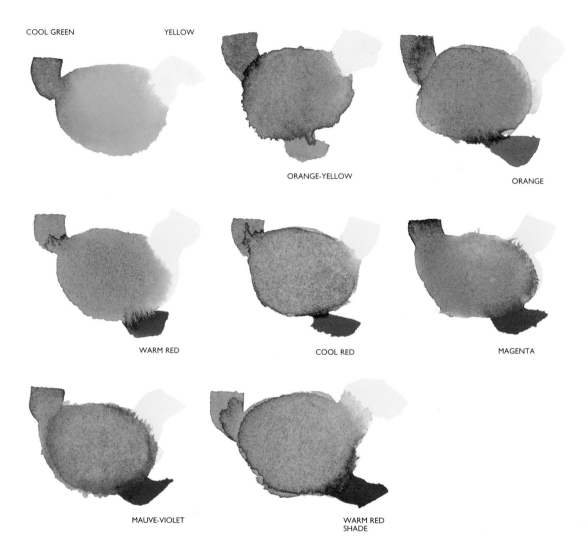

COOL GREEN   YELLOW

ORANGE-YELLOW   ORANGE

WARM RED   COOL RED   MAGENTA

MAUVE-VIOLET   WARM RED
                           SHADE

From our study of the pure hues we know that all colors from blue to mauve-violet to orange-yellow on the color wheel contain some percentage of magenta. Thus, adding any one of these hues to a mixture of phthalo green and yellow (top left) will give us a shaded green, because we're effectively adding only the magenta from each. These swatches show how this works with six different pure hues and, in the final example, with a shade of warm red. For an exercise you might try this: Experiment with juggling percentages (so that each shaded green has the same magenta, yellow, and cyan percentages) to obtain nearly the same shade each time.

BLUES, PURPLES, MAUVES, AND THEIR SHADES

Group 3 consists of the mixtures of cyan and magenta. Its shaded colors are those derived from mixtures of the pure hues from blue to mauve-violet on the color wheel and the "missing" primary, yellow, in varying proportions. I have placed these colors on the color wheel below relative to the primary, secondary, tertiary, and quaternary colors.

THE PURE HUES

The Group 3 pure colors are various percentages of saturation of the primary colors cyan and magenta. This means that they are either 100 percent magenta plus 0 to 100 percent cyan, or 100 percent cyan plus 0 to 100 percent magenta. None has the primary yellow in them. For example, purple, a secondary color, is 100 percent magenta and 100 percent cyan. Again, thinking of color in terms of cyan, magenta, and yellow proportions is the key to understanding how to mix colors.

Blue is a quaternary color: Its saturation proportions for the primaries are a 100 percent cyan and a 25 percent magenta.

Among artist's colors blue is best represented by paints made with the pigment cobalt blue PB28, traditionally the best of the lighter blues that are transparent. Unfortunately, cobalt blue is being viewed negatively nowadays because it carries a health warning; cobalt may pose some hazards. I therefore leave it off my personal palette.

Ultramarine Blue is a quaternary color: Its saturation proportions for the primaries are a 100 percent cyan and a 75 percent magenta. The paint is made with the pigment of the same name (also known as French ultramarine) PB29, and it is a good choice for your palette. Tests with a prism show no losers among the ultramarine blues available. I have picked Holbein ultramarine deep for my personal palette.

The pure hues of Group 3 are composed of various percentages of saturation of the two primary colors cyan and magenta.

Y YELLOW
C CYAN
B BLUE
UB ULTRAMARINE BLUE
P PURPLE
MV MAUVE-VIOLET
M MAGENTA
BSH BLUE SHADE
MVSH MAUVE-VIOLET SHADE

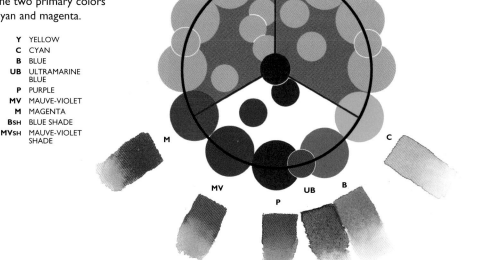

Purple is a secondary color: Its saturation proportions for the primaries are a 100 percent cyan and a 100 percent magenta. Made with a pigment called dioxazine purple RS (PV23), purple is directly opposite primary yellow on the color wheel and hence artists often exploit its usefulness as yellow's complement. I have chosen Holbein permanent violet for my personal palette.

Mauve-Violet is a tertiary color: Its saturation proportions for the primaries are a 50 percent cyan and a 100 percent magenta.

Two W&N Cotman paints, mauve and purple lake, are accurate mauve-violets and are the only paints I have found for this color. But they do have a drawback: They are both made with a blend of phthalo blue PB15 and a vivid magenta pigment, PV2, that is not lightfast. You may find mauves made with quinacridone, which is lightfast; however, these are properly considered mauve-violet shades, and we'll examine them in a moment. For my own palette, I mix mauve-violet using my cyan and magenta, as shown below.

Here are samples of the six pure hues of Group 3—the proportions of cyan and magenta indicated by the trios of circles (note the missing yellow in all cases). Below these I have blended Winsor & Newton permanent rose, my favorite magenta, with Grumbacher Thalo blue, my cyan, in the large pool of color and achieved these same hues. Observe, though, that the mauve-violets appear shaded or muddy-looking because of the presence of the primary yellow in the pigment of the permanent rose paint.

SHADED COLORS

The Group 3 shades are the pure blue to mauve-violet hues with the addition of the "missing" primary, yellow. If you wanted shades of ultramarine blue and purple, you would not look for premixed tube colors but would simply make shades of these yourself by adding black or yellow. As you probably know by now, a color containing yellow can also be the added color.

For instance, burnt sienna and lime green have a lot of yellow in their pigments. The illustration on page 56 shows that adding these two colors to a mixture of ultramarine blue and mauve-violet gives us shaded hues for Group 3.

But notice that Group 3 shades are different in nature from Group 1 and 2 shades—the browns and the olives. Shading blues and mauves doesn't yield different colors so much as dark or muddy-looking cousins. I have never wished to have any of these shaded colors on my personal palette.

I cannot even find a shaded purple among the paint companies surveyed in this book. If it were needed, you could mix a shaded purple, as shown below (second blended example).

Mixtures of ultramarine blue and black are additional shades of this group that you can obtain as Payne's gray and indigo—or you can duplicate them with your other paints. (We will deal also with mixing blacks and dark blues in Chapter 3.)

Blue Shade is a 100 percent cyan with about a 55 percent magenta and a 45 percent yellow.

Prussian blue, made with the pigment of the same name, PB27, is the only paint worth having for a premixed shaded blue. Still, it is unnecessary, in my judgment, because the pigments phthalo blue PB15 and PB17 are superior. Phthalo blue, you remember, is a paint you can select as a cyan: Lightened, it is true and vibrant for that use. But it is unusual in that it is as dark at full strength as Prussian blue. By contrast, Prussian blue is dull when lightened.

ULTRAMARINE BLUE   SHADE   YELLOW

PURPLE   SHADE   YELLOW

MAUVE-VIOLET   SHADE   YELLOW

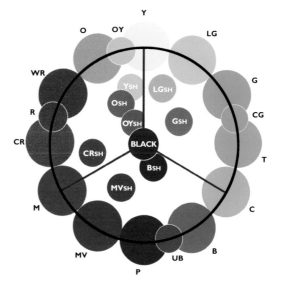

When you create shades of the pure hues of Group 3, add yellow, as was done here to ultramarine blue, purple, and mauve-violet.

Mauve-Violet Shade is 60 percent cyan, 100 percent magenta, and roughly 30 percent yellow. Two pigments used to make this color are quinacridone violet PV19 and thioindigoid red PR88 MRS (the MRS signifies a lightfast form of thioindigoid, which is otherwise unstable in light). Quinacridone violet PV19 is used in many brands, such as Winsor & Newton and Holbein permanent magenta and Daniel Smith quinacridone violet.

Thioindigoid red PR88 MRS is used in Grumbacher's Thio violet paint, which is dense and rich in color. The Da Vinci version adds to this the pigment PV19, a red-violet quinacridone.

I have picked the Winsor & Newton permanent magenta for my personal palette.

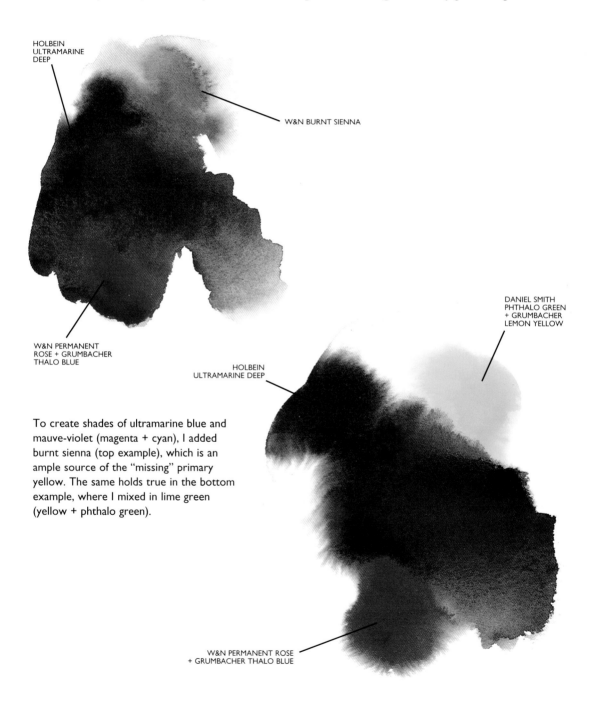

HOLBEIN
ULTRAMARINE
DEEP

W&N BURNT SIENNA

DANIEL SMITH
PHTHALO GREEN
+ GRUMBACHER
LEMON YELLOW

W&N PERMANENT
ROSE + GRUMBACHER
THALO BLUE

HOLBEIN
ULTRAMARINE DEEP

W&N PERMANENT ROSE
+ GRUMBACHER THALO BLUE

To create shades of ultramarine blue and mauve-violet (magenta + cyan), I added burnt sienna (top example), which is an ample source of the "missing" primary yellow. The same holds true in the bottom example, where I mixed in lime green (yellow + phthalo green).

MY PALETTE RECOMMENDATIONS

The paints I recommend here were chosen according to accuracy of color, lightfastness, and safety, as already detailed above. Despite all the restrictions, I think I have found a very good palette. Of course, I do allow myself to use other colors at times. Note again that I have not used all the colors that are available to me. I think it is better to mix certain colors, especially some of the greens—lime green, for instance. I have placed the colors in position on the color wheel; shown with it is a computer-generated wheel that shows which colors I use as packaged and which I prefer to mix myself (blank circles).

PRIMARIES
Cyan: Grumbacher Thalo blue
Magenta: Winsor & Newton permanent rose
Yellow: Grumbacher lemon yellow

GROUP 1 PURE HUES
Cool red: Winsor red
Warm red: Winsor & Newton bright red
Orange: Daniel Smith permanent orange
Orange-yellow: Daniel Smith Hansa yellow deep

GROUP 1 SHADES
Cool red shade: Winsor & Newton alizarin crimson
Orange shade: Winsor & Newton burnt sienna
Orange-yellow shade: Winsor & Newton raw umber
Yellow shade: Winsor & Newton raw sienna

GROUP 2 PURE HUES
Cool green: Daniel Smith phthalo green

GROUP 2 SHADES
Green shade: Winsor & Newton Hooker's green dark

GROUP 3 PURE HUES
Ultramarine blue: Holbein ultramarine deep
Purple: Holbein permanent violet

GROUP 3 SHADES
Mauve-violet shade: Winsor & Newton permanent magenta

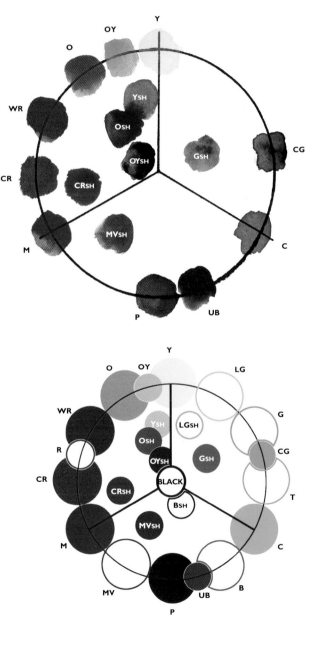

COMPARING PAINT BRANDS

The following charts list paints that I have studied with a prism and determined to be accurate in terms of the primaries cyan, magenta, and yellow. I focused my study on seven paint brands produced by five manufacturers: Winsor & Newton professional-grade Artists' Water Colours and student-grade Cotman Water Colours; Grumbacher professional-grade Finest series of watercolors and Academy student-grade series of watercolors; Holbein Artist's Water Color; Da Vinci Artist's Water Color; and Daniel Smith Extra Fine Watercolors.

I list those paints that appear equal in terms of the colors that end up on your paper. Again, I have not done any testing on the durability of paints; rating paints is not the function of this book. My technical information comes directly from the manufacturers. This type of informa-

PRIMARIES

COMPANY	CYAN	MAGENTA	YELLOW
Winsor & Newton	manganese blue PB33 • Yes • L cerulean blue PB35 • No • L Winsor blue PB15 • No • L	permanent rose PV19 • No • L	cadmium lemon PY37 • Yes • L aureolin PY40 • Yes • L
W&N Cotman	turquoise PB15/PG7 • No • L cerulean blue PB15 • No • L intense blue PB15 • No • L	permanent rose PV19 • No • L	lemon yellow hue PY3 • No • L cadmium yellow light PY37 • No • L
Grumbacher	cerulean blue PB35 • Yes • L Thalo blue PB15 • No • P	Thalo red PV19 • No • L	cadmium yellow lemon PY37 • No • L lemon yellow PY3 • No • L
Grumbacher Academy	turquoise PB15/PG7 • No • L Thalo blue PB15 • No • L	Thalo red PV19 • No • L	lemon yellow PY3 • No • L
Holbein	peacock blue PB17 • Yes • X cerulean blue PB35 • No • L	Opera PR122/PV10 • No • X permanent rose PR60 • No • L	cadmium yellow lemon PY37 • Yes • L permanent yellow lemon PY3/Y53 • No • L
Da Vinci	phthalo blue PB15 • No • L manganese blue PB33/B15 • No • L cerulean blue genuine PB36 • No • L	permanent rose PV19 • No • L red rose deep PV19 • No • L	Hansa yellow light PY3 • No • L
Daniel Smith	phthalo blue PB15.3 • No • L cerulean blue PB15 • No • L	quinacridone red PV19 • No • L quinacridone rose PV19 • No • L	Hansa yellow light PY3 • No • L cadmium yellow light PY35 • No • L

tion is helpful when making comparisons to consistently get accurate colors.

For each of the twenty-three colors already discussed, I list the various brands' paints. I also list the following for each paint:

- The manufacturer's color name (Hansa yellow light, Thalo blue, and so on).
- The *Colour Index* name.

- Yes or No as to whether the paint carries a health warning label.
- L for lightfast, or X for a problem with color durability.

If you are the type who likes to explore and stretch, some comparative study will be good for you. You'll decide on your own preferences for your personal palette.

GROUP 1:
COOL RED, RED, AND WARM RED

COMPANY	COOL RED	RED	WARM RED
Winsor & Newton	Winsor red PR2 • No • L	cadmium red PR108 • Yes • L cadmium red deep PR109 • Yes • L	bright red PR4 • No • L cadmium scarlet PR108 • Yes • L scarlet lake PR188 • No • L
W&N Cotman	cadmium red deep hue PR112 • No • L	cadmium red PR108 • Yes • L	cadmium red light PR108 • Yes • L cadmium red pale hue PR4 • No • L
Grumbacher	Grumbacher red PR112 • No • L	cadmium red deep PR108 • Yes • L cadmium red medium PR108 • Yes • L	vermilion deep hue PY3/R112 • No • L cadmium red medium PR108 • Yes • L cadmium red light PR108 • Yes • L
Grumbacher Academy	Grumbacher red PR112 • No • L	cadmium red deep hue R49:1/PY42 • No • X	cadmium red light hue PR112/Y1/O1 • No • X scarlet lake PR112/V19/O1 • No • X
Holbein	permanent red	cadmium red deep PR108 • Yes • L	cadmium red light PR108 • Yes • L
Da Vinci		cadmium red medium PR108 • Yes • L	cadmium red light PR108 • Yes • L vermilion (hue) PR188/O62 • No • L permanent red PR188 • No • L
Daniel Smith	perylene red PR178 • No • L pyrrole red PR254 • No • L permanent red PR170 • No • L	cadmium red deep PR108 • Yes • L	cadmium red scarlet PR108 • Yes • L pyrrole scarlet PR255 • No • L organic vermilion PR188 • No • L

GROUP 1:
ORANGE, ORANGE-YELLOW, AND YELLOW SHADE

COMPANY	ORANGE	ORANGE-YELLOW	YELLOW SHADE
Winsor & Newton	cadmium orange PO20 • Yes • L	cadmium yellow deep PY37/R108 • Yes • L cadmium yellow PY34 • Yes • L gamboge PY34 • No • L	raw sienna PY43 • No • L yellow ochre PY43 • No • L
W&N Cotman	cadmium orange PY37/R108 • Yes • L cadmium orange hue PY1/O13 • No • L	cadmium yellow PY37 • Yes • L cadmium yellow hue (azo) PY34 • Yes • L	raw sienna PY43 • No • L yellow ochre PY42 • No • L
Grumbacher	cadmium orange PO20/R108 • No • L	cadmium yellow PY37 • Yes • L	raw sienna PBr7 • No • L yellow ochre hue PBr7/Y42 • No • L
Grumbacher Academy	cadmium orange hue PO13/Y1 • No • L	cadmium yellow PY37 • Yes • L	raw sienna PBr7/Bk7 • No • L yellow ochre hue Y42 • No • L
Holbein	cadmium yellow orange PR108 • Yes • L	cadmium yellow deep PY37 • Yes • L	raw sienna PY43 • No • L yellow ochre Y42 • No • L
Da Vinci	cadmium orange PO20 • No • L benzinida orange PO62 • No • L	cadmium yellow deep PY37 • Yes • L	raw sienna PBr7 • No • L yellow ochre Y42 • No • L
Daniel Smith	permanent orange PO62 • No • L cadmium orange PO20 • No • L cadmium yellow pale hue PY1/PY3 • No • X	cadmium yellow PY37 • Yes • L Hansa yellow deep PY65 • No • L cadmium yellow deep PY37 • No	raw sienna PBr7 • No • L yellow ochre Y43 • No • L Mars yellow PY42 • No • L quinacridone gold PO49 • No • L

GROUP 1:
COOL RED SHADE, ORANGE SHADE, AND ORANGE-YELLOW SHADE

COMPANY	COOL RED SHADE	ORANGE SHADE	ORANGE-YELLOW SHADE
Winsor & Newton	**alizarin crimson** PR83 • No • L **alizarin carmine** PR83 • No • L	**burnt sienna** PBr7 • No • L	**burnt umber** PBr7 • No • L **raw umber** PBr7 • No • L **sepia** PBr7 • No • L
W&N Cotman	**alizarin crimson** PR83 • No • L	**burnt sienna** PBr7 • No • L	**burnt umber** PBr7 • No • L **raw umber** PBr7 • No • L **sepia** PBr7/PBk6 • No • L
Grumbacher	**alizarin crimson** PR83 • No • X	**burnt sienna** PBr7 • No • L	**burnt umber** PBr7 • No • L **raw umber** PBr7 • No • L **sepia warm** PBr7 • No • L **sepia natural** PBr7 • No • L
Grumbacher Academy	**alizarin crimson** PR83 • No • X	**burnt sienna** PBr7 • No • L	**burnt umber** PBr7 • No • L **raw umber** PBr7 • No • L **sepia hue** PBr7 • No • L
Holbein	**rose madder** PR83 • No • L **carmine** PR83 • No • L	**burnt sienna** PBr7 • No • L	**burnt umber** PBr7 • No • L **raw umber hue** PBr7 • No • L **sepia** PBr7/PBk • No • L
Da Vinci	**rose madder quinacridone** PV19/PB8 • No • L	**burnt sienna** PBr7 • No • L	**burnt umber** PBr7 • No • L **sepia** PBr7 • No • L
Daniel Smith	**carmine** PR176 • No • L **alizarin crimson** PR83 • No • X	**burnt sienna** PBr7 • No • L **quinacridone burnt orange** PBr7 • No • L	**burnt umber** PBr7 • No • L **raw umber** PBr7 • No • L **sepia** PBr7/PBk9 • No • L

GROUP 2:
LIME GREEN, GREEN, AND COOL GREEN

COMPANY	LIME GREEN	GREEN	COOL GREEN
Winsor & Newton		**Winsor emerald** PG7/PY1/PY3/PW4 • No • L	**Winsor green** PG7 • No • L **viridian** PG18 • No • L
W&N Cotman		**emerald** PG7/PY3 • No • L	**intense green** PG7 • No • L **viridian hue** PG7/PY1 • No • L **viridian** PG18 • No • L
Grumbacher	**Thalo yellow green** PG7/Y3 • No • L	**emerald green** PG7/PY3 • No • L	**Thalo green (BS)** PG7 • No • L
Grumbacher Academy	**Thalo yellow green** PG7/Y3 • No • L	**emerald green** PG7/PY3 • No • L	**Thalo green (BS)** PG7 • No • L
Holbein	**cadmium green pale** PY37/G18 • Yes • L **permanent green #1** PG7/Y53/Y1 • No • L	**emerald green** PY3/PG7/PW6 • No • L **cadmium green deep** PY37/PG18/PG7 • Yes • L	**viridian hue** PG7 • No • L
Da Vinci			**viridian green** PG18 • Yes • L
Daniel Smith		**permanent green** PY37/PG7 • No • L **permanent green light** PY3/PG7 • No • L	**phthalo green (BS)** PG7 • No • L **phthalo green (YS)** PG36 • No • L

GROUP 2:
LIME GREEN SHADE AND GREEN SHADE

COMPANY	LIME GREEN SHADE	GREEN SHADE
Winsor & Newton	sap green PG1/PY100 • No • L	Hooker's green dark PG1/PY100/PG7 • No • L Hooker's green light PG1/PY100 • No • L
W&N Cotman	sap green PG8/PY1 • No • L	Hooker's green dark PG1/PY100/PG7 • No • L Hooker's green light PG1/PY100 • No • L
Grumbacher	sap green PG7/PO48 • No • L	Hooker's green deep hue PB15/PY1/PBk6 • No • X Hooker's green light hue PB15/PY1/PO1 • No • X
Grumbacher Academy	olive green hue PG10/PBr7/PG7 • No • L	Hooker's green deep hue PG8/PY1/PO1 • No • X Hooker's green light hue PG8/PY1/PO1 • No • X
Holbein	sap green PG36/PY17/G8 • No • L	Hooker's green PY83/PG36 • No • L
Da Vinci		sap green PG7/PY42 • No • L
Daniel Smith	green gold PG8/PY1 • No • L sap green PG8/PY1 • No • L	

GROUP 3:
BLUE, ULTRAMARINE BLUE, AND BLUE SHADE

COMPANY	BLUE	ULTRAMARINE BLUE	BLUE SHADE
Winsor & Newton	cobalt blue PB28 • Yes • L	French ultramarine blue PB29 • No • L	Prussian blue PB27 • No • L
W&N Cotman	cobalt blue PB28 • Yes • L cobalt blue hue PB29/PW5 • No • L	ultramarine blue PB29 • No • L	Prussian blue PB27 • No • L
Grumbacher	cobalt blue PB28 • Yes • L	ultramarine blue PB29 • No • L	Prussian blue PB27 • No • L
Grumbacher Academy	cobalt blue PB29 • No • L	ultramarine blue PB29 • No • L	Prussian blue PB27 • No • L
Holbein	cobalt blue PB28 • Yes • L	ultramarine blue light PB29 • No • L ultramarine blue deep PB29 • No • L	Prussian blue PB27 • No • L
Da Vinci	cobalt blue PB28 • Yes • L	ultramarine blue PB29 • No • L	Prussian blue PB27 • No • L
Daniel Smith	cobalt blue PB28 • Yes • L	ultramarine blue PB29 • No • L French ultramarine blue PB29 • No • L	Prussian blue PB27 • No • L

GROUP 3:
PURPLE, MAUVE-VIOLET, AND MAUVE-VIOLET SHADE

COMPANY	PURPLE	MAUVE-VIOLET	MAUVE-VIOLET SHADE
Winsor & Newton	**Winsor violet** PV5/PB19 • No • L **mauve** PV1/PV10/PV14/PB15 • No • X		**permanent magenta** PV19 • No • L
W&N Cotman	**dioxazine violet** PV23 • No • L	**mauve** PB15/PV2 • No • X **purple lake** PB15/PV2 • No • X	
Grumbacher	**Thalo purple** PV23 RS/PV15 • No • X		**Thio violet** PR88 • No • L
Grumbacher Academy	**violet Thalo purple** PV23rs/PY42 • No • X **mauve** PV23rs • Yes • L		**Thio violet** PR88 • No • L
Holbein	**permanent violet** PV23 • No • L **mauve** PB29/PV19 • No • L		**permanent magenta** PV19 • No • L
Da Vinci	**permanent magenta** PV19/PB29 • No • L		**thioindigo violet** PR88/PV19 • No • L
Daniel Smith			**quinacridone violet** PV19 • No • L

PRACTICAL APPLICATIONS

In this chapter our lessons move from selecting and mixing colors to developing techniques for painting. A knowledge of the three primaries cyan, magenta, and yellow will be guiding you. The way to make color theory truly easy is to incorporate this knowledge into your work intuitively.

We'll see how to create pleasing passages of naturally muted color, nuanced grays, and rich darks. Then, employing a range of values from very dark to very light, we'll make color a tool at our disposal in building compositions. Modeling forms with lights and darks, we'll focus on mixing shades to create shadows. And finally, we will put our lessons on color to work as we create several complete pictures, including a landscape and several portraits.

USING COMPLEMENTARY COLORS

Almost every color we observe in the natural world from day to day is a shade. This means it consists of all three primaries at various percentages of saturation. If every color were pure, then we would see the world looking like a candy shop. The only pure hues we normally see are the colors of objects such as flowers and plastic toys, or colors we see on TV sets and neon signs. But mainly the world is muted—even grayish.

Every artist must therefore learn to mix a wide variety of shades. You will rarely find the occasion to use pure-hue paints straight from the tube in your paintings.

Shaded colors can be made four ways:

- By mixing the "missing" primary into a pure hue.

- By mixing pure-hue complements together and thinning with water.

- By mixing a pure hue with a paint that is premixed to a shade.

- By mixing a pure hue with a small amount of black and thinning with water.

Also, of course, you can use paints that are premixed to a shade, such as Prussian blue or burnt sienna, in and of themselves. I recommend that you experiment with all these methods and use whichever is best for you at any given time.

It's important that you have hands-on experience with shades so you can create pleasing passages of naturally muted color and nuanced grays. Let's begin with grays and black.

MIXING GRAYS AND BLACK

On the color wheel as we have constructed it of twenty-four colors (plus black), every pure hue plus its *complement* results in equal proportions

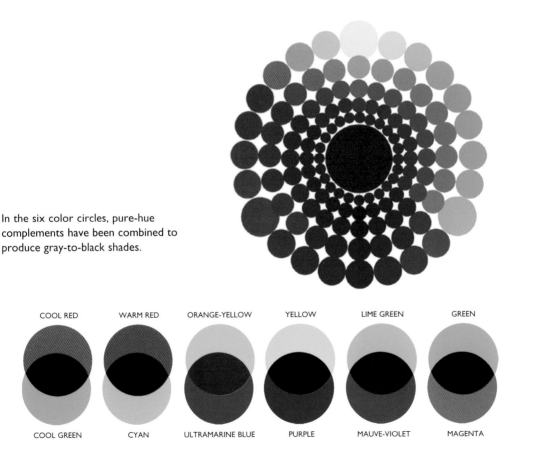

In the six color circles, pure-hue complements have been combined to produce gray-to-black shades.

COOL RED	WARM RED	ORANGE-YELLOW	YELLOW	LIME GREEN	GREEN
COOL GREEN	CYAN	ULTRAMARINE BLUE	PURPLE	MAUVE-VIOLET	MAGENTA

of cyan, magenta, and yellow. (A color's complement, you should remember, is one that is directly across the color wheel from that color.) A mixture of complementary pure hues at 100 percent saturation equals black. In other words, because of the equal proportions of the primaries cyan, magenta, and yellow, you will get black when you mix equal amounts of complements at full strength. Thin them with water and you get beautiful grays, as illustrated below.

| COOL RED | WARM RED | ORANGE-YELLOW | YELLOW | LIME GREEN | GREEN |

| COOL GREEN | CYAN | ULTRAMARINE BLUE | PURPLE | MAUVE-VIOLET | MAGENTA |

GRAY TINTS

Here, as in the preceding six color circles, complementary pure hues have been combined to produce blacks and grays. The gray tints reveal the color-rich grays you can achieve by mixing them.

Here, complementary pure hues create beautiful mixtures that will lend color richness to passages of gray in your work.

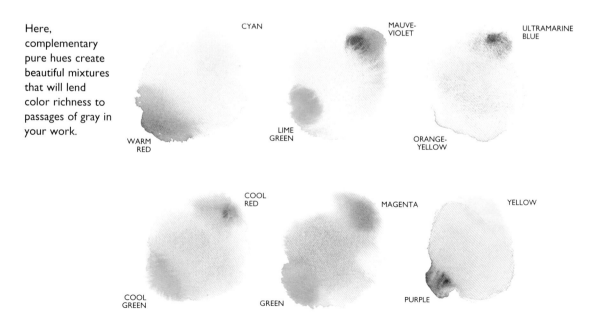

USING THE PRIMARIES FOR GRAYS

As I intend to show, your work achieves more character when you mix your grays by using the three primaries instead of complements or black paint. This is because the amounts of cyan, magenta, and yellow can be shifted and manipulated, giving you nuances of warm and cool that bring gray areas alive. I believe this mimics how we see color everyday. When you create gray areas by using any two complements you can create nuanced shifts in color only between the two hues you've used. For instance, a gray made from warm red and its complement cyan can only show reddish gray and bluish gray nuances.

Of course, a tube of black paint commonly has equal amounts of cyan, magenta, and yellow. There may be slightly more yellow if the black lightens to a warm gray, as ivory black does; or there may be more cyan if it lightens to a cool gray. But either way, the proportions of cyan, magenta, and yellow are locked into the pigment. Therefore, you get only uniform grays when you lighten black paint with water or white paint. This method yields a boring gray that lacks nuance and character.

Study the five painted subjects that follow: A man wearing a white shirt, a snow scene with storm clouds, trees in a foggy snowscape, a pewter teapot against a white background, and a white flower against a white background. For all of these, my cyan is Grumbacher Thalo blue, my magenta is Winsor & Newton permanent rose, and my yellow is Grumbacher lemon yellow. I painted the white and gray passages in these pictures with a wash of the three primaries and I allowed the hues to separate or diverge from the grays for nuanced effects. This is what I mean about moving color within color, giving your work more character even when muted colors predominate.

W&N PERMANENT ROSE

GRUMBACHER
THALO BLUE

GRUMBACHER
LEMON YELLOW

In this demonstration the dull "white" shirt on the left was painted with a thin wash of gray made from black paint. The shirt on the left, by contrast, was done with the three primaries. There you can see a movement of magenta and cyan, particularly, within the grays, making the right-hand example the livelier painting.

GRUMBACHER THALO BLUE

W&N PERMANENT ROSE

GRUMBACHER LEMON YELLOW

Both these snowy scenes are dominantly white and gray, yet I executed them with cyan, magenta, and yellow. My palette (center) consisted of Grumbacher Thalo blue, Winsor & Newton permanent rose, and Grumbacher lemon yellow. Notice that I allowed the three primaries to separate from my grays. Color nuances enrich the white and gray passages in each scene.

This teapot and white flower call for a technique for rendering "whites." Again, my palette is strictly Grumbacher Thalo blue, Winsor & Newton permanent rose, and Grumbacher lemon yellow. Observe that these primaries have been used to create grays and whites in which there is color movement. Though subtle, the movement is from cool cyan-tinged whites to warmer magenta tints and yellowish shades.

W&N PERMANENT ROSE

GRUMBACHER LEMON YELLOW

GRUMBACHER THALO BLUE

PAINTING "WHITES"

The best method I know for painting areas of white and shades of white involves the use of the three primaries, because they allow me the freedom of adjusting my colors from cyan to yellow—warm to cool—more easily.

In painting whites and off-white areas, use thin washes of the three primaries, allowing a light and very transparent gray to separate into passages of cool and warm colors. Look at the demonstrations on pages 70–72 and see how the "whites"—these very transparent washes of gray—come alive using this technique. Try this out for yourself and let the three primaries diverge from gray, creating hints of pink, violet, blue, yellow, and so on, throughout the painting.

Notice in the "white shirt" demonstration (page 70) the dull and listless shirt painted with a thin wash of gray made from a prepared black, as compared to the shirt painted with the three primaries. The movement of color that I was able to create in the shaded areas is a technique that Impressionist artists, such as Claude Monet, mastered. Using this technique will give your paintings vitality.

ATMOSPHERIC PERSPECTIVE

Temperature is a color trait that gives us advancing and receding color. Warm, brilliant reds, oranges, and yellows appear nearer to us than cool blues, greens, and violets seen from the same distance. Similarly, a pure hue will advance, whereas a muted, or grayed-down, color will recede.

You can give your pictures depth by exploiting this aspect of color in what is called *atmospheric perspective*. The principle is simple: Take the intensity out of any pure hue in those areas where you want an illusion of depth or distance. Grayed-down colors—shades—and lightened colors—tints—give the impression of distance because the atmosphere has a normally muting effect upon color, as do conditions such as haze, smog, and fog.

Colors look more distant the more shaded and lighter they are. This is called "atmospheric perspective" because the earth's atmosphere has a normally graying effect upon color. Here, the most intense color is burnt sienna, a shade of orange; it is used full strength in the foreground soil and thus appears close to the viewer. The distant mountains are grayer, lighter colors—tints of a cool green shade and of a mauve-violet shade.

MIXING SHADES FOR ATMOSPHERIC PERSPECTIVE

The four illustrations that follow show the same scene painted with four different palettes. To achieve an illusion of depth using atmospheric perspective I have employed shaded, grayish colors in the most distant areas of the scenes. Note, also, that the distant colors are cooler and/or lighter. For each, the palette is just three paints.

A problem beginning artists have is using too many colors in a painting—they feel they need to use all their paints. If you study the great masters you'll be surprised how few colors they used in a painting—exploiting a green, for example, using olive and grayish greens so that you see a predominantly green painting as full of variations in intensity and value.

Here the palette used is predominantly cool green and its complement, cool red, which warms the greens and contributes browns. I also added some orange-yellow. Notice the depth you can create by mixing complements. This grays down your colors to shades that will create atmospheric perspective. The small blocks of color are true shades because all three primaries are in them.

DANIEL SMITH
PHTHALO GREEN

WINSOR RED

DANIEL SMITH
HANSA YELLOW
DEEP

GRUMBACHER
LEMON YELLOW

HOLBEIN
PERMANENT
VIOLET

DANIEL SMITH
PERMANENT
ORANGE

My palette here uses the same cool green as before, but I chose an orange shade, burnt sienna, in place of the complement, cool red, to demonstrate that you can use shades to lower intensities for atmospheric perspective. Purple adds to the graying-down of the colors for this scene. As the small blocks of color show, I have progressively lightened my muted mixtures to create the illusion of depth.

DANIEL SMITH
PHTHALO GREEN

W&N BURNT
SIENNA

HOLBEIN
PERMANENT VIOLET

Here I use the complement of primary yellow, purple, to gray down the color to give atmospheric depth to the picture. A little orange adds interest to the muted colors I have mixed (small blocks of color). Observe that in the distance the colors are not only grayer and lighter but cooler as well.

The same technique has been applied now with cyan and its complement, warm red, plus a little cool green. Note that my emphasis here has been upon lowering intensities by lightening the dominant cyan shade, rather than by further graying it, as I move into the picture's distant areas.

W&N BRIGHT RED

GRUMBACHER
THALO BLUE

DANIEL SMITH
PHTHALO GREEN

A FORMULA FOR RICH DARKS AND BLACK

For years I've taught students to make black by mixing dark blue and dark brown. This was always a frustrating formula because the blacks always dried lighter than when applied, so you had to go over them again. Then one of my students showed me Christopher Schink's book *Mastering Color and Design in Watercolor,* in which full-strength phthalo blue (PB15) and phthalo green (PG7) were mixed with alizarin crimson (PR83), a cool red shade, to make black. So if you add Grumbacher Thalo blue and Winsor green to Grumbacher alizarin crimson, the result is that each of the three primaries is present in concentrated form. This makes for a very intense black that remains dark when it dries. (Thank you, Mr. Schink!)

You get rich transparent browns when you add burnt sienna to this formula. Use it as a base for rich, dark greens, blues, and reds. Study the examples shown below and try mixing your own dark colors and black.

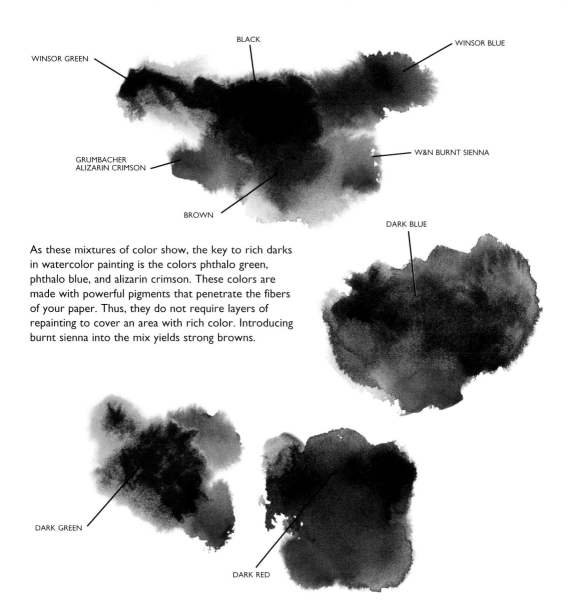

As these mixtures of color show, the key to rich darks in watercolor painting is the colors phthalo green, phthalo blue, and alizarin crimson. These colors are made with powerful pigments that penetrate the fibers of your paper. Thus, they do not require layers of repainting to cover an area with rich color. Introducing burnt sienna into the mix yields strong browns.

COLOR RELATIVITY

Whenever you use a color in a painting, it will be affected by the colors around it. There is a color-theory "rule" that is based upon an optical illusion: Because of our perception, a body of color will appear to throw its opposite value and its complement into the body of color next to it.

It is important that you understand this rule as an artist. Look at the illustration below. The top row shows six circles all of 30 percent gray. They are surrounded (left to right) by white, by 20 percent, 40 percent, 60 percent, and 80 percent grays, and by a black background. The black background, being utterly dark, throws its opposite value, which is white, into the 30-percent gray circle. This makes that circle look lighter than the one that is surrounded by a white background. By the same token, the white background throws its negative value, darkness, into the 30-percent gray circle, making it look darker than the one surrounded by black. Clearly then, our perception makes the appearance of the circle change relative to its background. Notice that the effects are similar in the illustrations below in which the circle is yellow.

In hue, intensity, and value, colors are relative to one another. This is one reason you shouldn't do a painting in sections. Painting is actually a process of making adjustments of hue, intensity, and value as you develop and arrange the colors and patterns of the picture. When you work back and forth throughout the composition, nothing gets "locked in" before all the elements are balanced.

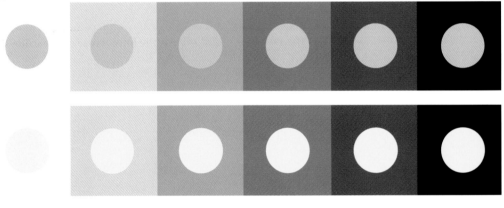

Because the primary-yellow circles are light in value—about the same in value as the 30-percent gray circles—the effect is similar when they are seen relative to their backgrounds: Though they are uniform, the gray circles appear to lighten as the background darkens, and the yellow circles appear to brighten.

Similarly, the cool green circles are both the same hue. The purple surrounding the left one throws its complement, yellow, into the green, which lightens and warms the green. The sap green background throws its purplish complement into the cool green, so that it looks even cooler. Lighter than the cool green, the sap green also throws a darker value into the circle.

WORKING WITH VALUE

As we've just seen, value is relative. Yet value remains the most important dimension of color. Mistakes in choice of hue are far less serious than those concerning value. Time after time the artist uses color well, only to have the painting fail because of an unsuccessful handling of a *range* of lights and darks.

All color has value, so to handle color effectively you must be able to recognize value differences in your subject.

The best way to work out value arrangements for a painting is to do thumbnail sketches in black and white (you can use black or any dark shade paint such as Payne's gray or sepia). The key is to simplify the areas in your painting, reducing them to basic light and dark shapes. You can squint at your subject to blur the details and see its overall arrangement of values.

Once you have mastered the ability to see value differences, you can become creative by adjusting the value of an area to make your painting more dynamic. Try to keep the range of values wide. A good range is: black, dark, medium, light, and white. Remember in com-

posing a picture that light values draw the eye more than dark values do.

I suggest that you do several thumbnail sketches to find the perfect combination of values for a picture. These sketches should take you no longer than a few minutes each. One problem artists have is "tightening up" and losing a rhythmic flow as they paint. This is because they do not want to make a mistake and mechanically try to manage every move in the painting. The sketches provide you a way to overcome this fear; failure isn't a problem because you know they are not the final product.

Once you have found the best black-and-white value scheme for your painting, you can redo it in color. Use simple colors that match the values you created in your sketches. Do not get involved in detail at this stage.

Admittedly, some artists have to skip the value sketches for fear of losing interest by the time they reach the final painting. But this does not diminish the importance of the value sketch. These artists have to visualize the values, holding them in their mind as they do the final painting.

The sketches in the top row show how flat a painting looks when you don't employ a wide range of values. In the sepia-and-white value sketches, my light-to-dark range is indicated by the small blocks. The value sketch in the bottom row shows how a wide value range gives the sketch greater depth. (Notice that I also changed the composition slightly to increase interest.) The final color version has some life to it.

VARYING VALUE AND INTENSITY

Intensity, as we saw in the first chapter, is the amount of brightness or saturation a color has. For variety, it is usually best to surround an intense color with shaded or tinted colors, keeping in mind that their values should fit the scheme you devised in your black-and-white sketch.

Artists often try to put two different colors of the same value and intensity next to each other. They do not realize the importance of varying the two colors. Look again at the samples on page 79, which show the weakness resulting from a lack of knowledge of value and intensity. You wouldn't paint a black-and-white picture of a 30-percent gray barn against a 30-percent gray horizon under a 30-percent gray sky, for the eyes don't distinguish the unvaried values easily. But working in color, making the barn red is not enough. If the red is the same value as the green of the trees and blue of the sky, the viewer will subconsciously reject the painting.

The same applies to the intensity of the colors. Look now at the sketch of the barn against a green horizon and a blue sky (below, left). It's a lot like the one composed of 30 percent grays

just described—the eye does not take pleasure in it. The picture's intensities of color must be varied. Some must be dulled by being used as shades or tints, and others can be employed as pleasing spots of brilliancy amid more muted colors. Such bright spots will draw the eye, just as light-valued passages do. A bright *and* light-valued area is the most powerful attention-getter you will have at your disposal, but only if it is part of a varied scheme. In terms of composition, these should become important factors in the arrangement of colors in your work.

These decisions are what make a painting personal to you. At first you may be a little shaky, but with time you will grasp these concepts and grow as an artist.

COLOR PROPORTION

You also need to consider color proportion in a composition. In the illustrations at the bottom of the page, the painting of the barn on the left is displeasing because the sizes of the color shapes are too equal and they are all intense pure hues. Changing the value and intensity helps, as in the middle painting. But unbalancing the color proportions also finally makes a painting that is strong and harmonious.

Two value sketches done in color: On the left, the colors are all of the same intensity and of mid-range value. On the right, the colors range from intense to very muted— a stronger design along with a wider range of values is obtained.

The sketch at the far left employs fairly equal amounts of warm red, green, cool green, and cyan at equal intensity. In the middle version, darks and lights give variety and improve the picture. Finally, proportions of the colors are varied for a more pleasing design.

MIXING SHADES FOR SHADOWS

The shadow on an object, which is called a *form shadow,* and the shadow the object causes to fall on another surface, which is called a *cast shadow,* will usually be painted differently. Sometimes it is taught that they should both be done in cool colors, but this is an unreliable concept.

Shadows follow a rule I call "opposite to opposite": When light illuminates an object, the color temperature of the shadows will be opposite to the color temperature of the light. For instance, if the light is warm, the shadows will be cool.

But keep this "opposite" in mind: If there is light reflected into a cool form shadow, then it will add to it some color that is opposite in temperature—a warm color (see cube, below).

The shadow's color will also be the complement of the light's color. The early morning sun is orange-yellow. The complement of this color is ultramarine blue. This is why in the early morning an illuminated fence post has a purplish-blue form shadow and casts a purplish-blue shadow on the snow.

A reflected light, besides being either warm or cool, will be affected by the color of the reflecting surface. This is often called "color bounce." If you place an object on several colored surfaces you can observe the reflected color in the object's form shadow (see illustration on page 82). Even when the light is neutral you may want to color the form shadow with some color bounce, just for a more pleasing effect. This is simple artistic license.

When light illuminates an object, the color temperature of the shadows will follow the "opposite to opposite" rule. These paintings demonstrate this in the case of shadows produced by a warm light, painted with a wash of orange-yellow (source at top left). One opposite is the cool color of both the sphere's form and cast shadows. A second opposite is the warm color of reflected light that is hitting the cool form shadow of the cube.

WARM ILLUMINATION

COOL FORM SHADOW

COOL CAST SHADOW

WARM REFLECTED LIGHT IN COOL FORM SHADOW

NEUTRAL ILLUMINATION

When the light is neutral—neither warm nor cool—the shadows are neutral gray. But reflected light that strikes gray shadow areas provides you an opportunity to enliven that shadow with color. On this sphere, I have put a reflection of warm color into the form shadow.

A cool light will produce an opposite warm shadow. The old man on the left appears in warm light with cool shadows. The old man on the right is illuminated by cool light with warm shadows. Just remember the words "opposite to opposite" and apply them.

WARM ILLUMINATION

COOL ILLUMINATION

The first cube, painted warm red, is on a magenta surface, so I have added permanent rose, for reflected light, to the form shadow of the cube. In the second example, a green surface reflects a small amount of green into the form shadow of the warm red. Green is close to warm red's complement, so the "color bounce" produces an area of gray. The third cube is on an orange-yellow surface, so I painted in a small amount of that color for the reflected light effect in the form shadow. In this case, the light is neutral, so the shadow is neutral gray where it runs off the color onto the white (see also page 81).

FORMULAS FOR TINTS AND SHADES

As seen in Chapter 1, you can describe, or model, forms by the way you handle color and value. You can now see that this means defining an object by the colors that indicate its illuminated and shaded surfaces. To model form that is lighted by a *neutral* light:

- First, determine an object's local color— in the examples below, the objects are warm red.

- Next, lighten the local color. With the resulting *tint* you will define the object's most highly illuminated surface.

- Darken the local color with its complement. With the resulting *shade* you will paint the object's form shadow.

This is a basic approach, which can be varied by the formula described on page 83 for objects lighted by a *warm* light.

The local color of the sphere and cube shown here is warm red (in this case, Winsor & Newton bright red). I have used the complement of warm red, cyan (Grumbacher Thalo blue) to make a warm red shade for the form shadows; with this I modeled the objects. I painted the highlighted surfaces with a tint of warm red.

WARM RED TINT

WARM RED SHADE

WARM RED

WARM RED TINT

WARM RED

WARM RED SHADE

W&N BRIGHT RED

TINT

SHADE

GRUMBACHER THALO BLUE

MIXING WARM TINTS AND COOL SHADES

When your subject is illuminated by *warm* light, create a tint for the highlight by adding yellow to its local color and lightening it. Darken the local color to create a shade for the form shadow. This shade will be a cool color and is best created by the following formula: Mix the local color plus a small amount of its complement *and* a small amount of its coolest neighbor on the color wheel. The coolest neighbor is always the color that is closest to purple, which is farther from the warmest primary, yellow, than any other color. For instance, orange's coolest neighbor is warm red; green's coolest neighbor is cool green, and so on. Move away from primary yellow toward purple. (For yellow's cool neighbor, select orange-yellow, and for purple's, use ultramarine blue.)

When your cast shadow falls on white, make it cool by adding a bit of blue to your gray.

WARM RED + YELLOW TINT

WARM RED SHADE

WARM RED TINT

WARM RED SHADE

WARM RED

WARM RED

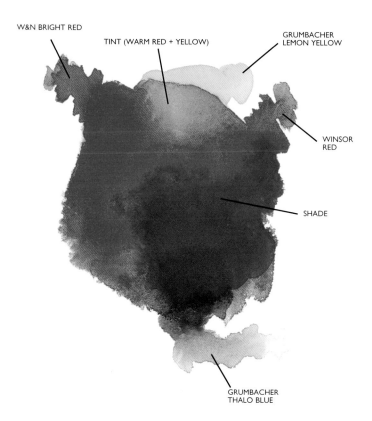

W&N BRIGHT RED

TINT (WARM RED + YELLOW)

GRUMBACHER LEMON YELLOW

WINSOR RED

SHADE

GRUMBACHER THALO BLUE

My local color is, again, warm red, and the illumination is a yellowish light. This time I mixed the form shadow color using the complement of warm red, cyan, *plus* the coolest neighboring color, cool red (in this case Winsor red). On page 84 are shown examples of the same principle applied to modeling spheres of different hues.

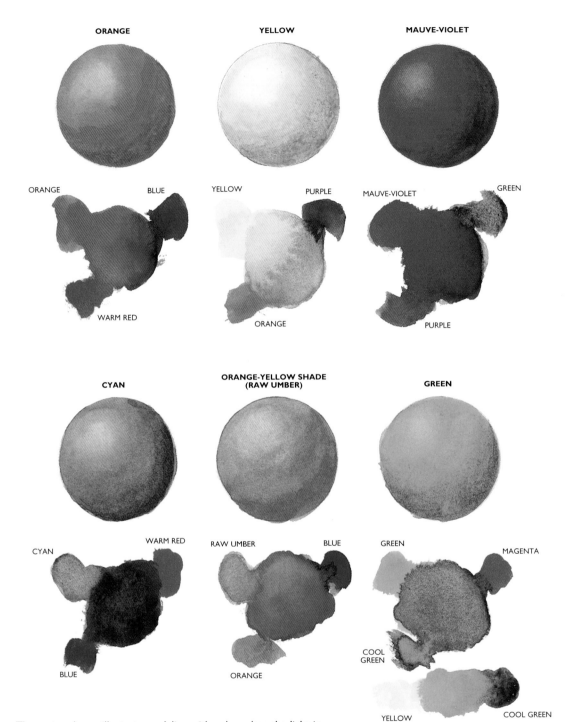

ORANGE

YELLOW

MAUVE-VIOLET

ORANGE · BLUE · WARM RED

YELLOW · PURPLE · ORANGE

MAUVE-VIOLET · GREEN · PURPLE

CYAN

ORANGE-YELLOW SHADE
(RAW UMBER)

GREEN

CYAN · WARM RED · BLUE

RAW UMBER · BLUE · ORANGE

GREEN · MAGENTA · COOL GREEN · YELLOW · COOL GREEN

These six spheres illustrate modeling with color when the light is warm. The local color of the fifth one is an orange-yellow shade (Winsor & Newton raw umber), demonstrating that the same modeling principle applies for shades, as follows: On the color wheel find the orange-yellow's cooler neighbor, orange. Mix this cooler neighbor with the local color and its complement, ultramarine blue. Model the sphere with the resulting color-rich shade. (Or, instead of orange, move farther to warm red—always be willing to experiment!)

MIXING COLORS INTUITIVELY

My teaching of a watercolor class makes me believe that many artists need the preceding formulas for mixing shades. It provides for an informed decision of what paints to use. Still, personally, I like a little more freedom in mixing my paints. We have already discussed creating a shade color by adding the "missing" primary to a pure hue. For example, for a shade of orange, you would mix orange and a touch of cyan. In Chapter 2, I showed you how brown is made by adding to orange any paint that contains the missing primary cyan—green, for instance. Keeping in mind the missing cyans, magentas, and yellows that can be added to a mix, let's create a shade and try to be more intuitive in our decisions.

Orange (see illustration) is 100 percent yellow and 50 percent magenta, so the missing primary is cyan. But because of that lower saturation of magenta, let's consider a touch of magenta as missing, too. A cool green, which has cyan in it, and a cool red, which has magenta in it, can be added to orange to get the orange shade.

Shaded colors work as well as pure hues, as we've seen. Try both: Add an orange shade, burnt sienna, and cyan to orange. This gives the desired results because all color comes from various combinations of cyan, magenta, and yellow.

This is how you can train yourself to think in mixing color. Don't be afraid to make a wrong decision. What you are doing is learning to respond intuitively. Try to improvise color. Through trial and error you'll be able to make correct decisions without deliberating over the color wheel.

Orange is 100 percent yellow and 50 percent magenta, so the missing primary, cyan, is added to orange plus cool red to mix a shade of orange. Here also, the cyan is substituted by cool green (left example), which contains a high proportion of cyan. You can also mix magenta as you explore creating orange shades. Adding magenta to orange and cyan amounts to a use of high proportions of all three primaries to make an orange shade.

SPECIAL SHADOW COLORS

Modeling certain subjects of the purest hues, such as bright red and yellow autumn leaves or flower petals, calls for special treatment. For shadow areas you need to avoid using true shades—any sombre colors that you'd get using the shade formula just described (page 83). This is usually because light is passing through such colored objects; they have an especially clean-looking quality because of their translucency.

Let's take flowers as an example. You should now restrict the use of the "missing" primary, for flowers are usually an intense pure hue. For instance, to get a cool shadow color for modeling a magenta rose (see illustration), avoid using the complement (green), which is loaded with the missing cyan. Try instead a shadow color made from the local color plus its cooler neighboring color—the color closest to purple. Remember: Don't become too restricted by the formula; this is only a rough guide.

On occasion the complement is called for, when the light makes a shadow neither cooler nor warmer, or when a rich dark is needed (see illustration on page 87). But be careful; that missing primary can dull your flowers.

It's important also that you use the purest colors on your palette and keep your water and brushes clean!

When painting translucent, pure-hued subjects like flowers, results are better if you avoid complements for shadow colors. Here I used Holbein Opera in my blends, even though it's not lightfast, because it is a strong, accurate magenta. In the case of the red flower (top), I mixed magenta (both Opera and Winsor & Newton permanent rose) with orange-yellow (Daniel Smith Hansa yellow deep) for red, then mixed red's cooler neighbor on the color wheel, cool red, instead of a shade. To paint the magenta rose, I mixed Opera and permanent rose, and to get my shadow I added mauve-violet (Winsor & Newton permanent magenta), magenta's cooler neighbor.

HOLBEIN OPERA

DANIEL SMITH HANSA YELLOW DEEP

W&N PERMANENT ROSE

HOLBEIN OPERA

W&N PERMANENT ROSE

W&N PERMANENT MAGENTA

A   B   C   D   E   F   G   H

This flower study relies only upon neighboring colors for the shadow colors, for direct complements would muddy the color—an effect totally at cross-purposes with my pure-hued subject. I first applied the local colors of the flowers without detail and let the paint dry. On this base I built the form of the flower with each local colors' cooler neighbor on the color wheel. (Most of the time you want the cool neighbor but sometimes the color of the illumination calls for the warmer neighbor.) Note how differing intensities have been used for their value differences in modeling—for example, in the yellow flower: A tint of the local color for the highlighted petals and an undiluted mixture of orange and yellow for the pure-hue shadows.

On my palette I did include cool green and cyan to mix a few shades for the darkest areas; I used a total of eight different paints: A—Winsor & Newton permanent rose; B—Winsor & Newton permanent magenta; C—Winsor & Newton bright red; D—Daniel Smith permanent orange; E—Daniel Smith Hansa yellow deep; F—Winsor & Newton alizarin crimson; G—Daniel Smith phthalo green; H—Grumbacher Thalo blue.

PUTTING COLOR TO WORK

At this point, let's explore the creation of some complete pictures with a focus on the specific problems and techniques we have covered. We'll start with making a "white" come alive in a study of a weatherbeaten barn. Grays and deeper shadow areas of lively color are the keys to doing this.

You may wish to paint your own version of this and the following pictures to develop your application of color techniques.

GIVING COLOR TO WHITES AND GRAYS

The siding of this aged white barn which has become tarnished by weather and sun does not need to look pallid if we use the three primaries to paint it. I have painted it with a thin layer of gray consisting of my cyan—Grumbacher Thalo blue; magenta—Winsor & Newton permanent rose; and yellow—Grumbacher lemon yellow. Notice how I have varied the gray by allowing other tints to separate from it: a pink, a violet, an orange, and so on. Moving color around in this way increases vitality. Next I added some orange to the shadow on the right side of the cupola. This was not necessarily "right," but it is artistically right to animate the color in a painting, especially in the darks. Always feel free to experiment and go with your hunches.

Finally, every time I paint outdoors there are birds in view, so I try to include them in my picture. Look carefully at the bird that is flying and you will notice that it's painted not just gray, but a violet-gray. A nice rule of thumb is to put color in the little details.

The mixture on the left uses the colors in the weakest intensities for thin, light-gray washes. Note the variously colored tints I obtained. The mixture on the right uses the colors in higher intensities for the dark grays. This enriches the shadows of the painting and dark details such as the birds.

W&N
PERMANENT
ROSE

GRUMBACHER
THALO BLUE

GRUMBACHER
LEMON YELLOW

GRUMBACHER
THALO BLUE

W&N
PERMANENT
ROSE

GRUMBACHER
LEMON YELLOW

When you are interpreting the whites and grays of your subject, don't get trapped by what you actually see, as in the photograph of this sheepdog. Do as the Impressionists did and add color to your whites and grays.

As in the previous painting of the barn, this technique enriches the whites and grays of the dog. Again, I have painted the whites with thin washes of gray using my three primary paints: cyan—Grumbacher Thalo blue; magenta—Winsor & Newton permanent rose; and yellow—Grumbacher lemon yellow. Notice how these colors, as tints, separate from the gray.

For the darker gray fur I used a different palette. Winsor violet and Winsor & Newton alizarin crimson became my source of magenta, and Winsor & Newton burnt sienna my source of yellow. Mixed with my cyan, these yielded colors that move around in the dark gray. The artist who uses only a black or a Payne's gray may have a more accurate painting, but it will also be a bit boring.

Observe in my painting (right) the color movement within the grays of this dog. On the whiter fur, thin gray washes shift from warm to cool for a pleasing interplay of tints. Changing from yellow ochre to cyan to pink on the dog's face also lends vibrancy to the picture.

W&N
PERMANENT
ROSE

GRUMBACHER
LEMON YELLOW

GRUMBACHER
THALO BLUE

W&N BURNT
SIENNA

GRUMBACHER
THALO BLUE

WINSOR
VIOLET

W&N ALIZARIN
CRIMSON

As an artist you need to train your eyes to see color where most people see only gray. In the photo below you can see some warm colors in the cat's fur; sometimes its flesh shows through the fur, as in the ear. There are even some suggestions of cyan and green.

I could have chosen the primary colors I used in the previous two pictures, but this time I changed the palette; you don't have to become stuck with one approach. My palette included Grumbacher Thalo blue and Winsor & Newton permanent rose again, but I chose a cooler yellow, Daniel Smith Hansa yellow deep (my favorite orange-yellow). Holbein permanent violet and Daniel Smith phthalo green contributed color richness as I created my grays for the cat.

For the stripes on the cat and the boy's hair I darkened my grays and brown with Winsor & Newton burnt sienna and Winsor & Newton alizarin crimson. The shaded area in the boy's face is given a glow of reflected color from his shirt—this called for Daniel Smith permanent orange.

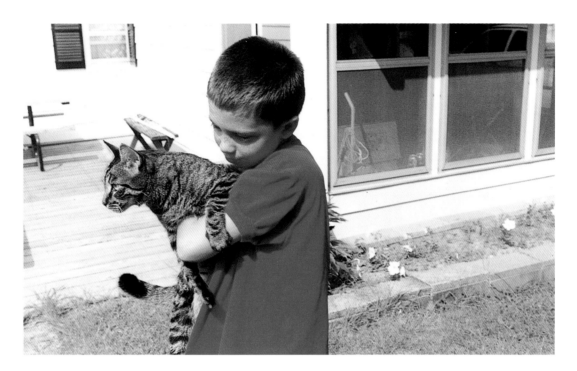

In doing this study I painted the cat without its stripes first, as you see below. I concentrated on values first to create the proper form and then applied various hues for movement within the gray. In the finished picture (right), note especially the magenta tints I have introduced to the cat's cheek.

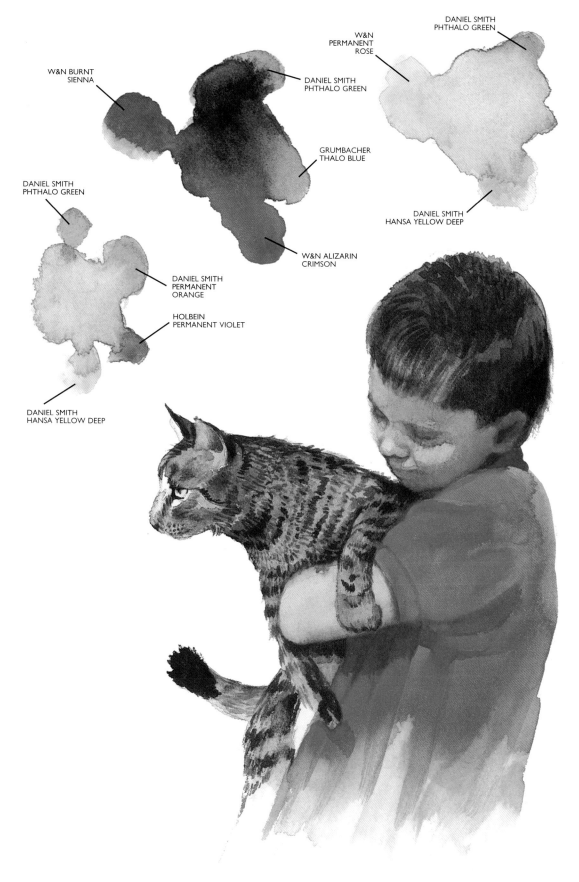

W&N BURNT
SIENNA

DANIEL SMITH
PHTHALO GREEN

W&N
PERMANENT
ROSE

DANIEL SMITH
PHTHALO GREEN

DANIEL SMITH
PHTHALO GREEN

GRUMBACHER
THALO BLUE

DANIEL SMITH
PHTHALO GREEN

DANIEL SMITH
PERMANENT
ORANGE

DANIEL SMITH
HANSA YELLOW DEEP

W&N ALIZARIN
CRIMSON

HOLBEIN
PERMANENT VIOLET

DANIEL SMITH
HANSA YELLOW DEEP

EXPLORING COLOR RICHNESS

We have seen how predominantly gray subjects can be infused with color to give more richness to a painting.

The first two scenes illustrated here are executed with a full-color palette—the paintings have a lot of hues from across the spectrum and look bright and lively.

In the first, below, the colors are mostly grayed down, but the principle of enlivening muted passages with color has been applied. Also there is color movement in the grass, which ranges from intense lime green to shaded greens, browns, and yellow-orange. The sky has a variety of pinks and even olive greens in its gray passages to lend it movement. Also notice the subtly colored flock of birds in the background and the hawk on the branch of the tree.

The second scene employs the full-color palette with less muting of the colors and illustrates further all the color variations you can get in gray rocks, blue water, and green trees.

W&N
PERMANENT
ROSE

DANIEL SMITH
PERMANENT
ORANGE

W&N
PERMANENT
MAGENTA

W&N RAW
SIENNA

GRUMBACHER
LEMON
YELLOW

DANIEL SMITH
PHTHALO
GREEN

GRUMBACHER
THALO BLUE

I did this scene with a full-color palette, most of them pure hues. Though I often muted these, I blended them right on the paper to achieve a lot of color interaction. Once again a gray barn has plenty of color in it: The shadowed side has purples and blues, and the lighted side looks warmer, with red and oranges in the grays.

| GRUMBACHER THALO BLUE | DANIEL SMITH PHTHALO GREEN | W&N PERMANENT MAGENTA | W&N ALIZARIN CRIMSON | W&N BRIGHT RED | DANIEL SMITH PERMANENT ORANGE | DANIEL SMITH HANSA YELLOW DEEP | GRUMBACHER LEMON YELLOW | W&N BURNT SIENNA |

This full-palette painting employs the pure hues and premixed shades shown here but with limited muting on my part. It is necessary to use colors at greater intensities to capture a sunny-day quality, as in this scene. As usual, I have painted the whites and grays of the rocks with tints and tinted shades. The sunlit surface of the lake required translucent color, so it is painted as an interplay of phthalo green and cyan (and, as they mix on the paper, their neighbors on the color wheel)—that is, the "missing" primary magenta was avoided. In the shadowed water, permanent magenta, my mauve-violet shade, is used nearly full-strength and blended in on the damp paper. Finally, note that for a clean look in the foliage I have modeled the trees in many places with full-strength phthalo green as a cool neighbor to the local color, lime green—again avoiding any muddiness that the missing primary might have lent to the shadow colors.

In the next two paintings observe how you can create a certain mood and harmony with fewer colors.

My personal preference is to work in this way with a limited palette. This approach isn't necessarily better—just a different viewpoint worth considering. The painting here leans toward gold and brown but still has little bursts of reds, oranges, and olive greens to give it life.

When you are working from a limited palette like this, it is important to create harmony throughout the painting. That's why my sky has an olive cast instead of the purer blue that I might have painted using a full-color palette. Because it is correct in terms of the color scheme of the whole painting, you still see it as sky although it isn't blue. There are only five colors used in this painting, as shown, and none of the brownish ones were created with brown paints.

In this limited-palette landscape, my cool phthalo green has contributed to the yellow-greens and olives, and my cyan serves only to mute the magenta-to-yellow warm hues. This sparing use of color gives unity to the scene and an autumnal mood.

DANIEL SMITH PHTHALO GREEN

GRUMBACHER THALO BLUE

W&N PERMANENT ROSE

W&N BRIGHT RED

DANIEL SMITH HANSA YELLOW DEEP

This painting done with only five paints leans mostly to the greens. The other colors are then used only as accents: Muted yellow and red and tints of orange shade are added in small touches that harmonize with the whole. Try this approach with a picture of your own.

Also notice that the sky in this picture is a pale green—not blue—in keeping with the overall scheme.

GRUMBACHER
THALO BLUE

W&N
PERMANENT
ROSE

DANIEL SMITH
HANSA YELLOW DEEP

DANIEL SMITH
PHTHALO GREEN

DANIEL SMITH
HANSA YELLOW DEEP

W&N BURNT SIENNA

DANIEL SMITH
PHTHALO
GREEN

GRUMBACHER
THALO BLUE

W&N BURNT
SIENNA

W&N
PERMANENT
ROSE

DANIEL SMITH
HANSA
YELLOW DEEP

It isn't necessary to have all kinds of green paints on your palette. You can create a variety of greens from phthalo green and/or cyan mixed with other colors. In a sense, the subject of this limited-palette painting is green; the other colors appear only as touches.

PORTRAIT PAINTING

One day my granddaughter Tiffany was wearing a big multicolored hat in a bright sun that produced strong shadows. I picked this subject because the hat contains the primary pure hues cyan, magenta, and yellow. I'm going to show you three different ways to paint it with just three paints.

The first version uses Grumbacher Thalo blue, Winsor & Newton permanent rose, and Grumbacher lemon yellow. With just these paints, I've created a full-color palette and painted Tiffany in all clean-looking colors.

W&N
PERMANENT
ROSE

GRUMBACHER
LEMON YELLOW

GRUMBACHER
THALO BLUE

W&N
PERMANENT
ROSE

GRUMBACHER
LEMON YELLOW

GRUMBACHER
THALO BLUE

GRUMBACHER
LEMON YELLOW

GRUMBACHER
THALO BLUE

W&N
PERMANENT
ROSE

W&N
PERMANENT
ROSE

GRUMBACHER
LEMON YELLOW

GRUMBACHER
THALO BLUE

For the initial version of the portrait I used the three primaries cyan, magenta, and yellow and painted Tiffany in all clean-looking colors—pure hues in the hat and very natural skin tones.

For the second version, my three colors are mostly shades with high proportions of the primaries: My strongly magenta shade is Winsor & Newton alizarin crimson; my strongly yellow shade is Winsor & Newton raw sienna, and my full-strength Grumbacher Thalo blue with slight muting acts as a Prussian blue. The result doesn't have the same brilliance because there are no pure hues used, but I still achieve an appropriate representation. This painting looks nearly as good as the first one because most of the colors we view every day are a mixture of all three primaries. Thus, for most colors we don't need pure-hue paints.

In the third version, I adopt Payne's gray for the palette, and it is my source of cyan. My magenta is mainly present in burnt sienna and my yellow in raw sienna. Each of these paints has a lot of the other two primaries in its makeup, so the overall coloring reminds one of an old Dutch master's painting with its muted golden-browns. It's still a three-color palette, still percentages of cyan, magenta, and yellow, and still a valid way of painting.

W&N RAW SIENNA

W&N BURNT SIENNA

W&N RAW SIENNA

W&N ALIZARIN CRIMSON

GRUMBACHER THALO BLUE

W&N COTMAN PAYNE'S GRAY

Notice that Tiffany's face and hair in the second version (left) are not unlike those of the first painting, but the hat takes on a different look altogether because the shaded paints won't give us the pure hues. In the third version (right), each of the three shades on my palette has a lot of the other two primaries in it, so the overall coloring is muted.

The variety of possible choices is endless and is what makes painting so interesting. But now let's look at the whole sequence for painting a portrait.

Since portraits aim at a specific likeness, I always start out with an accurate pencil drawing of the subject, either from life or from a photograph. This I do directly on the watercolor paper. I prefer a 2H or H pencil; they seem just right for watercolor paper. The 2H, in fact, melts away as you paint over it. (If you use an artist's 2B, it acts like charcoal and smears the watercolor.) In my drawing I ensure that all the major shapes and proportions of the head and hat are accurate.

With a snapshot of Tiffany as a guide, I pay special attention to the eyes and mouth because these are what capture an individual's personality.

Next, I wash in a light peach tint made from warm red mixed with orange-yellow and plenty of water. I usually wet the area where the skin and hair are to get a smooth underpainting. If the hair is light, the wash should not go over it. This is allowed to dry thoroughly.

Next, I put in any of the pure hues that are in the picture, such as you see in the multicolored hat. As we've learned, it's important to be engaged in painting the entire painting as you proceed because each color affects the color balance of the whole.

After these first colors have thoroughly dried, I go back in with the shades that define the forms. Shadows and highlights are necessary to model the face.

I paint the hair with blends of mauve-violet shade (permanent magenta), orange-yellow, cool red shade (alizarin crimson), and cool green. In the browns, no brown paints are used; as with grays, I can attain more color richness if I mix them than if I take them premixed from a tube.

DANIEL SMITH PHTHALO GREEN

GRUMBACHER THALO BLUE

W&N ALIZARIN CRIMSON

W&N PERMANENT MAGENTA

DANIEL SMITH HANSA YELLOW DEEP

DANIEL SMITH HANSA YELLOW DEEP

W&N PERMANENT ROSE

W&N BRIGHT RED

W&N ALIZARIN CRIMSON

W&N PERMANENT MAGENTA

GRUMBACHER THALO BLUE

DANIEL SMITH PHTHALO GREEN

As a final step, once the paint has thoroughly dried, I put in enough darks to give the painting the needed full range of values.

GRUMBACHER LEMON YELLOW

W&N BRIGHT RED

GRUMBACHER LEMON YELLOW

GRUMBACHER THALO BLUE

W&N BRIGHT RED

W&N PERMANENT MAGENTA

W&N PERMANENT MAGENTA	GRUMBACHER THALO BLUE	GRUMBACHER LEMON YELLOW	DANIEL SMITH HANSA YELLOW DEEP	W&N BRIGHT RED	DANIEL SMITH PHTHALO GREEN

In portraits, basically, skin tones require a tint which is a combination of warm reds and yellows; for the shadows, I mix shades by adding the complement of warm red, cyan, and a touch of mauve-violet. In doing a portrait you can apply the same techniques you'd use in other subjects. Here, for color richness, note that I applied a thin wash of cool green to the shadows on the head, and put in some touches in the hair as well. Remember, establish your base skin color, then do washes, letting pure hues mix with the base.

MASTERING SKIN TONES

Here is another example of how a six-color palette can be used to create subtle varieties in skin tones. I mixed a little Grumbacher Thalo blue and Daniel Smith permanent orange and phthalo green with Winsor & Newton permanent magenta to create shades for this portrait of a Masai man from Kenya. This gave me a medium brown that can shift between warm brown and a shade of violet.

I began with this pencil drawing, over which I put the first layer of colors, keeping the paints very wet and mixing them right on the paper.

W&N
PERMANENT
MAGENTA

W&N ALIZARIN
CRIMSON

GRUMBACHER
THALO BLUE

DANIEL SMITH
PHTHALO GREEN

DANIEL SMITH
PERMANENT
ORANGE

DANIEL SMITH
HANSA YELLOW
DEEP

W&N
PERMANENT
MAGENTA

W&N ALIZARIN
CRIMSON

W&N
PERMANENT
MAGENTA

DANIEL SMITH
PHTHALO
GREEN

DANIEL SMITH
PERMANENT
ORANGE

GRUMBACHER
THALO BLUE

DANIEL SMITH
HANSA YELLOW
DEEP

DANIEL SMITH
PHTHALO
GREEN

I made sure my mauve-violet purple shades were at the top of the head, which suggests a reflection of the cool light from a blue sky. Similarly, I allowed a dominance of alizarin crimson to suggest the translucency of the ear. Finally, I used a dry brush, once the paint was semi-dry, to wipe away paint to create highlights for the cheek bone and nose.

Once the shades of my underpainting had dried, my new washes were pure hues. For instance, a mauve-violet or orange wash over the brown gave me more color richness than if I had used a single complex violet-brown mixture.

On my palette with my magenta and cyan I put alizarin crimson and orange-yellow to do the underpainting for the face. I wetted the entire area of the face to prepare the watercolor paper and applied the base colors. I mixed the colors with plenty of water right on the paper and let them shift from warm to cool almost in an abstract manner. I am conscious of form and of value range in the head while doing this base painting (see page 106).

I let this underpainting dry before applying any more paint. Then I was ready to wash on colors to develop the detail. The most repeated statement made by student artists when I do a demonstration in class is: "I didn't realize how many washes it takes to create a painting." Watercolor portraits do usually take many washes of color. I always let the watercolors dry thoroughly before applying a new wash. You increase the chance of getting muddy color if you don't make this a rule. Of course, if you need a soft explosion of color, then you should purposely apply the paint wet-into-wet.

W&N PERMANENT ROSE

DANIEL SMITH HANSA YELLOW DEEP

W&N PERMANENT MAGENTA

GRUMBACHER THALO BLUE

DANIEL SMITH PHTHALO GREEN

I wanted to create a pinkish violet cast to get a sunset mood for this scene. On this palette, then, I used only five paints for a limited range of colors. Notice how I have moved from pinks to pastel greens in the background tints. I wanted the pink especially to move in and out through the entire painting.

MODELING TECHNIQUE

It's important that you think "form" as you paint. A skillful painting will give the illusion that you can actually put your hand around the subject. For this wildlife subject, a picture of a Canada goose, I established the basic forms and the balance of lights and darks first in my sketches (see the drawing below). I believe that if you think in terms of the shape and three-dimensionality of your subject your mind will respond and you'll model form as you mix and apply color.

Think about the lessons presented earlier on how shadow colors can be varied from warm to cool. In the illustration opposite, observe how the raw umber and alizarin crimson, which are warmer, advancing colors, helped me to model this bird's bulging breast. Cyan and phthalo green added to these warm colors give me cooler shades for the shadows.

I always recommend to my students that they use the paints that fit their style. For instance, I love raw umber, a shaded orange-yellow. Color theory helps me understand its makeup, so I know its limitations—one of which is that it cannot give me clean oranges because it has some cyan in its makeup. For this painting raw umber suited my purposes perfectly, so I included it on my palette without hesitation

In my drawing I first established the shape and roundness of the body, as indicated by the arrow.

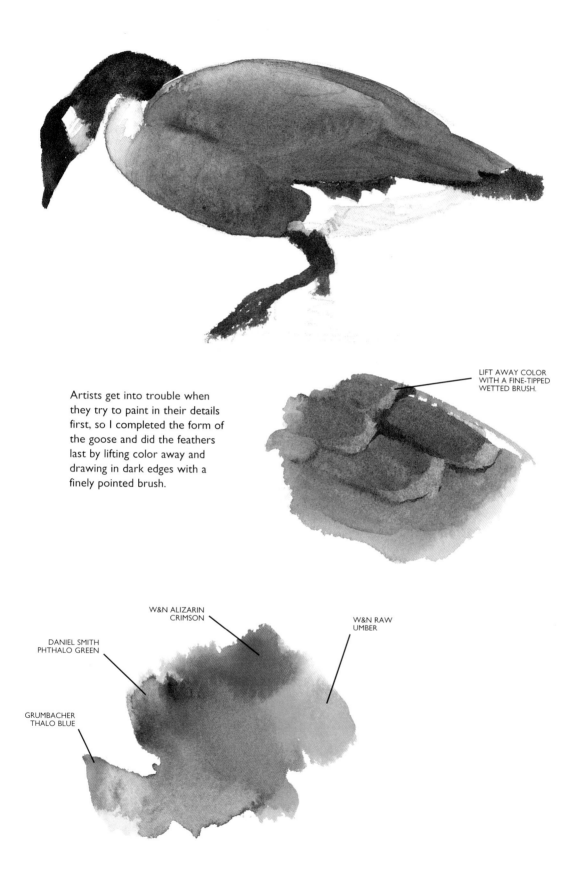

Artists get into trouble when they try to paint in their details first, so I completed the form of the goose and did the feathers last by lifting color away and drawing in dark edges with a finely pointed brush.

LIFT AWAY COLOR WITH A FINE-TIPPED WETTED BRUSH.

W&N ALIZARIN CRIMSON

W&N RAW UMBER

DANIEL SMITH PHTHALO GREEN

GRUMBACHER THALO BLUE

| W&N BURNT SIENNA | W&N ALIZARIN CRIMSON | W&N PERMANENT ROSE | W&N RAW UMBER | DANIEL SMITH PHTHALO GREEN | GRUMBACHER THALO BLUE |

Even if your subject is basically black, white, and brown, keep your colors moving, as I did here. Remember to mix deep, rich darks and to separate and recombine colors in a subtle interplay—taking advantage of the fact that all color derives from the primaries cyan, magenta, and yellow.

INDEX